DUBČEK'S BLUEPRINT
FOR FREEDOM

D1345940

DUBCEK'S BLUEPRINT FOR FREEDOM

His original documents
leading to the invasion of
Czechoslovakia

Profile by
HUGH LUNGHI

Commentary by
PAUL ELLO

WILLIAM KIMBER · LONDON

First published in Great Britain by

WILLIAM KIMBER & CO. LIMITED

6, Queen Anne's Gate, London, S.W.1

© 1968 by Paul Ello

Introduction © 1969 William Kimber & Co.

Standard Book No. 7183 0231 1

Printed in Great Britain by Billing & Sons Limited
Guildford and London

NOTE ON THE DOCUMENTS

The documents reprinted in this volume are facsimile reproductions from the original papers as translated by Czech linguists in Prague without changes, including the various imperfections present in the original copy, in order to retain their full original authenticity.

ACKNOWLEDGEMENTS

This book was prepared with the assistance of Messrs. Joseph Pelton, Henry Kenski and Miss Cathy Pearson. I am especially indebted to my wife for her patience and encouragement. As usual, errors of fact and judgment in the commentary are my own.

PAUL ELLO

PREFACE

This volume is published for scholars and laymen alike.

In the case of the former, the significance of the documents presented here will be obvious. As well as their intrinsic importance as basic source material, these documents offer what amounts to a blueprint for the further development of a Socialist political order.

As such, not only do they shed considerable light on the present state of affairs in Czechoslovakia, but, more importantly, they provide some indication of the direction which Communist Party State Systems will have to move if they are to survive. The layman will also find much in these documents which is of value.

When read in conjunction with the accompanying introduction and analysis, the documents help to explain a good deal of what has recently occurred in Eastern Europe. In particular, they offer a perspective hitherto unavailable for viewing the Soviet decision to intervene militarily in Czechoslovakia.

The documents are arranged in chronological order. To preserve their value for the research scholar, they are reproduced in their entirety in the original form.

Students of the Soviet Bloc are likely to experience no difficulty in ascertaining the substance of these documents. The average reader, who, either because he is unfamiliar with the current state of affairs in Eastern Europe, or because he is unaccustomed to the style employed in these documents, is likely to find the going a bit more difficult. Hopefully, the burden will be eased somewhat by the commentary which accompanies each of the documents.

CONTENTS

A CHRONOLOGY OF EVENTS

1967

June 27-29   The Czechoslovak Writers' Union criticizes openly the domestic and foreign policies of the régime.

October 30   First open student demonstrations caused by bad conditions in student hostels

December 8   Visit of the First Secretary of the CPSU, Leonid Brezhnev, in Prague.

1968

January 5   Antonin Novotny replaced as First Secretary of the CCP by Alexander Dubček, who attempts a party-purge.

March 5   First steps towards a relaxation of censorship.

March 22   Novotny is forced to resign as head of the state. General Ludvik Svoboda is appointed as his successor on March 28.

April 3   Government promises investigation of the death of former Foreign Minister Jan Masaryk, said to have been murdered by Stalin's agents.

April 4   Oldrich Cernik appointed Prime Minister. New Cabinet formed.

April 5   Action Programme published. Extensive civil rights and reforms promised.

May 4   Dubček visits Moscow.

May 8   Conference of East German, Polish, Hungarian and Bulgarian Party leaders in Moscow.

May 10   Soviet military manoeuvres commence in Poland near the Czechoslovakian border.

May 17   Alexei Kosygin, Premier of the Soviet Union and Marshal Andrei Grechko, Minister of Defence and former commander of the Warsaw Pact armed forces, visits Prague. Czechoslovakia agrees to Warsaw Pact manoeuvres on Czechoslovakian territory.

May 30   Antonin Novotny ousted from the Party.

July 9   Prague denies necessity of convening a Warsaw Pact summit meeting because of its reforms.

July 10   Concern voiced about the stay of Russian troops in Czecho-
              slovakia after the end of the Warsaw Pact manoeuvres.

July 15   Warsaw Pact structure criticized by Czech General Vaclav
              Prchlik. New leaders ignore criticism.

July 17   Letter of the other Warsaw Pact members criticizing Czecho-
              slovakian reforms published.

July 29-31   Talks between the Czechoslovakian leadership with members
              of the Soviet politburo at Cierna and Tisou.

August 3   Meeting of Warsaw Pact members and Czechoslovakian
              leaders in Bratislava. Soviet troops withdrawn.

August 9   Yugoslavian President, Marshal Tito, visits Prague.

August 10   Soviets resume manoeuvres in the Ukraine, along the Czecho-
              slovakian border.

August 11   East German leader Walter Ulbricht is given a cool reception
              in Prague.

August 14   Soviet press violently attacks Czech reforms.

August 15   Nicolae Ceaucescu, President of Rumania, is given a hearty
              welcome in Prague.

August 20   Soviet and Warsaw Pact forces invade Czechoslovakia after
              a secret meeting of Soviet leaders. Dubček arrested.

INTRODUCTION

Why Dubcek?

"Public opinion has promoted Dubcek overnight from First Secretary of the Communist Party to First Secretary of the nation"—so said a broadcast on Prague Radio a week before the first confrontation of Czechoslovak and Soviet leaders at Cierna on July 29th, 1968. While the leaders faced each other at Cierna and a few days later at Bratislava, a demonstration unprecedented in a Communist country took place: people in their hundreds of thousands throughout Czechoslovakia spontaneously began signing resolutions of support for Dubcek and his team and the signatories included even Russian, East German and Polish tourists. Earlier in the summer the new Czechoslovak Institute of Opinion Research and the Communist Party daily *Rude Pravo* had each conducted opinion polls to test support for Dubcek and the Action Programme. The results were overwhelmingly in his favour, showing over 90 per cent support, an unprecedented outcome for a political personality poll. During the Soviet invasion virtually all the conscious population was wholeheartedly behind Dubcek. But the invasion merely consolidated the feeling for Dubcek who had, long before, become a symbol of the people's aspirations. And yet prior to January 5th of the same year, when he replaced Antonin Novotny as First Secretary of the Czechoslovak Communist Party (CCP), Dubcek was hardly known to the general public.

Why did he become the people's hero and how? Above all, perhaps, because he said he wanted to "give socialism back its human face," a slogan which on the television screens—one of the potent forces in Czechoslovakia's fight for freedom—Dubcek's own appearance, with his wide grin, somewhat awkward manner but patent sincerity seemed to personify. From the documents here reproduced and from his subsequent speeches it can be seen that Dubcek has been consistent in maintaining that the goal must be achieved by purifying the Communist Party and making it worthy of the people, by making it demonstrate that it deserved the "leading role" it held in society. But the people backed him in spite of the Party's monopoly, not because of it. They backed him because they saw the need to rally round a single and effective leadership, a leadership which had set them on the path to a truly open society. The years under Novotny when the Party had been one of the most sub-servient of Moscow's satellites had long ago brought disillusionment with socialism itself. The disenchantment was expressed throughout Czechoslovakia in the classic "theory": there are three roads to Socialism. The first, the Leninist road, is like being in a long tunnel and seeing only a spot of light at the end. Then there is the Stalinist road—that is like being in a tram-car, where half the people are "sitting" (i.e., in prison) and half are shaking. And thirdly, there's the post-Stalin road—that is like travelling in a Soviet Ilyushin airliner, where everyone feels like vomiting but nobody can get out. It is a measure of Dubcek's stature, and that of his colleagues it should be said, that after the Soviet invasion a larger number of people joined the Czechoslovak Communist Party out of a genuine desire to support it than ever before in such a short period. Who was this man to whom people, unasked, remained devoted even months after Moscow had tried every trick to discredit him?

Alexander Dubcek was born into a poor home on November 27th, 1921, in the western Slovak village of Uhrovec. His father, a joiner, had emigrated in search of work to the United States before the First World War. He had returned not long after its end to the newly created Republic of Czechoslovakia. Alexander, the second of two sons, was born three years after its foundation. His father, Stefan, was one of the first to join the Communist Party of the new State and was carried away by enthu-siasm for that other young régime, the Soviet Union. In response to an appeal by the Comintern Congress for concrete assistance by the inter-national working class to the Soviet economy, Stefan joined a group of qualified artisans in an international co-operative farm venture they called *Interhelpo*. This group, consisting of 106 families, including the Dubceks, mostly Slovaks and a few Czechs, Germans and Hungarians, set out in March, 1925, for Pishpek, a tiny market town in Kirghizia on the desolate border of Sinkiang, later to become Frunze, the capital of the Kirghiz Republic. When Alexander was 12 the family moved to Gorkiy, about 300 miles east of Moscow, where his father found work in the important automobile works and where Alexander completed his secondary schooling in 1938. In that year all foreign workers in the U.S.S.R. were given the choice of taking Soviet citizenship or leaving. Stefan Dubcek left with his family. Back in Slovakia Alexander became a skilled lock-smith in the Skoda factory at Dubnica. Their experiences in Russia, where they had lived through the bloodiest of Stalin's purges, the "Yezhov-shchina," did not deter his father, his elder brother Julius nor Alexander himself from joining the underground Slovak Communist Party in 1939, illegal under the German puppet Slovak State. With his brother he joined a partisan brigade in the Slovak uprising in August, 1944. His brother was killed, he himself was twice wounded. His father was deported to the Mauthausen concentration camp, where he found Antonin Novotny in the privileged position of *Kapo*, helping to control the other prisoners. His father did not see Slovakia again until several weeks after the end of the war. He is still an active Party member, but has not held high office. After the war Alexander worked as a locksmith in Trencin in Slovakia where he became a district Party official. He became a full-time Party official in 1949 and quickly rose to membership of the Slovak CP Central Committee and leader of the Regional Party Committee of the important town of Banska Bystrica by 1953. He failed to be re-elected to the Central Committee two years later, but it is not clear whether this was because of disagreements with the then leaders of the Slovak CP in their policy of subordinating their Party to Prague or simply because he had won the privilege of a three-year post-graduate course at the Higher Party School in Moscow. These three years until 1958 must have been crucial. It was the traumatic period of the denun-ciation of Stalin by Khrushchev and his followers in 1956. And later that same year came the even more agonizing and shameful period for Soviet Communism, the rape of Hungary. It was followed by the beginning of the most liberal years of the Khrushchev era. These years and those of his adolescence in Stalin's Russia, when no family was left unscarred by the terror, and friends of the highly suspect foreigners least of all, must have given Alexander Dubcek an insight into Russian mentality and the methods of totalitarian Communism such as no other Czech or Slovak leader enjoyed.

During his studies at the Moscow Party academy he and his fellow students must have compared the tragic case of Hungary with the then hopeful prospects of the Polish 1956 Revolution and drawn their own conclusions. Dubcek graduated with honours in Moscow. On his return to Slovakia he found that the de-Stalinization ferment had made little impact. On the contrary, the first rehabilitation commission, reluctantly set up by the Party, had merely sustained most of the charges against the victims of the 1951-54 purges and trials. Dubcek, with his fine record at the top Party academy in the Soviet bloc, was appointed the leading regional Party Secretary, in charge of the Party in the Slovak capital, Bratislava. In 1960 he rose to the highest Party establishment at the centre in Prague when he became one of the Secretaries of the Czecho-slovak CP Central Committee and two years later a member of the ten-man Party Presidium.

In 1963 Dubcek became the virtual governor of Slovakia, succeeding, as Slovak First Party Secretary, the Stalinist Bacilek whom Novotny had reluctantly thrown overboard. According to an account published in the Bratislava *Pravda* in April, 1968, Novotny, in protest, left the meeting before Dubcek's election. This was one of the first of Novotny's fatal errors in his mishandling of the Slovaks and henceforth he refused to attend meetings of the Slovak Central Committee. In 1963 Dubcek clashed with Novotny, though undramatically and by implication only, over disciplinary action to be taken against two outspoken Slovak journalists and to a lesser extent over the rehabilitation of Slovak nationalist Communists. On the latter issue Dubcek took a cautious stand, probably calculating that impetuosity over this symbolic issue would merely ruin any chances of winning a measure of real autonomy for the Slovak Party later. Like Novotny, Dubcek in 1966 had identified himself with the new economic reforms. Unlike Novotny he did not equivocate. On another economic issue, the demand of Slovak repre-sentatives for a preferential investment rate to equalize Slovakia's lagging living standards with those of the Czech lands, Dubcek took a statesman-like attitude, allowing that there was a case but showing no favouritism.

Although Dubcek now walked the corridors of power and by virtue of his "governership" of Slovakia exercised considerable influence, he never sought, or at least never caught the limelight outside Slovakia or even there, until last year. He seemed to follow an orthodox line, though in his approach to individuals he was more human than the usual Com-munist *apparatchik*. Perhaps it was this quality which drew his associates to choose him as a compromise candidate to replace the discredited Novotny in the outcome of the climacteric Central Committee meetings at the end of 1967. What exactly occurred at these meetings is not yet known publicly, since the official records are so far unpublished. But the three issues at stake were, first, the implementation of the economic reforms, then freedom of expression and, finally, effective autonomy for Slovakia. It is known that Dubcek came into direct conflict with Novotny over the second. The kind of arguments he used can easily be gathered from the documents published here and from a statement published in the Bratislava *Pravda* at the end of 1967 where he called on the Party to resist attempts to make its influence felt by authoritarian means. Dubcek believed, and still believes, the Communist Party must lead, but his theme is: government by persuasion not by force. He has constantly deplored what he called "the arrogance of authoritarian rulers."

When the Soviet First Party Secretary, Leonid Brezhnev, appeared at one of the December sessions of the Central Committee he apparently refused to intervene on Novotny's behalf. According to some reports, he relied on the army coup which Novotny was preparing. But, in fact, the Kremlin attitude to Novotny has been consistent, before, during and since the invasion. As they did with the notorious Rakosi in Hungary in 1956, the Russians not only abandoned Novotny, regarding him as expendable once he was unable to carry his colleagues with him or keep them in order, but have on several occasions publicly stated they did not want a return to the conditions prevailing under his rule. In December, 1967, the Czechoslovak Central Committee had voted to remove Novotny as First Party Secretary, though not as President, but had not agreed on his replacement. It is highly unlikely, in view of Dubcek's liberal record, that Brezhnev suggested him. In any case, Brezhnev is said to have refused to intervene at all. By the time it adjourned for Christmas the Central Committee had still not decided on a successor. A commission was appointed to submit proposals urgently in the New Year. According to reports, there were two main candidates, Oldrich Cernik, at that time a Deputy Premier, in charge of economic affairs, and the Slovak Jozef Lenart, the Prime Minister under Novotny. The liberals advanced the former, the Novotnyites the latter. But the commission proposed Dubcek. Perhaps because it was a surprise candidacy, it was accepted: by the liberals because of his record, by the Slovaks because he was their man and by the conservatives because, as a relative newcomer without a faction, providing a power base, he seemed to represent no threat and appeared manageable. What to the power-seekers was Dubcek's weakness was, in fact, his strength: as far as can be ascertained, Dubcek had not indulged in personal intrigues.

The three dark ages Dubcek had lived through—the bloodbaths of Stalin's Russia in the 'thirties, the purges of good Slovak Communists under Novotny and his predecessors and, back again in Russia, the Soviet invasion of Hungary, must have inoculated him against totalitarian Communism. Other Communist leaders in East Europe had been through similar experiences but would not learn the lesson for fear of losing power. The secret of Dubcek's outlook, as of his later popularity, seemed to lie in his genuine humility. He is not an intellectual, but neither is he anti-intellectual. He is without humbug. He does not pretend to be an "ordinary working chap," but he is more ready than any of his predecessors to go out and meet the people. He expects to be taken at face value. He has never encouraged others to make him out to be a whizz-kid or a worker of economic or any other miracles. Though a life-long Communist, a career-Communist, neither his manner nor his words suggest the ruthless, Soviet-style *apparatchik* with the self-confidence born of ignorance. Even during the fairest days of his country's high summer, he displayed a disarming diffidence, never losing his courteous humility. There is no trace in him of that mock-modesty which Stalin used to assume for foreigners. Yet Dubcek is also a man of steel and courage, as well as tenacity and statesmanship, as he proved at his confrontations with the Russian leaders and by his endurance of the physical violence and psychological pressures which he endured at their hands. The fact that he is one of the few Communist leaders in East Europe who have come to power neither sitting on Soviet bayonets, nor inheriting the system of those who did, accounts for his unsolicited popularity among non-Communists as well as among his fellow Communists. Whatever his ultimate fate, Dubcek, with his tall figure, his beaky eagle-profile softened by a huge and, at one time, often smiling mouth, his sober family devotion to his wife and three sons, established in the course of eight frenetic months an honourable and genuinely respected place in history such as perhaps no Communist leader in the world has yet achieved.

Why Invasion?

To be fair to Dubcek himself, as well as to his colleagues, many of the reforms associated with his name were not initiated by him but by his partners, as these documents show. It was merely that Dubcek symbolized for all his countrymen, as for many outside, the spirit of those reforms. Therefore, in analysing the reasons for the Soviet invasion of Czechoslovakia and Moscow's subsequent policies, it is convenient to refer to Dubcek's policy statements, middle of the road though they are and often overtaken by events. It is useful also to establish what Dubcek did not stand for. He did not regret the Communist take-over of his country in 1948, on the contrary, he described it as "the decisive landmark of our history." He did not intend to weaken "the leading role of the Communist Party." Though he spoke of "flexibility" in foreign policy outside the Soviet bloc, he did not intend to reverse the foreign policy of his predecessors: at no point did he even imply that Czechoslovakia should desert the Soviet alliance or the Warsaw Pact or default on Comecon, the bloc's "common market." He did not encourage the talk of diplomatic relations with West Germany and Israel, which, in the event, became of less than academic interest early in the year. He did not suggest that the Party should leave the arts and literature alone: he was for "Communist persuasion" but against "administrative guidance" in cultural matters. He did not step outside the limits of orthodox Marxism-Leninism, though Lenin had a far more cynical concept of the use to which the Party apparatus should be put than did Dubcek. On his appointment to the highest post in the country Dubcek proclaimed his loyalty to Marxism-Leninism and he never suggested a revision of Marxist doctrine. Dubcek's stern reactions to the growing anti-Soviet outbursts in Czechoslovakia during the summer of 1968 stemmed not just from the statesman's need to reassure the great neighbour but from a realization that if the Soviet Union were totally discredited so would be the Czechoslovak Communist Party. The Party had to dissociate itself from the aberrations of the past, including the slavish copying of the Soviet model, but this must not lead to the discrediting of the Party as a whole. To preserve the Party's leading role Dubcek would not allow the revival of non-Party organizations representing different interests, in which he genuinely believed, to take place outside the Communist dominated National Front.

In the face of such a record the Soviet *Pravda's* attempt on the second day of the invasion to discredit Dubcek in the eyes at least of good Communists suffered from a marked credibility gap. *Pravda* wrote that while a minority of the Czechoslovak CP Presidium members "led by Dubcek" had adopted "frankly right-wing opportunist attitudes," the majority had spoken of the need for a resolute campaign against "reactionary anti-Socialist forces. . . . The right-wing revisionist elements in the leadership of the Central Committee," continued *Pravda*, "were in fact playing for time while conniving at counter-revolution. As a result of their perfidious, treacherous activities," *Pravda* declared, "a real threat arose to Czechoslovakia's Socialist achievements."

For "Czechoslovakia's achievements" one should perhaps read here "the Soviet Union's." But what were the "perfidious activities" which Moscow saw as a threat? Of course, it may have been that the Kremlin saw Dubček as a prisoner of his own extremists, unable to control events, whatever the good intentions he proclaimed. But in that case the Soviet leaders would not have committed the incredible folly of treating Dubcek brutally, as a common criminal, allowing physical assault to be committed against him and having him brought to Moscow in handcuffs. Instead, they would have treated him as the potential leader of a new régime against the extremists.

Looking at the events of 1968 in the longer perspective it seems there were three "perfidies" committed by Dubcek and his colleagues which were basic and unforgivable and which, apart from the military-strategic considerations, perhaps weighed most in the decision to invade. First, Dubcek showed he meant what he said when, on February 22nd, 1968, the Twentieth Anniversary of the Communist take-over of the country, he summed up his policies in his promise of "the widest possible democratization of the entire socio-political system." Every Communist leader in power, from Stalin onwards, had made similar noises. Stalin, indeed, had given the Soviet Union "the most democratic Constitution in the world." No Soviet leadership had ever intended that the rights enshrined in it, least of all freedom of speech, should be enjoyed by the people. Dubcek knew that the press, radio and television—the information media he intended to liberate—were demanding and would continue to insist on no more than the rights embodied in Czechoslovakia's Soviet-modelled Constitution. This alone would and did result in a revolution endangering by its example the other countries of the Soviet bloc, all of which had similar, unimplemented Soviet-model Constitutions. What made Dubcek's folly, if not perfidy, worse in Soviet eyes was that he resolutely refused to use unconstitutional methods even against his political opponents: he could easily have removed as early as the spring of 1968 the adherents of Novotny, the so-called hard-liners, from the influential party and state posts they were still occupying, by using their own methods against them, or even simply by demanding their resignations. Public opinion was against him for failing to do so. In the Soviet view Dubcek's refusal to use the methods of the police state was at best weakness, at worst an ostentatious reflection on the Kremlin's political habits. What was perhaps worse, Dubcek openly pointed out that the failure of the economy was due to "the deformations in the political system," explaining that the latter meant the vested interests of the "new class" of Party functionary (see p. *132*). This point, strongly argued under Novotny by the author of the economic reforms, Professor Ota Sik, was particularly dangerous to the power monopolies in the Kremlin and the rest of the Soviet bloc. For the main theoretical justification for authoritarianism in Communist countries, and one always adduced by apologists of the system, is that it produces economic results. Another myth destroyed by Dubcek and his associates is a lynch-pin of socialist philosophies and political strategies even outside the Communist systems: namely, that the various classes of society are in constant opposition to each other and should be constantly provoked against each other in the interests of party political advantage. Dubcek's Action Programme "resolutely condemns" attempts to do so (p. *135*).

So while Dubcek did not want the basic régime changed in Czechoslovakia, he wanted to see the implementation of human rights and freedoms which were embodied in the Constitution. But the Communist Party had to prove it could provide and safeguard those freedoms. According to the Action Programme (p. *144*), and this was the second basic threat the Russians saw to the survival of their own and other oligarchic parties, the Party could not give this proof as long as its leading role was "conceived as a monopolistic concentration of power." This, of course, is precisely how Lenin conceived the Party and how the Soviet Communist Party still operates today. Indeed, of the ruling Communist Parties in Europe at the present time only the Yugoslav and the Czechoslovak (and Slovak) do not, or at least in 1968 did not, see their role in that way. So, Moscow's view of a Communist Party is diametrically opposed to Dubcek's. The conservative Soviet attitude is still coloured by the old-fashioned Lenin concept of the Party as a conspiratorial band consisting of a professional élite. Hence the danger from an open society, with freedom of expression, where the Party's "secrets" can be discussed in public. Moscow betrayed its fears most openly on the day after the invasion: in its editorial article entitled "The Defence of Socialism is a Supreme International Duty" *Pravda* of August 22nd, 1968, maintained that "certain leaders of the Czechoslovak CP Central Committee" instead of "resolutely stopping the attempts to destroy the Party" had continued "transforming the Czechoslovak CP into an amorphous organization incapable of action, *a sort of debating society*" (my italics). Moscow had used the identical phrase to describe the degeneration of a Party during its justification of the Soviet invasion of Hungary in 1956. Novotny had been unable any longer to invest a Soviet-modelled Party with credibility nor sell it as a continuing necessity to the people of Czechoslovakia. That was the main reason why the Russians abandoned him, as they had the Hungarian Rakosi. After the invasion the Russians vainly attempted, through the die-hard ex-Party *apparatchik* Antonin Kapek and others to restore this concept of the élite Party with its *esprit de corps* and its close similarity to the Nazi Party.

The third unforgivable sin committed by the Dubcek leadership and embodied in the Czechoslovak blueprint for freedom is one to which little attention has been paid hitherto, but which was regarded by Moscow as the gravest and probably tilted the balance in favour of those in the Soviet Politburo who counselled invasion. And yet it was one which Dubcek and his fellow-reformers could not have avoided without abandoning the very essence of their grand design for "socialism with a human face." Dubcek's constantly reiterated promise that the Party would relinquish its main instrument of power, the security apparatus, and turn it into a constitutional organ for the defence of the country instead of only of the Party, must have filled the Russians with far more alarm than any other "threat." The alarm was intensified by the official promises given to the people of Czechoslovakia that the secret police officials guilty of what is always euphemistically referred to in Communist countries as "violations of Socialist legality" would be brought to account and given the fair trial they had denied others. Such trials and investigations which, under the conditions of freedom from censorship prevailing in Czechoslovakia, would have been carried out in public, would have revealed a great deal about the Soviet involvement in the secret police operations of an ostensibly sovereign country.

After the last World War Moscow had imposed Communism on the countries of East and Central Europe in two overlapping stages: first, through the physical presence of the Soviet armed forces and, secondly, through the creation in those countries of a secret police apparatus and maintenance of control over it. In a totalitarian state the principal lever of power, often dominating the Party, is the secret police apparatus. This was why Moscow insisted that the Communists who participated in all the post-war coalition governments in East Europe demanded and obtained the Ministries of the Interior as a first step in creating and establishing control of the security apparatus. This in turn eventually gave the Russians control over every Ministry and the whole civil service in the satellite country, since all appointments were subject to the over-riding approval of the secret police. There is a clear reference to this omnipotence of the secret police in the Action Programme (p. *165*): after declaring that the Party's policy is to be based on the principle that no undue concentration of power in the State must be allowed, the docu-ment notes: "This principle is infringed mainly by undue concentration of duties in the existing Ministry of the Interior" (i.e., the one inherited from the Novotny régime). The Ministries of the Interior in the countries of East Europe were, and some of them still are, staffed by personnel appointed more or less directly on Moscow's orders. Many of them were men and women of dual nationality, being Soviet citizens as well as nationals of their own countries or they assumed local nationality if they did not already hold it. Czechoslovakia was no exception to this Moscow control of the security apparatus, though it took a little longer to establish it there during the country's brief spell under a non-Com-munist government from 1944 to 1948. Only Yugoslavia, under Marshal Tito, was able to withstand the wholesale penetration of its secret police by the Soviet NKVD (as the Soviet police chief Beriya's apparatus was then known). Tito's resistance to the Soviet attempts to infiltrate his security apparatus was one of the principal issues of his quarrel and break with the Moscow-controlled Cominform.

Against this all-important background it is easy to imagine the con-sternation with which the leaders in the Kremlin regarded the references made by Dubcek and in the Action Programme to the inadmissibility of "police methods" and the need to take the machinery of State out of the hands of State Security. Even more alarming to Moscow was the defiant yet confident assertion in the reply to the Warsaw letter that the Czecho-slovak CP was trying to prove that it was "capable of a different political leadership and management than by means of the condemned bureau-cratic-police methods" (p. *327*).

If the Action Programme is the central document of this collection, then the chapter headed "For the development of socialist democracy" and especially the section entitled "Guarantees against highhandedness" (p. *164*) must have been seen in Moscow as the key to the document and to the reforms, since it envisages the end of the police state. In May, 1968, a drastic purge of the secret police had been carried out by the new leaders in Prague. In this Moscow undoubtedly lost many of its placemen. It was probably the reason why Moscow in its various demands to Prague had kept insisting that it would agree to the restoration of the position "as it was before May," when beside this loss of its own agents in the security apparatus the dismissal from the top Party ranks of several leading conservatives had been small beer. There was little likelihood of Moscow taking over the secret police again and, even if Moscow did succeed, that body was never likely to exercise the same influence again. Did not the Action Programme state unequivocally: "The irreparable losses suffered at that time (of suppression of democratic rights) . . . will remain for ever a warning against similar methods" (p. *129*)? And: "The Party declares clearly that this apparatus (the Security service) should not be directed and used to solve internal political questions" (p. *166*).

But Moscow's concern was not only over the possibility of losing control, however indirect, of the Czechoslovak security apparatus and so of the machinery of State. Dubcek kept promising a thorough cleansing of the Augean stables. The Party, he said at the May Plenum, had to dissociate itself from the faults of the past. Among these faults were the violations of human rights committed by the security organs. Direct responsibility for these "deformations" rested with "specific culprits of the Security Force, as well as in judicial, State and Party bodies" (p. *243*). While the security apparatus would be strengthened "in the spirit of the Action Programme"—that is, given responsibilities in its proper sphere of securing the safety of the State against outside enemies—"a consistent reconstruction of the security organs and their purging of all responsible for the aberrations" of the past was necessary to make them effective in the proper way (p. *248*). Moscow must have realized that any investigations of the "specific culprits" who were "responsible for the aberrations" would be bound to produce incriminating evidence against the Soviet secret police operations in Czechoslovakia. The "culprits" would, in self-defence, involve the Russians. Furthermore, the investigations might make public vital information about the Soviet operations against other Soviet bloc countries. There have been persistent reports that, under the Novotny régime, the Soviet secret police had used Prague as a forward base for their operations in the other countries of the bloc. The ferocious Soviet reaction to the investigations in the spring of the death in mysterious circumstances of the Foreign Minister Jan Masaryk in 1948 and to the article on June 13th in the Czech writer's paper *Literarni Listy* commemorating the Soviet abduction and execution of the Hungarian leader Imre Nagy, had already betrayed Moscow's extreme sensitivity in this area of examination of the past. And in June, for example, other papers, in Bratislava first and then in Prague, published an interview with the infamous former head of the Interrogation Department of the Ministries of Security and the Interior in the 'fifties, Bohumil Doubek, in which he recalled the Ministers ordering him to submit interrogation material to "the Soviet experts" before bringing them to the Ministers themselves. Clearly, as far as Moscow was concerned, and in view of the paramount position occupied by the secret police apparatus (now known as the KGB) in Russia, a vital Soviet interest was being threatened by these revelations and the prospect of more to come. It was a factor not to be lightly dismissed by those in the Soviet Politburo who might have been inclined to hesitate over the decision to invade Czechoslovakia.

The Invasion and After

Moscow's objective, then, was to halt these dangerous processes and to restore a leadership in Prague which would control the population through a Soviet-style Communist Party using the proper lever of power —a pervasive and omnipotent secret police, with no nonsense about "democratization of the socio-political system." This did not mean a restoration of the discredited Novotny. But the Kremlin calculated that there were enough men and women throughout Czechoslovakia who would be only too glad to have their jobs, which as good Party members they had held by favour of the Party, restored and secured to them under the Soviet umbrella. The Soviet leaders thought there were certainly enough high Party and Government officials who had lost their jobs or were in imminent danger of doing so and would see nothing unusual in getting them back by the grace of Moscow. So sure were they of these "healthy forces" as they called them that they announced that the armed forces of the Warsaw Five had been summoned by them to "save Socialism" in Czechoslovakia. This was the greatest miscalculation by Moscow. The "healthy forces" never materialized except as a frightened handful of Central Committee members, and could not even be named when Russia was challenged to do so in the United Nations Security Council. Moscow failed to form the puppet government it so desperately needed to give its invasion a cloak of legality. Except for a few traitors, including a deputy Minister of the Interior called Salgovic, even the formerly Soviet-infiltrated security police refused to collaborate with the invaders. Their attitude was illustrated by the action taken by them against Soviet KGB men brought to Prague with the invasion forces to arrest liberals and issued with passes printed in Czech, identifying them as members of the Czech Secret Police. The forgeries were easily detected from their bad Czech; the Czech Secret Police rounded up the KGB men and, handing them over to the Soviet High Command, commented that they must be American spies as they were using obviously forged identity documents.

The Kremlin had been misinformed by its representatives in Prague about the extent of the support for Dubcek's reforms. In particular, the Soviet ambassador Chervonenko had completely failed, it seemed, to realize that the great majority of the Communist Party itself, notwith-standing the vested interests it had at stake, was wholeheartedly and enthusiastically behind Dubcek. Even the workers, who stood to lose by the proposed economic reforms initially, were solidly behind Dubcek, as they had shown in numerous resolutions from the factory floor and through the trade union organizations which gave Dubcek full backing all the time. The remarkable solidarity of the workers behind the Dubcek leadership was most vividly illustrated during the invasion when the emergency 14th Congress delegates numbering 1,200 met secretly from the invaders in the largest factory in Prague, assisted by thousands of the factory workers, not one of whom, as far as can be judged from the success of the Congress, informed the occupying forces.

It was obvious that psychologically Moscow had been simply in-capable of comprehending the significance of Dubcek's inspiring and wholly truthful assessment made in July in a television appearance responding to the Warsaw letter where he had correctly pointed out that "after many years an atmosphere has been created in which everyone can speak his mind without fear." The Soviet Union had never experi-enced such a situation: under Khrushchev people saw signs of it on the horizon. It was just not within the Kremlin's experience and the Soviet leaders were unable to gauge the extent of the popular revolution it represented.

There were, of course, two other important reasons why the Russians failed to establish the puppet government they had planned to set up on the pattern of the Kadar government after the Hungarian Revolution in 1956. The first factor was the heroic behaviour of the 72-year-old President, General Ludvik Svoboda. In Moscow he had insisted on the release and reinstatement of Dubcek and his colleagues, threatening to commit suicide on the spot if the Russians refused. The second factor was the surprisingly long-lasting unity of the Czechoslovak leadership in the face at first of Soviet threats and later of Soviet attrition. Some three weeks after that brutal confrontation in Moscow the popular Chairman of the National Assembly Josef Smrkovsky, addressing a meeting of chemical workers at the Zaluzi chemical works, underlined the importance of that unity like this: "The unity of the leaders today is an arch from which not a single stone must be allowed to fall and which is best symbolized by the personalities and relations of Comrades Svoboda and Dubcek." No little credit, too, must have been due to the intimate knowledge and understanding of the Russian mentality displayed in their dealings with them by both Dubcek and Svoboda—the former as a result of his upbringing and later studies there, and the latter from his service there at the end of the First World War and during the Second World War when he was decorated as Hero of the Soviet Union. It was true the invasion had come as a surprise to Dubcek: but this was not so much a miscalculation of the Soviet mentality as a justified, though in the event mistaken, gamble on which faction in the Soviet Politburo would prevail. In any case, even when faced with overwhelming force, Dubcek seems to have been able to drive a hard bargain with the Russians.

Having failed to replace the Dubcek leadership with a puppet government, partly because no Czech or Slovak politician dared to play the traitor in the face of the people's remarkable resistance to the invasion and its aims and realizing the extent of the popular support for Dubcek, the Russians attempted to discredit him in the eyes of the people by slowly squeezing him to accept increasing restrictions on the programme of reforms. The erosion of the reforms was formally promulgated by the three Moscow Agreements of August 27th, October 4th and October 16th. The Russians presented them as settlements to "normalize" the situation. They were negotiated under duress, with the Czechoslovak leaders on the first occasion being the prisoners of the Russians. In Orwellian terms the Russians indicated that they would accept the "post-January reforms" in Czechoslovakia—except in so far as they presented opportunities for "anti-Socialist forces." They claimed there would be no interference in Czechoslovak internal affairs. On the other hand the October 4th Agreement obliged Czechoslovakia to "intensify the struggle against anti-Socialist forces" and to take the necessary steps to "place all the mass media at the service of Socialism and to strengthen the Party and State authorities with men firmly adhering to positions of Marxism-Leninism and proletarian internationalism." Proletarian Internationalism is the term adopted by Moscow in the 'twenties and the days of the Comintern to indicate unswerving obedience to the U.S.S.R. even at the cost of loyalty to one's own country. It was the very core of Stalin's policy of subservient Communist parties. The Agreement of October 16th imposed the "temporary" stationing of Soviet troops in Czechoslovakia. In May, 1957, a similar agreement was concluded with Hungary for the "temporary" stationing of Soviet forces in that country, and the even earlier December, 1956, treaty with Poland allowed Soviet troops there "temporarily." They are still in both those countries. In several practical details the terms of the Czechoslovak Agreement are harsher than either of the other two. The three Moscow-dictated Agreements with Czechoslovakia marked the end of the post-Stalin assurances of the possibility for Communist countries to choose "different roads to Communism" which were enshrined in so many "Moscow Declarations" and which were a concomitant of the doctrine of "peaceful co-existence" between countries of "different social systems."

Erosion
Moscow's attempts to erode the freedoms won by Czechoslovakia since January began immediately after the return of the Dubcek leadership from their imprisonment by the Kremlin. But, having failed so disastrously in their political objective of overthrowing that leadership, Moscow now trod more circumspectly. Instead of relying on the incompetent ambassador Chervonenko, the Kremlin despatched, on September 6th, one of its most experienced and widely travelled Foreign Ministry officials, First Deputy Foreign Minister Vasili Kuznetsov, to Prague. On the same day the Czechoslovak Party Presidium announced its opposition to "extremes in politics, irresponsible tendencies of any kind, efforts to endanger the post-January policy and the conclusions of the Moscow negotiations, from whatever side." From that time until the end of the

year every major policy decision and step taken by the Dubcek leadership was marked by the same cautious balance and sense of reality. Dubcek had returned from Moscow the uncontested leader of the country as well as of the Party. Although he warned the nation that the facts of the invasion and occupation would have to be faced, he continued to maintain that, in spite of the temporary suspension of some of its goals, the blueprint for freedom would not be abandoned. Most important of all was his pledge, made in a broadcast on September 14th warning against clashes with the occupying forces, that there would be no return to the pre-January conditions, nor a repetition of what had happened in the 'fifties; in other words there would be no return to the secret police terror. About a month later, on October 11th, Dubcek repeated the pledge in a major speech in which he explained why the Czechoslovak leadership had refused to authorize a programme of unjustified arrests and dismissals which "some Communists" (he did not specify in which country) demanded for anti-semitic and other reasons. "Some individuals," said Dubcek, "think this is now the time to move towards excesses similar to those of the 'fifties, that this is a time to return to the deformities of sectarian non-Leninist methods." Communists should understand, continued Dubcek, that "socialist thought in our country is not deformed— *for example, by anti-semitism* . . . " (my italics). In the same speech Dubcek confirmed the refusal of the Czechoslovak leadership to go back to the smothering of free discussion inside the Communist Party: they all had fresh in their memories the period in which anything that challenged the opinions of certain leaders was immediately branded as anti-socialist. That sort of atmosphere stifled thought. They could not tolerate, Dubcek declared, the stagnation of society that ensues, which bred boredom about public affairs, for that would do irreparable harm to Socialism. "And we said so to the Soviet comrades more than once," Dubcek revealed. It was significant that the Soviet *Pravda* in its report of Dubcek's speech published on October 14th conspicuously omitted these two key passages. It was on these and several similar pledges that the information media in Czechoslovakia doubtless relied when they courageously continued to write and discuss in a remarkably open manner internal developments in their country. They had been told they would not be allowed to criticize their Warsaw pact allies who had invaded them and they abided by the prohibition. On the other hand they also kept to their self-imposed pledge: "If we cannot tell all the truth, at least we shall not tell any lies."

[29]

With the passing weeks, however, Dubcek and his apparently lone uncompromising supporter, the National Assembly Chairman Josef Smrkovsky, still seemed to adhere to their principles. But other voices began to be heard in the top Party leadership calling for greater "realism" towards Moscow—the voices of such men as the highly ambitious Slovak First Party Secretary Gustav Husak, his fellow Slovak Sadovsky, even the Premier Cernik, the ex-Social Democrat Erban and the colourless but dangerous former Interior Minister Strougal.

Certain concessions were made to Moscow quite early on, including the dismissal from office of persons whom the Kremlin particularly feared and disliked, some of them for reasons of thinly-veiled anti-semitism. Among them were prominent reformers, including the father of the economic reforms Ota Sik, the Foreign Minister Jiri Hajek who had addressed the United Nations Security Council with the information that the invasion had been carried out without the knowledge of the legal authorities; others were the Chairman of the National Front Dr. Frantisek Kriegel (branded by the Russians as a "Zionist), the Minister of the Interior Josef Pavel, and Zdenek Hejzlar and Jiri Pelikan, Directors respectively of Czechoslovak Radio and Television whose media had played so great a role in the peaceful revolution and an even more courageous part in maintaining the unity and morale of the nation during the invasion. But to balance the removal of the progressives, other reformers were brought into leading positions—for example, the liberal-minded Jan Pelnar took over the important Ministry of the Interior—and some pro-Soviet neo-Stalinists were dismissed. The latter included a former Director of Radio and latterly Chairman of the Central Board for (Tele-)Communications Karel Hoffman who had played the traitor at the beginning of the invasion by vainly attempting to transmit to Moscow and to foreign news agencies the fake call from the "healthy forces" to the Warsaw Five. Another figure suspected of collaboration, Party Secretary Drahomir Kolder, was sent off as economic adviser to the embassy in Sofia. Another suspected collaborator, Party Secretary Alois Indra, reported to have suffered a heart-attack during the August talks in Moscow, returned to Prague from Moscow on September 28th and was retained in the leadership, presumably on Moscow's insistence. His colleague, Vasil Bi'ak, was also retained, having denied, in a statement published on September 18th, that he had had advance knowledge of the invasion and stating that he had refused to join the small group who wanted to remove Dubcek. On the other hand, the traitor and neo-Stalinist editor for ten years of the Party daily *Rude Pravo*, Oldrich Svestka, was dropped from the Party Presidium.

Under the first Moscow agreement the XIVth Party Congress, which had met in secret during the invasion, had to be repudiated and the convocation of the new XIVth Congress postponed. Nevertheless, the Central Committee Plenum convened on August 31st was augmented by delegates who had been elected to the XIVth Congress during the summer, eighty of whom were co-opted to the Central Committee, the majority being progressives. The Plenum elected a Presidium of 21 members, compared with 11 previously and, significantly, 13 of the new Presidium had been elected at the extraordinary XIVth Congress during the invasion. However, when the Central Committee met again in the middle of November a less unwieldy body, an eight-member Executive Committee of the Presidium, was created which appeared to lean towards a "realist" position. It included the 44-year-old Lubomir Strougal whose star had been steadily rising. Strougal had been Minister of the Interior under Novotny from 1961 to 1965, a period when admittedly this Ministry had begun to soften some aspects of its rule by terror. Nevertheless, during his tenure Strougal must have worked very closely with Moscow and, almost certainly, would have taken direct orders from Moscow on many issues. In the post-January period Strougal did not take a "conservative" attitude but appeared to be a neutral but obedient official. He was made Deputy Premier and Chairman of the Economic Council. During the invasion he supported the legal Government and was reported to have been arrested by the invaders, possibly by mistake or as a blind. He was, therefore, an uncompromised but, from the Russian point of view, reliable bureaucrat from the Novotny era whom they knew well from his tenure of the Interior Ministry. At the November Plenum Strougal was given the potentially vital post of Chairman of the Bureau for Czech Party Affairs. This was the only counterpart to the existing Slovak Communist Party which Moscow would permit. Under the proposed federal structure of the country the formation of a Czech Communist Party would be required to provide the necessary "symmetry." But only a Congress of the whole Czechoslovak Communist Party, banned by Moscow, and a constituent Congress of the Czech Communist Party could establish such a body with all its organs. Moscow was well aware that elections to a Congress of any kind, in the prevailing conditions of relative freedom, would result in the overwhelming return of liberal delegates. Whether the Russians would insist on Strougal heading a Czech Party, when it was eventually allowed, was an open question; what was now certain was that Strougal was one of the most influential men in the country, holding, besides his two posts of Executive Committee member and Czech Bureau Chairman, that of a Secretary of the Central Committee. At the November Plenum Strougal made statements which dangerously undermined the position of the Dubcek leadership, criticizing it for adopting even the draft of the Action Programme in April—though it had been made clear that it was to be submitted to the XIVth Party Congress—on the grounds that it was too drastically different from the directives of the XIIIth Congress, held under Novotny, and was without the sanction of a full Congress. Some days after the November Plenum Strougal blamed, in a television interview, the Dubcek leadership for what he called the excesses of the information media. Wittingly or not, Strougal was playing the Soviet game. About a month before the November Plenum a pre-war Party official and former member of the Ministry of Interior under the Communists, Miroslav Jodas, in conjunction with Antonin Kapek, former Party manager of one of Prague's largest engineering combines CKD and a strong neo-Stalinist, and Karel Mestek, Novotny's Agriculture Minister, had organized meetings in various cities, the largest being in the Liben district of Prague, at which attempts were made to discredit the Dubcek leadership, whom they censured in a resolution for "ideological softness, weakness and incompetence." The meeting also demanded much closer control of the press and radio and the dismissal of many of their staff. Between 300 and 600 Communists attended the meeting, though exact numbers were not known. A Lieutenant Korolenko and several other Soviet Army officers were present and spoke at the meeting, thereby violating the Moscow Agreement clause stipulating no interference by the occupation army in the internal affairs of the country. Then, a week before the November Plenum, the pro-Soviet elements staged a meeting under the auspices of the Czecho-slovak-Soviet Friendship Society in honour of the Soviet October Revolution anniversary. At this meeting similar sentiments were expressed, one of the principal speakers being Novotny's Foreign Minister, Vaclav David, a man of notoriously limited intelligence. Only Soviet journalists and cameramen were allowed into the meeting, but as the 3,000 invited guests left the hall they were greeted by the crowds outside with shouts of "collaborator" and "traitor." It was perhaps because of the utter failure of these old-guard Communists to command any significant following and, on the contrary, because they caused such revulsion among the population as to be counter-productive, that Moscow decided to cultivate instead the neutral political figures like Strougal.

One major task of the November Plenum was to produce a programme revising the April Action Programme. In fact, the resolution produced at the end of the Plenum as the revised programme bore signs of countless rewriting and was full of compromise declarations clearly intended to please all sides; it suspended rather than nullified the Action Programme. The resolution closely followed Dubcek's opening address to the Plenum on November 14th. It admitted that "right-wing forces and opportunistic tendencies" had complicated the post-January course, but at the same time matched warnings against these right-wing tendencies with similar ones against sectarianism and dogmatism, that is neo-Stalinism. It recalled that the Party's crisis had been caused by its failure to carry out de-Stalinisation. Significantly, it repeated the promises that the Party would "in no circumstances again permit the violations of Socialist legality or deformations" and, in a reference to the rehabilitations, that it would "continue to make good injustices against Communists or other citizens." It reiterated several times the need to "unite the whole Party upon the positive foundations of the post-January policy," and to develop exchanges of ideas between all groups of society on the one hand and the Party and Government on the other. But it warned too, that the Party must strengthen its leading role and observe "democratic centralism," that is strict Party discipline. Another threatening note in this "revised programme" was the emphasis placed on the need for the press, radio and television to be "instruments for the promotion of the policy of the Party and State," an injunction bearing the clear hallmark of the Kremlin

Soon after the publication of the results of the Plenum, university students throughout the country called for a three-day sit-in strike in support of Dubcek and against the apparent imposition of new restraints. In a ten-point resolution issued on November 18th, they declared that freedom of the press and of assembly were inalienable rights. The Party and State leadership, however, appealed to them to stay off the streets and avoid violence, and the students co-operated. Writers and journalists expressed understanding of the leadership's difficulties, but declared themselves unwilling to accept any watering down of the programme of reforms embodied in the Action Programme.

In the middle of December the Central Committee held another Plenum at which it discussed economic reform and the new federal system which came into effect on January 1st, 1969. During September, groups of economists had, on two occasions, issued carefully reasoned statements supporting Professor Ota Sik, in exile since the invasion first in Yugoslavia then in Switzerland. Sik wanted to return to Prague to attend this Plenum but was given spurious messages originating in Moscow to the effect that disciplinary action would be taken against him if he returned. By the time the faked nature of the message had been discovered the two-day Plenum had ended. Presenting the report on the economy to the Plenum Oldrich Cernik, the Prime Minister, declared the economic situation to be very serious, with the economic "imbalance" worse than the previous year. But, he said, the policy of economic reform would be continued. However, this could not be done in haste. The greatest risks lay, according to Cernik, in the field of foreign trade. Czechoslovakia's markets would remain primarily in the Comecon countries, but "mutually advantageous" trade with non-Communist countries would be developed also. Cernik's statement appeared to confirm the affirmation made by Dubcek to party officials in mid-October that Czechoslovakia would continue to trade with the West. Problems of management would continue to be one of the main spheres of activity of the State, now about to be reorganized along federal lines. This sounded as though the suggestions for decentralizing management proposed in the reforms were being eroded. However, there was no immediate reaction from the trade unions, who had been issuing resolutions demanding that the economic reforms be implemented, nor from other bodies. Much more concern was expressed over the reports that the Plenum would announce dismissals of reformist leaders. The reports had arisen from the absence of Smrkovsky from the top-level meeting of the Czechoslovak leadership with the Russians held in Kiev during the first week of December and the omission of Smrkovsky's name from the Soviet reply in an exchange of messages. During the December session workers at several factories threatened strike action, and the trade union daily *Prace* published a resolution from one factory mentioning the possibility of a general strike to prevent Smrkovsky's dismissal. Other factories published resolutions in the press protesting against the whittling away of the January reforms and against the lack of information on such important events as the Czechoslovak-Soviet talks in Kiev.

Reaction

There were other cases of strong reaction to what the population saw as Moscow's attempts to deprive them of all the fruits of their glorious year. So, while the leadership was compelled to make cautious and statesman-like pronouncements as they strove to restore government after the invasion and to keep the country running, within the limits permitted by Moscow, the people were by no means submissive. By the year's end there was still no collaboration with the occupying forces, except for some isolated groups of Novotnyites who had lost comfortable posts. In spite of the restrictions imposed on the information media by the establishment in early September of an Office for Press and Information and the amendment in the same month of the Press Law of June guaranteeing freedom of expression by a paragraph reintroducing censorship, the press, radio and television continued to comment freely and even to criticize the leadership and its policies when they were regarded as a betrayal of the reforms. For example, the restrictions imposed on foreign travel in mid-November were severely criticized in public and in the press. In the same month a newspaper complained that the leaders were losing touch with the people. As already mentioned economists defended the Sik economic reforms and early in December a distinguished economist pleaded in a scholarly analysis published in the press for the implementation of the economic reforms planned before the invasion. The radio carried similar open discussions, including a suggestion by one writer that the proper course was to carry on "as though nothing had happened in August." Above all, the population complained of the growing secretiveness in the highest circles of the country. Press and radio, under instructions, refrained from polemics with the Warsaw Pact "allies." But on October 14th the workers of the CKD factory protested against Soviet breaches of the Moscow agreement, namely dismissals of Czech and Slovak politicians under pressure from Moscow, attacks on Czechoslovak leaders and the distribution of the news-sheet *Zpravy*, published in Czech in East Germany and distributed in Czechoslovakia by the occupation forces. Complaints against this anti-Czechoslovak publication which had first been distributed by the invasion forces and carried no imprint or address of publishers, and against its companion radio organ, Radio

Vltava, which had broadcast from East Germany since the start of the invasion, grew in the following weeks until in early December the chairman of the governmental committee for press and information, Deputy Premier Petr Colotka, stated on television that he had recommended that the question be taken up through diplomatic channels. Two days later Colotka was relieved of his post on the committee, probably because of Soviet objections to this recommendation and to his generally liberal approach to censorship. But if the people saw that some of the policies of the reform leaders had to be compromised, most still recognised at the year's end that at least Dubcek, Smrkovsky, Svoboda and Cernik had not compromised their reputations. They and other leaders and various committees had made courageous declarations since the invasion which still gave hope for the future. In the first place, they had never accepted the Soviet thesis that a counter-revolution had existed in Czechoslovakia since January: they would never allow Moscow to claim the blood victims it wanted on that score—nor, it seemed, on any other. Perhaps the most important declaration was the one signed by the above-named leaders and Husak and issued on September 10th, which reaffirmed the inviolability of Czechoslovak laws, forbade any return to illegality against the personal security of citizens who did not infringe the laws, promised freedom of artistic creation and scientific research and appealed to all who were abroad to return and use their talents for the good of the country. Four days later Dubcek made the speech pledging there would be no repetition of "what happened in the 'fifties." On September 19th the CP Central Committee announced its determination "to create a complete system of legality and to prevent any infringement of legality by methods of closed-door justice."

On another subject, the leading role of the Party (with which Moscow was so obsessed), a progressive Party Secretary and Presidium member, Josef Spacek, wrote in the party daily *Rude Pravo* that he saw it as a "leadership of society, based on a voluntary and constantly renewed support for party policy by the entire public." The public had seen similar sentiments expressed in the Soviet *Pravda* in the past, but it felt that Spacek really meant what he wrote.

Again, in spite of indications from Moscow that it did not want the rehabilitations of victims of the purge killings of the 'fifties to continue for fear of embarrassing revelations, the Minister of Justice, Dr. Bohuslav Kucera, reaffirmed in the press on October 9th his intention of adhering to the original rehabilitation programme, due to be completed in two or three years.

At the end of October the Czechoslovak Academy of Sciences produced a 12,000-word document analysing the Soviet pamphlet "On Events in Czechoslovakia" and rejecting its justifications for the invasion as based on falsehoods. The Academy document described Moscow's ideas, particularly on "different roads to Socialism," as "dogmatic, primitive and alien to scientific Socialism."

Clearly the information media had not reverted to the pattern of those in the totalitarian societies of the Warsaw Five which had invaded Czechoslovakia. At the beginning of December the director of the Press and Information office, Josef Vohnout, explained to the National Assembly's cultural committee that his office was not a successor to the Central Publications Administration—the notorious censorship organ of the Interior Ministry abolished after the January changes—nor was its main purpose repressive. His organization, he said, was bound to orient information media towards protecting State interests, but it would render "preventive assistance" to the press. A negative side to this relative freedom of the press was the suppression after the invasion of two radical publications of high standard, namely the Slovak writers' weekly, *Kulturny Zivot*, and the university students' weekly in Prague, *Student*. Later the journalists' weekly, the outstanding *Reporter*, was suspended for a month and the Czechoslovak CP Central Committee weekly *Politika*, also of high standard, was suspended indefinitely.

Profit and Loss
And so at the end of 1968, a year which should have seen the proud and joyful celebration of the 50th anniversary of the Czechoslovak Republic but instead saw Czechoslovakia occupied again as it had been under the Nazis thirty years previously, it was possible to assess the gains and losses to each side.

On the profit side for Russia, the Soviet Union had demonstrated, particularly to the other Warsaw Pact countries, that it was prepared to use force in its imperial interests: it had thus brought to a halt the ideological ferment in East Europe. The presence of Soviet troops in Czechoslovakia ensured close control of the country, not only internally but over its relations with the non-Communist world. After a period of settling down, Moscow could intensify its own secret police activities inside the country and in the neighbouring countries, again using Prague as a forward base. The invasion had demonstrated the efficiency of the Warsaw Pact military machine and the unwillingness of the Western powers to act, thus impressing Communist and underdeveloped countries with Soviet might.

On the other hand, the Soviet invasion and, indeed, the occupation up to the end of the year had utterly failed in its principal objective of removing the Dubcek leadership and replacing it with a puppet government. It had succeeded in turning an erstwhile ally—at one time the most dependable in the Soviet bloc—into an inveterate enemy, probably for centuries to come. One of Czechoslovakia's brilliant broadcasters expressed the feeling vividly in a broadcast on the first Sunday of the invasion: "In 1938," he said, "the Nazis were our enemies and they invaded us. Britain and France were faithless allies, but they did not attack us. In 1968 Soviet Russia, our ally, invades us." But it was not only Czechoslovakia that the leaders in the Kremlin had turned against the Soviet Union. The people of the invading partner states had their mistrust and hatred of Russia intensified. Yugoslavia was driven into closer relations with the West and the work of years of rebuilding bridges between Moscow and Belgrade ruined or severely retarded. Albania finally broke, formally, with the Warsaw Pact as a direct result of the invasion. The majority of the world's major Communist parties turned against Moscow in an unprecedented condemnation of the Soviet action. Many of the Soviet-created and controlled Communist international front organizations, including the Secretariat of the most important, the World Federation of Trade Unions (WFTU), condemned the invasion and demanded withdrawal of the occupation troops.

In the non-Communist world the condemnation was virtually universal. At the United Nations General Assembly Debate in October over sixty of the eighty delegates who spoke deplored and condemned the Soviet aggression against Czechoslovakia. Public and government reaction in the developing countries of Africa and elsewhere was outspoken in castigating the Soviet invasion. Several official spokesmen, and not only the Chinese, referred to a "fascist-type" invasion. Perhaps the greatest damage done to the Soviet cause by Mr. Brezhnev and his colleagues was this identification of Soviet Communism with Nazism, as equally vile totalitarianisms. In the press photographs and the television films of the invasion the world had seen this identification made symbolically as children and students in Czechoslovakia boldly chalked the Nazi swastikas on the Soviet, East German, Polish, Hungarian and Bulgarian tanks and vehicles. Another symbol used by the victims of the invasion for the same purpose was to underline the letters *SS* in the Latin letter form of U.S.S.R.

So unfavourable was world reaction to the Soviet Union that it had two important effects, among others on Soviet policies. First, it undoubtedly restrained the rigours of the occupation of Czechoslovakia. Secondly, it compelled Moscow to propound a highly damaging doctrine of intervention to excuse its actions retrospectively. This was the so-called doctrine of the "socialist commonwealth" which stated that the Soviet Union had a right to intervene in any country of that "commonwealth" where it judged that a "threat to Socialism" existed. The doctrine was first advanced by S. Kovalev, head of the Soviet *Pravda's* propaganda department, in an article in that daily on September 26th. It was reaffirmed by Brezhnev at the Polish CP Fifth Congress which he attended in November.

On the Czechoslovak side the immediate losses were, of course, greater than Russia's. Apart from anything else, the material losses directly attributable to the invasion by the 650,000-strong invasion force were considerable. *Rude Pravo* as early as September estimated that the damage to heavy industry in loss of production alone was some £95 million (at the low official rate of exchange). Of course, the cost of invasion to Russia and her partners had also been high, and the reason why the Czechoslovak Government was probably allowed considerable latitude in carrying out its economic policies was that Moscow did not want Czechoslovakia to become an economic liability to Russia or to the Comecon. Next to the loss of life, which was probably not more than about 200 Czechs and Slovaks killed, the most serious damage to the country was the tragic loss of its new-won freedoms and human rights. And yet there were compensations. The country was united as it had not been for almost thirty years or more. For now, unlike the time under the Nazis, and barely even between the wars, the Czechs and the Slovaks were closer to each other in spirit than they had ever been. The federation of the country, longed for by the Slovaks, had, at last, been achieved, in the face of the Russians who wanted to keep the two nations divided and at logger-heads. During the invasion the Russians had put about the totally false rumours that some Slovak provinces wanted to become

"Soviet Republics." Symbolically, the legislation creating the Federal State was enacted to coincide with the 50th anniversary celebrations on October 28th. The Communist Party was genuinely stronger than ever but knew it had to prove itself to the country and said it was prepared to do so. The morale of the labour force, including intellectuals, almost completely broken under the mismanagement of the Novotny régime, was high again and even received a boost from the invasion: people gladly pledged themselves to work an extra "Dubcek shift" to make up the losses. Not unnaturally, this was a wasting asset as people began to feel they were again working largely for the Soviet Union. In spite of this, the spirit of the country revived at the beginning of the year after its twenty-year sleep, emerged from the ordeal of the occupation with added lustre and still burned brightly at the end of the year that marked fifty years of the Republic's existence. It may be cold comfort to the people of Czechoslovakia today but it needs little prophetic skill to foresee that generations to come will look on the year 1968 as one of the most glorious in the long history of the Czech and Slovak peoples. Certainly in the long tally of history the losses suffered by Russia will far outweigh the gain of holding Czechoslovakia captive.

HUGH LUNGHI
December 19th, 1968.

COMMENTARY

COMMENTARY

IN the evolution of the Soviet Bloc there are those events which, for
for one reason or another, stand out more vividly than others.
The dispute between Stalin and Tito, for example, followed in February
of 1948 by the coup in Czechoslovakia, set the stage for five years of
rigid Soviet domination of Eastern Europe. Similarly, Stalin's death in
1953, followed by the adoption of the so-called "New Course" and
Khrushchev's speech to the XXth Party Congress ushered in a period
of transition which, although temporarily halted by Soviet intervention
in Hungary, has continued up to the present time.

Although separated in time, these and other events such as the split
between Moscow and Peking, the ouster of Albania from the bloc, and
now, Soviet intervention in Czechoslovakia, are not unrelated. Taken
together, they attest to an ongoing, if somewhat disjointed and not
always predictable, process of change and accommodation.

It is in the context of this process that the documents presented here
must be read. For it is this process, and not the struggle between freedom
and slavery, or the contest between nationalism and internationalism,
which thus far has dominated the evolution of the bloc.

The Stalinist Era

From the time the Red Army first arrived in Eastern Europe until Stalin's
death in March, 1953, the process appears to have worked rather smoothly.
In a system organized around the twin principles of Soviet primacy and
the universal applicability of Soviet experience, there was never really
any question as to who was responsible for initiating change. Nor, for
that matter, was there ever any doubt as to where the obligation for
accommodation lay. Decisions made in Moscow were by and large
simply implemented throughout Eastern Europe.

That the process worked so smoothly can be attributed to a number of
factors. There was, in the first instance, the visible presence of the Red
Army in Eastern Europe. In addition, there was the fact that those

responsible for implementing the policies laid down by Moscow had been handpicked, for the most part, by Stalin. Lacking any substantial basis of popular support, they were hardly in a position to emulate the independent posture of Tito. Then there was, of course, Stalin himself. As Lenin's successor, he had a legitimacy second to none. Moreover, there was the "Cold War," with its attendant rigid division of the world into opposing camps. Finally, there was the fact that the system, although favouring the Soviet Union, did not work to the total disadvantage of the other members. This is neither the time nor the place to undertake an accounting of the benefits which accrued to the countries of Eastern Europe during the Stalinist era. Suffice it to say that the material advantages of membership in the bloc were not entirely one-sided.

The Transitional Phase
With the death of Stalin in 1953, the process of change and accommodation began to show signs of breaking down. Although the Red Army was still in Eastern Europe, the death of the Soviet dictator confronted his successors with the difficult choice of either continuing the policies of the past or, barring that, of working out a different sort of arrangement for holding the bloc together. That they opted for the latter is hardly surprising. Five years of rigid Soviet domination, coupled with Stalin's insistence on slavish emulation of Soviet economic and political experience, had produced mounting political unrest and growing economic stagnation throughout most of Eastern Europe—a situation which, it should be noted, was not only recognized by Stalin the year before he died, but which was vividly confirmed by the uprising that occurred in East Germany during 1953.

The necessity for developing a new arrangement was, in part at least, also a function of the situation that obtained within the Soviet Union following Stalin's death. In the ensuing struggle for power, elements wedded to the policies of the former dictator were defeated by those whose commitment to economic reform and, in a more limited sense, political liberalization, appears to have extended not only to the Soviet Union but to Eastern Europe as well. For the victors in this struggle the prospect of working through individuals whose loyalty to Stalin was exceeded only by their close identification with his policies could not have been very appealing.

In addition, there was the problem of China. As long as Stalin was alive, his personal stature ensured that the process of change and accommodation which characterized the relationships between the Soviet Union and the countries of Eastern Europe would also operate, if in a less effective fashion, in the dealings between Moscow and Peking. The men who followed Stalin to power had no such guarantee. As men of lesser stature, they would, moreover, have to deal with a China which in 1954-55 was considerably more capable of independent action than had been the case in 1949. Confronted with the prospect of being responsible for behaviour over which they would be able to exercise only limited control, they undoubtedly found much to be said for a modified process of change and accommodation.

Finally, there was the international situation, or, to be more precise, the "Cold War." For Stalin, the deterioration in East-West relations which occurred after 1947 served to justify the imposition of rigid controls both at home and throughout the bloc. His successors, however, were primarily concerned with consolidating their power as well as with introducing political and economic reforms. It is little wonder, therefore, that in the years immediately after Stalin's death the Soviet Union sought to effect a gradual reduction in the level of international tensions. It is even less surprising that, having once decided to modify its position of implacable hostility towards the West, the leadership of the Soviet Union would, in time, also find it necessary to modify the process of change and accommodation which had controlled the evolution of the bloc during its formative years.

Towards a New Order

Although the impact of these factors was immediately apparent in terms of Soviet behaviour toward the rest of the bloc, their impact upon the process of change and accommodation was neither as direct nor as obvious. Thus, for example, in the three years following the death of Stalin, we find the Soviet Union moving to correct many of the problems associated with the previous era. Among the steps taken in this connection were: an end of one-man rule in Hungary, which resulted in a loss of power for the pro-Stalinist elements headed by Rakosi; sale of the joint stock companies to the governments of Eastern Europe; dissolution of the Cominform; an attempted reconciliation with Tito; the promise of further economic credits for China coupled with an agreement to abolish the Sino-Soviet joint stock companies and to return both Port Arthur and Darien to Chinese control; institution of the Warsaw Treaty Organization; and, in February 1956, the denigration of Stalin in a speech delivered by Khrushchev before the delegates assembled for the XXth Congress of the Communist Party of the Soviet Union (CPSU). In reviewing these and other developments of the period it is important to recognize that the initiative for change came, in each instance, from the Soviet Union. With the notable exceptions of Moscow's fleeting courtship with Tito and the concessions made to China, accommodation appears to have remained the exclusive obligation of the other members of the bloc.

More important than the specific measures taken during this period, however, was the move, again initiated by the Soviet Union, to develop an alternative basis for the conduct of intra-bloc relations. Initially, at least, the movement took the form of vague pronouncements concerning the creation of a "socialist commonwealth," and assurances to the governments and people of Eastern Europe that the new order did not constitute a return to Stalinism. Capping this effort was the publication in October 1956 of the "Principles of Development and Further Strengthening of Friendship and Co-operation Between the Soviet Union and Other Socialist States." Following as it did the intervention in Hungary, this document called for the building of relations among the members of the bloc "on a basis of full equality, respect for each other's territorial integrity, independence and sovereignty, and non-interference in each other's internal affairs." Taking note of past abuses, it went on to express regret over the necessity of having had to intervene in Hungary, and pledged a willingness on the part of the Soviet Union to "discuss with the other socialist countries measures to ensure the further development and strengthening of economic contacts between socialist countries with a view to eliminating any possibility whatever of violation of the principle of national sovereignty, mutual benefit and equality in economic relations." Finally, the Declaration offered to discuss with the other members of the bloc the status of Soviet advisers and Soviet military units stationed in Eastern Europe.

Needless to say, in the years which have elapsed since the publication of this Declaration the gulf separating promise and performance has remained substantial indeed. Yet the fact remains that after 1956 the process of change and accommodation did undergo a gradual modification. In part at least, the modification appears to have been intentional—that is to say, it reflected a conscious decision on the part of the Soviets to rely on institutional integration and ideological supremacy as the primary instruments for holding the bloc together. Whereas Stalin relied principally on the force of his personality and the force of the Red Army, and whereas he insisted on keeping the members of the block divided through a system of bilateral arrangements, Khrushchev and the men who succeeded him have consistently stressed the benefits of integration and, to that end, have encouraged greater participation in various multilateral arrangements within the overall structure of the Council of Economic Mutual Assistance. In so doing, of course, they have had to face the prospect of institutionalized opposition grounded, as it were, in the legitimate pursuit of "many roads to socialism."

To much greater extent, however, modification of the process of change and accommodation can be characterized as unintentional. To be sure, in the period after 1956, the Soviet Union demonstrated an increasing willingness to tolerate national diversity. Political as well as economic deviation from the Soviet model was, or at least seemed to be, viewed by Moscow as an essential prerequisite for the maintenance of the bloc as a functioning system. What Moscow did not seem to recognize, initially at least, was that change initiated from within has a way of getting out of hand; particularly where permissible limits of diversity are ill-defined and external constraints are susceptible to evasion by one or more of the members.

Prior to 1961, and the open break with China, the gradual nature of the changes taking place throughout Eastern Europe—and, for that matter, within the Soviet Union itself—seemed to have kept pace with a gradual reapportionment of the responsibility for accommodation. In other words, change initiated by individual members of the bloc did not pose a threat to the integrity of the system. As a result, the Soviet Union, for its part, appears to have been willing to bear a greater part of the obligation for accommodation.

Crisis in the Bloc
After 1961, however, the precarious balance that had characterized previous efforts to modify the process of change and accommodation began to deteriorate. On the one side, there developed mounting pressures for internal reform. Although such pressures were neither universal nor uniform in their intensity, they nevertheless manifested themselves

against a background of worsening relations between Moscow and Peking. On the other side, there developed added opportunities for initiating change—opportunities which appear to have been, at least in part, related to the effort of the Soviet Union to enlist support of the other members of the bloc in its ongoing struggle with the Chinese.

The convergence of necessity and opportunity seems to have placed the Soviet Union in a position where the initiation of change increasingly favoured the other members of the bloc, while the obligation for accommodation became more and more a responsibility of the U.S.S.R. Confronted with this situation, Moscow nevertheless continued to temporize, except, of course, in the case of Albania where the challenge to Soviet authority—assuming as it did a pro-Chinese orientation—was so obvious that it could not be ignored. In the case of Rumania, however, the U.S.S.R. clearly adopted a wait-and-see policy, apparently on the assumption that the Rumanian Communist Party not only had an interest in making sure that the internal reforms did not get out of hand, but more importantly, that the Party was strong enough to deal with any and all internal challenges to its authority.

Then, in January of 1968, the situation in Czechoslovakia began to change. The fall of Novotny, followed by the adoption of the Action Programme by the Central Committee of the Czechoslovakian Communist Party (CCP) on April 5th, presented the Soviet Union with a situation that was both unique and—from the point of view of the bloc—potentially very dangerous. The uniqueness of the Czech situation lay in a number of factors. First, there were the contemplated reforms, the extent of which, as can be seen in the documents presented here, went far beyond anything previously attempted in the bloc. Secondly, and probably even more disquieting, was the anti-Soviet character of the popular response to the promise of reform. Thirdly, whereas the Rumanian Communist Party had consistently demonstrated an ability to regulate both the character and extensiveness of its reform programme, the CCP, and more particularly Alexander Dubček, projected a much less reassuring image. With its members divided between Czechs and Slovaks on the one hand, and pro- and anti-Novotny elements on the other, the Party appeared to be experiencing considerable internal dissension. Its image certainly was not helped either by Dubček's apparent inability to eliminate all supporters of Novotny from positions of authority or by the continued expression of anti-Soviet sentiment in the face of official pleas for moderation. Fourthly, there was the fact that Czechoslovakia does share a common border with West Germany and, as such, has traditionally occupied a position of special importance in the eyes of the Soviet Union.

For the Soviet Union as well as for other members of the bloc, the situation as it developed in Czechoslovakia after January must have appeared doubly dangerous. At worst, there was the distinct possibility that the reforms would get out of hand and that, in time, this would lead to pressures for withdrawal from the bloc. Should that happen, disintegration of the system would be just a matter of time. At best, there was the equally distressing possibility that, given Czechoslovakia's economic potential, the reforms could be successfully carried out without jeopardizing the position of the Party. Should that happen, the Soviet Union would then be faced with the equally unpleasant choice of acknowledging the legitimacy of not only the economic but the political reforms as well. The implications of such a choice both for the bloc as a whole and for the internal political situation in each of the member countries—particularly the German Democratic Republic—are so obvious as to preclude further elaboration.

Crisis in Czechoslovakia

Considered in this context, the military intervention initiated on August 20th is not surprising. What is surprising is that it did not occur sooner.

Although no one can say with certainty why the Soviets waited eight months to intervene, the delay would seem at least in part to reflect the degree to which the process of change and accommodation has actually been modified in the years since Stalin's death.

In reconstructing the events which preceded the intervention, one finds, for example, that the removal of Novotny did not evoke any significant reaction on the part of either the Soviet Union or the other members of the bloc. In fact, considering the conditions in Czechoslovakia at the time of his ouster, it is quite probable that his removal met with the full approval of the Soviet leadership. Whether Moscow actually gave prior consent is a matter of some speculation. Nevertheless, the change in leadership was carried out in the absence of any public opposition from the Soviet Union. However, in the months following the January plenum of the Central Committee of the CCP, the public reaction of the Soviet Union to developments in Czechoslovakia became increasingly hostile. At first the Soviets seem to have reconciled themselves to the necessity for, and the legitimacy of, the reforms set forth in the Action Programme adopted by the CCP in April. Judging from the statements in *Pravda* and *Isvestia* during the period immediately preceding and following adoption of the Programme, Moscow's principal concern seems to have been less with the reforms than with the ability of the CCP to maintain effective control over the situation. Thus we find, for example, the appearance of articles supporting the right of the CCP to initiate change which also contain warnings about the danger of counter-revolutionary activities and an insistence upon the primacy of the CCP as the vanguard of the working class within Czechoslovakia. Between April and mid-July, mounting Soviet concern over the course of events in Czechoslovakia appears to have been characterized by a continued willingness to tolerate reform and by an increasing uneasiness over the danger of a counter-revolution led by so-called "anti-socialist" elements. Throughout this period, however, the Soviet press continued to make a clear distinction between the CCP and forces in the country who were hostile to socialism. Accordingly, in reporting publication of the statement "2000 Words to Workers, Peasants, Employees, Scientists, People in the Arts, to All Citizens" in the Czech press, *Pravda*, on July 11, noted that the statement "does not conceal its sympathies for the capitalist system." This same article went on to comment, however, that "healthy forces in the party and in the country view this document as an overt attack on the socialist system, on the CCP's guiding role and on Czechoslovakia's friendship with the Soviet Union and other socialist countries."

The practice of distinguishing between the "anti-socialist" elements in Czech society and the CCP was, however, gradually abandoned by the Soviets in the weeks that followed. In a series of attacks directed first against "some Czech leaders" and then against the Central Committee of the CCP, Moscow went to great pains to point out that the U.S.S.R. felt conditions in Czechoslovakia were getting out of hand and that, unless corrected, they would constitute a threat not only to the CCP but to the rest of the bloc as well.

From the middle of July until the intervention on August 20th, articles in the Soviet press alternately emphasized the need for corrective action and the danger of "imperialist intervention." Although the attacks abated somewhat following the conferences at Cierna and Bratislava, they resumed with an even greater intensity shortly thereafter.

What emerges from this brief review is the fact that it was apparently not the initiation of change by the CCP which prompted the military intervention on August 20th, but rather the inability of the CCP to convince the Soviet Union that the changes being initiated did not constitute either a threat to the survival of Communism in Czechoslovakia, or a danger to the rest of the bloc. In retrospect, Moscow appears to have been willing to accommodate itself both to the fall of Novotny and to the prospect of internal reform. What it could not accommodate, however, was the initiation of change by elements within Czechoslovakia whose aims included the termination of Communist rule in that country. Initially, at least, the Soviet Union apparently thought that the CCP could handle the situation. Thus, it sought to emphasize the danger without indicting the CCP. When it became apparent that Dubček and his supporters were either unable or unwilling to move decisively against these elements, Moscow decided to drop this polite distinction and launched instead a series of direct attacks against the CCP. Even so, care was taken to accuse the Czechs of nothing more than a failure to understand the gravity of the developing situation. In return for its moderation the Soviet Union received assurances from Prague that it did not consider the danger of counter-revolution to be very real. These assurances, coupled as they were by publication of the so-called "Statement of 2000 Words" and General V. Prchlik's subsequent comments concerning the ineffectiveness of the Warsaw Treaty Organization, probably convinced the Soviets of the need for more strenuous measures. Although the agreements reached at Cierna and Bratislava have never been fully revealed, it would seem safe to conclude from what is known that the purpose of these meetings was to impress upon the Czechs the importance of curbing what the Soviets and other members of the bloc undoubtedly viewed as a very dangerous situation. That they failed to accomplish this purpose is attested to by the subsequent intervention which began on August 20th.

Conclusion

The purpose of this analysis has been twofold. On the one hand, I have sought here to provide a perspective for viewing recent developments in Czechoslovakia. To that end I have tried to emphasize the ongoing process of change and accommodation which has characterized the evolution of the Soviet Bloc. Caught up, as it were, in the press of recent events, it is easy to lose sight of the fact that the bloc has come a long way since the Stalinist era. No longer does the initiative for change reside solely with the Soviet Union and no longer can the obligation for accommodation be said to lie entirely with the other members of the bloc. The years that have elapsed since Stalin's death have witnessed a gradual sharing of the power which once resided almost exclusively in the Centre. As a consequence, responsibility for initiating change, particularly after 1961, has become increasingly more of a shared responsibility. In the process, so has the obligation for accommodation.

This is not to suggest that the bloc is today a system composed of members who are equal in all respects. The Soviet Union, if only by virtue of its size and power, remains pre-eminent. Nor is it to suggest that there are no limits to the modification of the process of change and accommodation. The intervention in Czechoslovakia, like the earlier intervention in Budapest, indicates that limits do exist, even if vaguely defined, and that these limits are transcended at the point where the initiation of change is likely to require that the Soviet Union accommodate itself to the dissolution of the bloc.

Herein, or so it seems, also lies the real significance of the Czech experience. The intervention, coming as it did after eight months of attempts by the Soviet Union and other members of the bloc to pressure the CCP into action, was probably occasioned less by fear of reform than by a genuine concern that in the absence of a strong Communist Party, responsibility for initiating change within Czechoslovakia would gradually fall to those identified as "anti-socialist" elements, and that, as a consequence, the CCP would eventually find itself in the position of having to accommodate itself to its own extinction. For the Soviet Union and other members of the bloc, the intervening months between January and August witnessed in Czechoslovakia the evolution of a process of change and accommodation not unlike that which had been operative throughout the entire bloc in the period since Stalin's death. When viewed in this context the intervention thus appears to have had a dual function. Not only did it serve to re-establish the permissible limits of diversity for the bloc as a whole, but within Czechoslovakia itself it sought to ensure that in the future change would be initiated by the CCP. Whereas the obligation for accommodation would continue to reside with rest of Czech society.

The second, and related, purpose of this analysis has been to set the documents that follow in perspective. Read against the background of the developing crisis within the bloc and within Czechoslovakia itself, the documents serve to illuminate the full extent of the modifications wrought in the process of change and accommodation throughout the bloc. More importantly, they attest to an initial modification of this same process within Czechoslovakia. In the case of the former, military intervention in Hungary merely halted for a time the modification. Whether the same will be true within Czechoslovakia is something which the reader must decide for himself. These documents will provide a basis for his decision.

I

DUBČEK'S SPEECH
APRIL 1, 1968

THIS document, like those that follow, is probably best understood as an exercise in simultaneous communication with several different audiences. There is, in the first instance, the internal audience; an audience composed of the "masses" (Czechs, Slovaks, workers, peasants, intellectuals, etc.), the Czechoslovak Communist Party (CCP), and the Czech Government. In addition, there is the external audience. Here it is useful to distinguish between the Soviet Union, members of the bloc and other "fraternal parties," on the one hand, and the non-Communist world on the other.

Reading and, more importantly, interpreting a document of this type presents a number of problems which, for the most part, are inherent in any effort to communicate: they involve the meaning of words, the constraints of the media, the intentions of the speaker and the values of the audience. To try to resolve these problems in the limited space available here would amount to an exerise in futility. Nevertheless, in order to better understand what follows, they should be identified.

Let us recognize at the outset that words are value-laden symbols. As such, they may have one meaning for a Marxist, let us say, and a completely different meaning for one who is wedded to liberal democracy. Traditionally, the Communists have exploited this feature in instances where. communication among the "initiated" has been involved. Not only does the use of what we would regard as jargon facilitate communication but it offers the added advantage of privacy—a necessary factor when sensitive issues are aired in a public forum. For men like Dubček it is difficult and, in this case at least, probably unnecessary to abandon the practices of a lifetime. He is communicating with those who understand only too well the numerous references to "some comrades" or to "anti-socialist elements."

In a related vein, let us also acknowledge the fact that here, as anywhere else, "something is lost in the translation." Although reproduced in its entirety, the speech was obviously not delivered in English. The "cost" of translation is probably not very high, however, if only because of the fact that this speech, like the other documents, originated with the Czechs themselves. Presumably, it reflects careful scrutiny by the powers that be.

A more serious problem is that which attaches to the limitations or constraints of the media; in this case, an official speech intended for public consumption. As a formal statement of intent, the speech was undoubtedly made with the understanding that it would receive careful scrutiny by all concerned, including, it might be added, the Soviet Union. That knowledge, together with the realization that, once made, a public statement is difficult to repudiate, almost certainly accounts for the moderate tone of the speech and the conciliatory nature of references made to the past. To expect otherwise would be asking for the impossible.

Then, of course, there are the problems associated with the audience or, to the extent that more than one audience is involved, with the necessity for simultaneous communication with divergent groups whose interests, attitudes, and expectations do not always converge. For the speaker, the problem is essentially one of balancing the need to communicate with the need to conciliate. Thus, we find criticisms of the past coupled with praise for accomplishments of the present; the promise of democracy coupled with the insistence that it be "socialist democracy"; the awareness of alienation coupled with commitments to humanism; assertions of independence and sovereignty coupled with the pledge of greater support for the cause of "socialist unity." Whether Dubček succeeds in carrying off his "balancing act" is a matter of opinion. For the reader, however, the attempt makes it difficult to establish with certainty when he is speaking to the internal audience and when he is not.

Finally, there is the problem of objectivity: the speaker's, the reader's, and my own. For myself, the notion of total objectivity, like that of total rationality, is nonsense. We all have our value preferences and I certainly am no exception. The most I can do is make explicit that which is implicit in this and succeeding commentaries. To that end let me say that I carry no brief either for the "captive nations" school or for the "convergence" theorists. To assume, as in the case of the former, that Communist political systems are founded on "error," presided over by cynical opportunists who, in a somewhat detached fashion, manipulate entire populations for their own selfish ends and therefore cannot endure, is to ignore the history of the last fifty years. For those who wish to read this speech as the death knell of Communist rule in Czechoslovakia, I would recommend they reflect upon the source and the nature of the proposed reforms. I would offer the same advice to those who might interpret the speech as another instalment in an inevitable process of convergence. In particular, I would urge that they give thoughtful consideration to the references made to ideology, the role of the Party, and the nature of the political system.

For myself, I prefer to see this speech and the documents that follow as a sign of maturity on the part of a developing political system; a system which up to now at least has demonstrated not only a significant capacity for making mistakes but, and more to the point, an equally significant capacity for being able to live with its mistakes. This is not to suggest that the system lacks either the ability to correct its mistakes or the capacity to initiate change. It is to suggest—and here I part company with the "convergence" theorists—that the initiation of change, in Czechoslovakia as in other Communist political systems, has been promoted not by pressures from below, although, such pressures have, and still do operate, but *primarily* by a desire on the part of those who as the principal beneficiaries of the system believe in and work for its survival. To argue differently is, or so I would contend, to confuse liberalization with liberalism, reform with renunciation and superficial similarities born of parallel development with a merger of identities. It is, in addition, to misread the principal message of this speech. That message, simply stated, is that elements within the CCP had decided the time had come to initiate change; that having made this decision they and nobody else would preside over its implementation; and, that as a result they and the system would emerge stronger, not weaker.

The Internal Audience

In presenting this message to the internal audience, Dubček manages what amounts to a skilful orchestration of variations on a common theme; namely, unity, socialism and humanity. First there is the past or, more specifically, the period prior to the January plenum of the Central Committee of the CCP. In dealing with this period, he fully admits that errors were committed; errors which, among other things, served to divide the Party from within, the Party from the "masses", Czechs from Slovaks, the Party from the Government and the Government from the people. As might be expected, his criticism is both selective and, judging from what is known of the conditions which obtained throughout Czechoslovakia at the time of Novotny's fall, relatively mild. Thus, the audience is pointedly reminded that while mistakes were made, they were accompanied by many accomplishments. It is also reminded of the fact that the mistakes of the past occurred as a result of individuals in the Party and the Government who, for one reason or another, failed to apply socialist principles in their dealings with the "masses." In this way he establishes two points: first, that responsibility for the economic stagnation, political oppression and growing alienation which had developed in Czechoslovakia prior to the January plenum lies whit individuals—particularly Novotny, although he is not singled out by name—and not with the Party; second, that the belief system or ideology which, it should be noted, serves to legitimize the primacy of the CCP, is still relevant to the organization of life in Czechoslovakia. The implication in each instance is quite clear. On the one hand, he has by his acknowledgement of error committed in the past established the need for reform. On the other hand, by linking these errors to individuals who failed to follow the principles of socialism, he has also established the right of the CCP to continue to preside over the initiation of change.

This, of course, is the same message that is conveyed by his assessment of the present, i.e., the period of time between the convening of the January plenum and the delivery of the speech. In dealing with this period he again emphasizes the theme of unity, socialism and humanity. The variation is, however, slightly more optimistic. Thus, he stresses not the widening gulf between the Party and the "masses," but a convergence born of reforms carried out in the best socialist tradition. Despite the gains made, he is careful to point out that progress has been slow. In part, this is attributed to the complexity of the problems; problems which he suggests have been carefully analysed by the CCP as a prelude to the proposal of the Action Programme. In part, the limited progress made during this period is seen as the fault of "some comrades" who are reluctant to accept the onset of a new era.

In analysing events since the January plenum, Dubček once more emphasizes the need for reform. The gains recorded during that period are presented as proof of the willingness and ability of the CCP to guide the future development of Czechoslovakia. Failure to resolve all of the problems confronting the country is not the fault of the CCP. Again it is the individual who is to blame; the individual who as a Party member cannot or will not conduct himself in accordance with the principles of socialism. Yet the Party will not be deterred from pushing ahead. For those who might doubt either its sincerity or ability in this regard there is the Action Programme; the end-product of careful scrutiny by the CCP of the problems confronting Czechoslovakia. There are, moreover, assurances to recalcitrant members who will not conform that the Party understands and speaks for the "masses," and therefore it is acting in the highest traditions of socialism. The implication is, of course, that those who wish a return to the old ways are acting against the "masses" and are therefore in "error."

Once again the message is driven home. Reform is essential. Moreover, the Party recognizes the need for change and is prepared, despite the opposition of a few die-hards, to carry on with its efforts to lead the Czechoslovakian people to a better future under socialism.

Dubček concludes his message to the internal audience by outlining in general terms the provisions of the Action Programme. The reforms contained in the Programme itself will be dealt with in a subsequent commentary. For now, it is sufficient to note that the speech, in dealing with the future, continues to emphasize the theme of unity, socialism and humanity. The variation of that theme when projected against the future is, if anything, even more optimistic. Thus the audience is offered the promise of reforms which, if implemented, will help to bring the Party and the people even closer together. Reforms, moreover, that will help to heal old wounds between Czechs and Slovaks in the crucible of federalism; open government to the people; free the economy from the mistakes of the past; and, in the context of a socialist democracy, create opportunities for personal fulfilment that will eliminate alienation once and for all.

To be sure, the road ahead will not be easy. The problems to be faced are complex and the solutions are difficult. Moreover, there is the danger that elements in the society will seek a return to the old ways or, what is even worse, reject the promise of a future under socialism for the decadence of bourgeois democracy.

Yet, or so the audience is told, the road can be traversed. The CCP, as the Action Programme amply demonstrates, is fully aware of the problems, and has already begun devising solutions. Together with the "masses" it will in the future, as in the past, continue to deal "scientifically" with the difficulties facing the nation. This will require that changes be made. It is, however, important that these changes be carefully considered. To move too quickly would be to give the anti-socialist elements in the society an opportunity to sabotage the work of the Party and the "masses." It might also give those who are disturbed about developments since the January plenum an opportunity to turn the tide in their favour. Again, the CCP is aware of the danger and, with the help of the "masses," will see that neither danger ever materializes.

The message for the future, as for the past and the present, is one of change; change initiated and presided over by the CCP. It is a message not of repudiation but regeneration. It is a message which offers liberalization, not liberal democracy. Finally, it is a message of strength and belief, not of weakness and denial.

The External Audience
The projection of this message to the external audience is keyed to a somewhat different theme. That theme, in the case of the Soviet Union, other members of the bloc and "fraternal parties," invokes a plea, a promise and a warning. The plea is for understanding and is most prominently reflected in those portions of the speech that purport to deal with the need for change. It is there that he describes the shortcomings of his predecessor. It is there too that he speaks of the accomplishments of the past and the wishes of the "masses." Leaving aside the internal implications of these comments, it would appear that his aim here is to convey to the "socialist camp" the necessity for initiating change. By emphasizing the gravity of the situation he seems to be suggesting that the CCP and, by implication, he himself, acted out of necessity as much as choice. Whether this was indeed the case is another matter. The point is that if the CCP could accommodate itself to the will of the "masses," why then should not the rest of the bloc accommodate itself to the CCP.

The promise is an assurance that the changes contemplated in the speech will no no way jeopardize either the primary of the CCP as the "vanguard of the masses" or the integrity of the Soviet Bloc. Viewed in this context, the explanation of the term "socialist democracy" as well as the comments concerning the unwillingness of the CCP to tolerate "anti-socialist" elements, the retention of the People's Militia and the National Front, the need for moderation, etc., were probably intended as much for external as for internal consumption. The same can surely be said for his references to proletarian internationalism, his remarks concerning the Warsaw

Treaty Organization and his statements dealing with the Vietnam conflict, and the German question.

The warning is more implicit than explicit. It is a warning against interference in the internal affairs of the CCP. Thus, for example, we find references to the principles of equality, sovereignty, and non-interference are accompanied by the assertion that "the socialist elaboration of our future road is inviolable." Similarly, in commenting on the outcome of an earlier meeting in Dresden with other leaders of the bloc Dubček takes care to point out that the "exchange of opinions must be understood in the sense that the principle of non-interference in the internal affairs of other parties will continue to be valid."

This message, when projected to the non-Communist world, assumes the character of an illusion. It is the illusion of "freedom." For the western reader, it is easy to be misled by this speech. The reforms proposed here seem, on the face of it, to mark the creation of a democratic political order. Yet, as I have tried to show, the message of the speech is not one of rejection but of renovation. Dubček is not a liberal-democrat, he is a Communist. As such, he undoubtedly believes in the capacity of his system to provide a better future for the people of Czechoslovakia. Careful analysis of the speech certainly gives us no reason to assume otherwise.

Conclusion

In sum, the message of this speech is the same for both the internal and external audience: that elements within the CCP, for whatever reason, had decided the time had come to initiate change; that having arrived at this decision they, and they alone, had decided to preside over the process of implementation; and that as a result they, and the people of Czechoslovakia, would be better off for the effort. Internally, the message is presented as a call by the CCP to a better future under socialism. To the Soviet Union, members of the bloc, and other "fraternal parties" it is a plea for understanding, a promise of internal stability and continued loyalty to the "socialist camp," and a warning against interfering in the internal affairs of the CCP. To the non-Communist world it is the illusion of "freedom" projected against the substance of an abiding belief in the ability of the prevailing system, once modified, to provide a better future for the people of Czechoslovakia.

This is my interpretation; the reader, here as throughout, is invited to provide his own.

THE SPEECH DELIVERED BY COMRADE ALEXANDER D U B Č E K
AT THE PLENARY SESSION OF THE CENTRAL COMMITTEE OF THE
COMMUNIST PARTY OF CZECHOSLOVAKIA

on April 1st 1968

A p r i l   1968

THE SPEECH BY COMRADE

ALEXANDER D U B C E K

Dear Comrades,

We were asked by the January plenary session of the
Central Committee of the Communist Party of Czechoslovakia
to work out an action programme that would ensure the attain-
ment of objectives set by that session. Our draft programme
should also prepare the ground for the elaboration of a long-
er-term programme of the Party. We wish to submit our draft
action programme to you today together with other materials.

Let me give you, by way of introduction, a short explanation of the materials, an appraisal of their importance
and ideas, and also submit a brief report as to how the Central Committee presidium of the Communist Party regards the
development which our society and our Party have been going
through since the January plenary session.

Naturally this evaluation of the development can only
be of a preliminary character in view of the dynamism, scope,
and depth of the movement after the January plenary session.
You, members of the Central Committee gathered here, will
surely make your own addition and improvements to it.

However, one thing is obvious and indisputable: the
movement since the January session is undoubtedly socialist
and democratic, called to life by our Communist Party, and

a   [65]   3

is also characterized by an unwonted activity of our citizens.

It is clear that, from the point of view of our long-term prospects, the period we have been going through since January is extremely important. It has not only been a very serious test of values, but even a telling proof of the ability of our Party to imbue the social development with a new spirit. The situation deserves and undoubtedly will call for a profound analysis and explanation. Today, however, it requires a great concentration of efforts, sacrifice, will and singleness of purpose, patience and perseverance of the avant-garde party of the socialist society.

The process of new tasks and methods of fulfilling our mission, encountering old attitudes and habits, full of contradictions in intself, surges through the whole Party. That is right. We could not start on new roads otherwise.

On the one hand we can witness new hopes of the really broad masses, an unexpected activity of social organizations and of the Party in the first place, an activity admired even abroad, but was surprising even for us at home, which greatly enhanced the attractivity of our country and of our policy. However, many are wondering and so surprised as to express fears whether the Party has not been recoiling under the pressure, whether it is not being driven by the development and whether it will be able to oppose wrong actions, harmful demands that always crop up during such a process.

We must seek answers to all these questions, we must go into their causes and judge them correctly, The Central Committee presidium has reviewed the situation, at least for operational purposes, several times lately and published its attitude.

We must, however, try to grasp more profoundly the meaning of the development of the past months. I think we are most likely to come near to this if we understand the most

4

a

essential characteristic of the dispute which has been growing in the society and in the Party during the last few years.

The essence of the dispute lay in the appraisal of
the social and economic situation as it developed in Czechoslovakia after the political and economic defeat of the bourgeoisie, and after laying the political and economic foundations of socialism. The putting into effect of a new phase
of the socialist revolution at the stage of non-antagonistic
relations necessitated, at the same time, the development,
further shaping, and establishment of a political system to
meet this new situation. The problem is one of intensifying
the role of the Party and generally its attitude to the present tasks of social development. We have to apply to a fuller extent, the basic principles of the theory of Marxism-
Leninism, the principles of socialist construction in which
we have already achieved outstanding successes, the principles
of the leading role of the Party. It was and it is a matter
of marching forward, of unfolding these principles. We are
beginning a new stage of our proletarian socialist revolution, we have to set up such a political structure, to
adopt such political methods of work that will correspond
to the new conditions which **we have so far been lagging** behind. We have to set purposefully to elaborate and realize
such a role of the Party in society which will establish –
and it has done so already in this short time – the Party
as the vanguard of society and its progress, as a political
leading force of this society, to restore the confidence of
people in it.

We were right in stressing the political aspect of
the present problems. Otherwise we could hardly proceed
successfully in fulfilling the policy of the 13th Congress,
and this is our main concern, that we want to put into

a

5

practice, that we shall continue to elaborate. The Party is
thus taking an ever more marked and convincing stand in the
forefront of the movement and is not only defending the
stage achieved. This, I think, is a sufficient retort to
those who feared lest the new attitude should weaken the policy of the 13th Congress. We are bound to say publicly and
clearly that the Central Committee of the Communist Party of
Czechoslovakia stands and will continue to stand for the concentrated fulfilment of this Party policy. It was just this
conviction and resolve that urgently called for an intensification of socialist democratism, for an explanation of
the new conditions and tasks of our socialist society. It
is with regard to the binding conclusions of the 13th Congress and experience from their being put into effect that
we have to formulate even such tasks that have already been
overcome and thus add new touches to emphasize the basic
line in the period between congresses and prepare a new formulation answering the experience and the new conditions.

It should be said - and you will certainly have a
vivid memory of the origin of the events at the last three
plenary sessions - that the Central Committee of the Party
could not channel the actual course, vigour, and complexity
of the events of the past three months into a definite pattern either at the January plenary meeting, or before the
district Party conferences. You, members of the Central Committee, know very well what it was like when we were part-
ing in January, that the Party leadership which opened the
door to this process and put itself at its head did not and
could not have any time schedule for the development of the
events.

The peculiarity of this process is actually that it
was mostly, especially in the speed of its flow, called
forth by a creative and, at the same time, spontaneous activity of the broad masses led by communists, which thus acted
in the sense and in accordance with the conclusions of the

[68]

plenary meeting of the Central Committee without any insti-
gation and ordering about from above. This, too, bears out
the correctness of the January decision. It was therefore
necessary, even desirable, to know better the opinion of
the Party rank and file and of the broad masses of inhabitants, which made itself heard so conspicuously at the annual
meetings and conferences in basic organizations, and especially at district conferences. To do anything before the
Party conferences would have meant interfering with the
process without having more profound knowledge of Party
opinion.

We are more and more confirming that social movement
cannot be simply decreed, that reason cannot be imposed upon
it from outside, but that under our conditions this reason
lies first of all in the knowledge, interests, and movements
of the broad masses, and that it is the task of the Party to
discover this reason, to give it final shape, to improve it,
to emphasize progressive thinking and deeds, to oppose incorrect views, and to return the knowledge thus enriched to
the social movement of the broad masses, to point it out to
them, and so raise them to a higher social level. This difficult task must be borne by the whole Party.

There is therefore nothing more and nothing less at
stake than a full application of the fundamental Marxist
concept of the role of the broad masses and the role of the
Party and of politics. The Party can play its role only if
it fully leans on the interests and experience of the really
broadest masses and on a scientific understanding of their
application. Also in our latest political movement it was
and is practice that helps from below to put finishing touches to the programme of a new political system. This movement seized the existing political and social forms and,
where these forms proved to be capable of absorbing the new
contents, it made use of them. If, however, the existing
forms were insufficient, this democratic movement of the

a

7

broad masses started to break them.

Let us not fear this wave, but let us take it as a lesson. Let us adopt and apply, in every more important social issue, the principle of tackling weighty problems in time and with the assistance of people. Only they will help us to get near to the truth and to truthful conclusions, only with them, and if it is their cause, can we achieve something, can we make changes and attain some goals. The Party can only carry out this essence of political activity well if it makes it, that is conceives it and puts it into practice, as a whole, together with communists in the appropriate fields - in production, culture, government - if it makes it jointly with the communists in the particular fields of work or walks of life. It may be more difficult, more complicated, but it is the only correct political procedure.

Such an attitude is welcomed by an overwhelming majority of communists and the population at large. This is borne out by the results of public opinion polls, thousands of resolutions, letters, conclusions of annual meetings and district conferences. What is important is not figures, but the tendency: confidence in the Party is growing, and so is self-confidence inside the Party.

Activity is evident in all social categories, among workers, the intelligentsia, agricultural workers, though still characterized with a certain irregularity and sometimes spontaneity. It is our duty, the duty of the whole Party and of all communists, to imbue this activity with a really creative character. A revival can be witnessed also in the inner life of large social organizations - in the trade unions and among the young people.

Economic results of the first two months of this year show that the hectic period of discussions, polemics, appraisals, and resolutions did not leave any unfavourable signs on the working morale. On the contrary, we are being increa-

8   a

singly convinced that the development of democracy is the
only way of strengthening a conscious discipline. We also
have full confidence in our working people to be able to understand that the newly started tendency of development can
be effectively supported by deeds, by purposeful work in
factories, in the fields and workshops as well as in scientific thinking and in the arts.

We can, therefore, say quite unambiguously that the
decisions and conclusions of the January plenary session
proved to be correct, and also absolutely necessary, because
the state as it existed – accumulation of many ripe and un-
tackled problems – threatened an acute political crisis. The
vehemence of the whole society's response supplies a proof.
At the same time, of course, it is a commitment for the whole
Party and for us in the Central Committee to apply all our
efforts to a resolute realization of socialist democracy, to
analyze this decisive positive development and to carry it
on. On the other hand not to ignore the extremes which harm
the movement, and thus to be at the head of a further development of this socialist democracy. Everybody in this Republic, all the more so a Party member, must be aware that
we do not have in mind just any sort of democracy, but socialist democracy. That this cannot mean a weakening of the leading role of the Party, but only a new adaptation in the spirit
of Leninism, effective, purposeful, meeting the new conditions. That there is no question of an impairing of the influence on and tasks towards the socialist state, but of the
best expression of the principle of democratism and the necessary centralism, so that the democratic element of the
development of our society, inherent in the socialist state,
might find an ever better expression.

We see the essence of socialist democracy in that it
directly affects all social strata, in that it is democracy
not only in respect of institutions, but that it governs
also all other provinces of the social life of people.

a

9

Freedom of speech is a very important precondition
for expressing opinions and interests. These, however, will
necessarily clash with each other and with the social reality. Institutional safeguards of their objective appraisal
and solution is a further necessity which must be thoroughly
elaborated and put into legal form. All of this would have
no sense, of course, if the submitted and recognized problems
were not tackled, if they were not grappled with in the social sphere at all, and in economy in particular, if the social activity were not transformed into economic activity.
The wealth of thoughts must be reflected in a growth of cultural and material wealth. It will always be, again and again,
the honest, purposeful and good work that pushes us forward.
Nothing else can be promised.

We consider socialist democracy to be a system in which
the working man has his own standing and value, his security,
his right, and his future. It is based upon human participation, coherence, and cooperation. We wish to meet people's
longing for a society in which they can feel to be human among
humans. This active, humane, integrating part of socialism,
a society without antagonism, that is what we want to realize
systematically and gradually, serving the people. It is a very
gratifying task to serve humanity, one which has been waged
by Marxist revolutionaries for more than a hundred years. We
are carrying on their work and want to link up imaginatively
with everything that is progressive and positive in the history of our nations.

If we want to make socialist democracy a living thing -
and let there be no doubt about that - we must and we shall
be guided in our work, by the living theory of Marxism-Leninism and shall actively defend its ideology against various
attacks. We shall fight for its purgation, for its realization in the full sense of the term, and thus we shall best
enhance the attractiveness and convincingness of socialist

10

a

ideas in our class-split antagonistic world.

The main bearer of ideas of a further and full realization of the socialist revolution is the working class
which was and still remains the pillar of social progress.
It is most, socially and politically, interested in an all-
round development of our society, it is part and parcel of
social progress which can bring it and hence the whole society a further general liberation. The speed of changing
the whole society depends on its revolutionary self-surpas-
sing.

It is as true, now as in the past, that the working
class will have to find its way - again and again, in every
new situation - to understanding its role in society, and
it is the duty of the Party to be its friend in this respect
to help the working class better understand its tasks at the
new stage of development. We have to keep in mind, of course,
that just as the whole society, even the working class is
differentiated by the varying attitude of its members to the
spirit of political progress of social development.

In view of the Party being armed with scientific
theory, in view of the whole historical achievement of our
Party and in view of the fact that the revitalization process
and the opening of a new stage in our country was initiated
by our Party, we think we have the right to declare: the Communist Party of Czechoslovakia continues to be, and is now
even more rightly, the decisive, organized, and progressive
force of our society. The main method in the activities of
the Party must be such a political practice in which the
Party will continuously seek public control and make full
use of the results of science and erudition and of the inspiring existence of the arts. This too will be a permanent
well of fresh water upon which the Party may draw for a constant progressive development and against stagnation.

The tasks facing us, the socialist, non-antagonistic

a

11

character of our society, and the longing to satisfy, to the highest possible extent, all the needs of our society, preparation of the scientific and technical revolution, all this makes it possible, but also demands, a strengthening and development of the unity of our society. One of the main tasks of the Party at present and in the future, all the more so is that we understand this unity dialectically. We have to respect the increasing differentiation, and achieve unity by meeting specific requirements. In addition, we have to overcome whatever is bad in the heritage of the past as regards relations among individual classes and social categories, between the nations.

When going over to a new chapter of the socialist revolution, I think we have to thank all those who for tens of years took part in its preparation by carrying on a revolutionary fight for a remoulding of society. It was an immense task, hard, full of searching, often accompanied by misunderstanding, self-denial, sacrifice, personal courage. Not only we, but history will surely appreciate that period of the birth, preparation, and putting into practice of socialist ideals in our country as a period literally bursting with historical events, a period of an immense activity of communists-revolutionaries.

I also wish to thank all of those who, in the past twenty years, honestly and boldly carried out their tasks, who make up an overwhelming majority of our society, and whom we have chiefly in mind in our strivings. Without the honest and meticulous work of millions it was not possible in the past, and it will not be possible in the future, to bring the present intentions of the Party to fruition - to meet the longings and realize the ideas of our nations.

In the interest of the future we shall try to get rid of everything that has become obsolete or that has proved to be incorrect. The Central Committee gave impulse to this,

12

a

at its January plenary meeting, by the self-criticism then applied, and it accelerated the process. The idea is to further develop and strengthen everything positive that has been accomplished. It is really unfounded if this process is used by individuals for a sweeping rejection and debasement of everything done before. We cannot reject and debase a bold and honest work because of faults and of achievements that have become anachronistic. We shall consider and rectify the wrongs and faults of the past, but that does not mean to disparage and slander the past which is bound up with officials and members of the Party, economic workers, antinazi fighters, workers, peasants, citizens of our Republic. Our thanks are due to them and to their efforts for everything positive in our past.

Now, together with these unambiguous conclusions and standpoints we must at least try to judge how in these past three months the Party as a whole has carried on, the practical part of political management, how we have managed to understand the ideas and moods of the working people in the various social categories, how we project them into our policy, put the finishing touches to them and realize them, where we see the problems of that period.

A really new situation has emerged. Instead of one apparently homogenous social interest in the country which coincided with the ideas of some leading comrades, we are now faced with many differentiated, overlapping and mutually clashing interests and attitudes expressing various short- and long-term partial interests of the most varied social categories.

It is my opinion that the Central Committee of the Communist Party of Czechoslovakia can at this very stage commence the task of fulfilling the real mission of the Party as the leading force in our society. It can start with an analysis of the people's real interests, with evaluating their common and their differing aspects, their

[75]

a

13

expressions of progressiveness and conservatism, to make clear what of these real interests are part of the interests amd requirements of the whole society, to arrive at conclusions in the strategy and tactics of its advance with regard to individual social categories. In carrying through the logical development of society as a whole the Party may consciously place itself at the service of the real needs and interest of the people, solicit their confidence in materializing them.

Naturally, in the short time we have so far had at our disposal, these ideas can hardly be more than an outline of a programme. People therefore ask for guarantees that this process will not stop. Although we are still only at the beginning of our revitalizing process, some personnel and institutional guarantees of its further development have already been created.

What, in our opinion, is the main problem now, at this moment? I should say the main problem of the moment is to trim our revitalization process, to make it more concrete, to consolidate it. So far all the attention is centred around personal changes, but a more substantial stage is already in the making. A mere change of persons is no way to reach the fundamental goals, but at the same time the fundamental change cannot be forced along hastily, in an improvised way and at the speed characterizing the past few weeks which neither we nor the public can bear indefinitely.

A period is just beginning when a system of safeguards and stimuli of an organized progress is to be set up, when a mechanism must be developed to achieve our aims not in a haphazard and catastrophic way, but calmly, smoothly, and democratically. Our plenary session is sure to play a great role in this respect, insofar that it will be the first step towards fulfilling the action programme. Here, in

14

a

preparing the action programme - we have, I think, fulfilled
the objectives of the January meeting within a short and bu-
sy period. We thought them to be decisive at this stage.
A Central Committee plenary meeting without planning further activities, for which an action programme would provide
preconditions, would only complicate and hamper the materialization of the conclusions of the last three meetings, all
the more so because the level of today's knowledge, based
upon district conferences, provides scope for developing
the spirit of the conclusions of the past meetings and enables dissociation from some expressions of demagogy, anarchy, and various extremes which could only interfere with
the process of democratization. Nobody and nothing can halt
the creative development of our socialist society. It can,
however, be slowed down and affected by impatience, subjectivism in reverse and other extremes alien to this socialist development.

Our political work, however, will not be easy either
tomorrow or in the future. The criticizing ferment of the
past few months indicated the way our political work has to
take. Apart from undoubtedly positive features the democratization process brought up many old, and also some new weak
spots and shortcomings. Evidently this process of criticism
has not yet touched all the old features we have to overcome
come but, what is more important, it does not always touch
the essentials of our social life, but very often only its
superficialities. The criticism, it is true, reached and rea-
ches almost all spheres of our social life, but it often concentrates only on the consequences without taking into account
the causes. And so various faults and shortcomings are simply stated and more or less put in connection with certain
persons. Meanwhile it is clear, that we have to lay stress
on an improvement of methods. We are lacking a more profound
historical and analytical survey on the origins of these
faults and shortcomings. I think, especially in connection

a 15

with the preparations for the 14th Congress, that for a
further positive course of democratization of our social
life, it will be necessary to get down to a really thorough
analysis of the entire economic and political development
to date in our socialist society.

It is, of course, not only a matter of the past. The
analytical method must be concerned especially with the present. Today, tomorrow, and in the future, the development will
be controversial, the new will clash with the old. It is
essential to recognize in time what is what and where to go
in for greater, more general details. Such a deeper sounding
is imperative for all those who have a say in social processes.

Hand in hand with this programming role of the Party,
the Party activity proper and political work as such, political influencing, must return, at all levels and in all sectors, to a more consistent organizational work among the
people, to a more lively contact with the people, to a direct investigation of their real views. This applies to Party officials, but it also applies to every Party member, as
this is the essence of his Party membership - to get to know
the Party policy, to take a part in its shaping, to participate in its being put into effect, in explaining it.

This activity in the Party has become very weak. In
appraising the upswing of Party life these days we have to
realize that a return to such a concept of the duties of the
Party member will be complicated and strenuous. We are resolutely criticizing the haughty and administrative methods in
Party work which paralysed the activity of members. We must
at the same time realise that it has left deep marks, consequences in practice, habits and, with some people, even
a tendency to seek alibis, to rely on instructions. This is
true also of members in all spheres of social activities.
Contact and understanding with people whose social-political

16   [78]   a

interests and problems are being tackled are indispensable.
To order people about is not possible and right no matter what
form may be used, administrative or theoretical postulates,
or means aimed at affecting public opinion. This must be
faced not only by members drawing the attention of various
Party bodies up to the Central Committee to the wrong opinions but by opposing them ideologically themselves. They
are expected to defend the Party policy, to explain it, to
win people over for its realization.

I think that from our plenary meeting, we must address
with full confidence and also with exacting requirements, the
ranks of our membership who must get our full support, the
basic organizations committees elected at annual meetings,
the district Party committees elected at annual conferences.
We must not chicane and scandalize, without reason, the work
of thousands who, consciously, full of loyalty to the Party,
courageously and mainly honestly fulfilled the tasks of our
socialist construction. We are asking the active Party members, the overwhelming majority of our members to which the
Central Committee looks for support - and we are convinced
that this request will be met - to show their self-sacrifice
again as it was always so typical for them and to develop
activity among workers in factories, fields, building sites,
and all other working places. This is the direction our socialist policy for the people must take with more vigour
than ever before. It is their interests and worries that we
must pay attention to in the first place, it is they whom
we must understand, in good or bad situations. I think that
every communist, every democratically thinking person understands that he can realize his ideals only in unity with the
life of our working people. Every type of sectarianism is
harmful.

Important in this respect is the role of district
committees which, after the district conferences and backed
by the realistic content of our policy, will do a good deal

a

17

of work among the citizens, especially in securing the fulfilment of economic tasks which should get much more attention in pre-election political activities, no matter whether
the elections take place in June or in the autumn. This important task would be jeopardized if the conclusions of some
district conferences were to be questioned. If it is found
that some replacements of officials are necessary here or
there, no new conference is required, especially if the call
of some individuals is not in harmony with the opinion of
an overwhelming majority of Party members. Democracy does
not mean never-ending conferences. The discussion and consultations must be followed by a conclusion binding for all
members, and then by the deed. Conferences were and are the
highest Party organs in the districts, and in the periods
between the conferences it is the district committees elected by the conferences. The principle of democratic centralism, which must be fully respected in the intra-party life,
without which the Party would lose its capacity of action,
requires the minority to submit to the conclusions, to the
decisions of the majority, and to apply its opinion by adhering to intra-party rules.

Just a little note. There are rumours, a sort of
doubting, as to whether the people's militia should continue
to exist. Of cours it should. The people's militia is firmly
incorporated in a uniform system of the country's defence,
it has its own share of duties which it will certainly carry
out. Doubts about its role are quite unfounded.

I think, comrades, that generally speaking, in pushing
through democratic relations their scope and depth must be
observed to a greater extent. This especially refers to personnel and cadre problems. We must establish an atmosphere
that would make it possible for Party officials to be criticized, to make this a natural feature, to prevent criticism
breaking out only when things have gone to the extreme, and then
using force. At the same time, however, we must reach a state when

18

a

the criticized persons can take a stand, when they can explain untruthful or incorrect reproaches. A mass obsession in this respect or even its inciting can only bring tragic consequences, as we were able to see for ourselves in the past. Wrongs cannot be undone by causing new wrongs. In the struggle of the new with the old we must do all possible to rally the Party of the platform and around the goals submitted by the Party Central Committee. Here, in this political scope, let differentiation and unification take their course.

We do not want and cannot proceed so that the rectification of shortcomings would be contrary to our basic principles of ethics, we do not want to have to rectify the rectifications. We declare this idea binding on the communists in all sectors and in all Party bodies. We know our people well, and even if some individuals might succumb to their passions, organizers of an incorrect course which would not comply with the ethics of our Party work would never find understanding with our public.

A further problem, lesson, and requirement to be met - and this will be among the first for us to strive for at a further stage of our socialist democracy, is really to develop an ever richer content - that is the knowledge that the criticism bore the stigma of one-sidedness practically right through. For a long time it was a monologue as it hardly found any opponents either from the ranks of the conservative wing, or even from the progressive wing. It found its expression, among other things, also in the fact that, even though there are both objective and subjective reasons for it, little was heard from the technical and economic intelligentsia. It is necessary to take into fuller account the desirability of a larger share of the public expression of the attitude of workers and peasants for the future course of this democratization process. The reasons are

a

19

of course various. A role was played in this respect by information available, its speed of supply and its level, immediate availability of public involvement and so on. It
resulted in a certain perturbation and fears with some of
the comrades in factories and agriculture because their
interests were left unheeded. We have to keep this in mind
at all levels of Party activities, in the economic life,
in trade unions, in the youth movement, and to redress the
situation. Our journalists, radio and television workers
must realize this in order to improve their very useful and
beneficial work and, by giving more attention to the thoughts
and opinions of workers and peasants, to improve to an even
greater extent our capacity of rallying for action.

People working in this field and communists did much
in accomplishing our aims through the mass media of information. They correctly used the conclusions of our January
plenary meeting in preventing people getting informed by a
whispering propaganda or from abroad. This is enhanced by
supplying information on discussions going on in the Central
Committee presidium and the secretariat. They may feel rewarded by an immense interest shown in their work. However,
this interest binds them, at the same time, to a very high
political or even a statesmanslike responsibility as every
wrong or unobjective news or transmission has a mass reper-
cussion, calls for a standpoint, an explanation. If we want
to refine, and we shall do so, democratism with a clear socialist tendency, then responsibility for its good functioning and for preventing anybody from meddling with it rests
indeed on all component parts, all levels of management.

It is necessary to appreciate the self-evident truth
that the speed in submitting problems may be easily increased,
but their solution, their realization - unless we indulge
in subjectivism in reverse has its own objective limits and
requires a good classification of tasks. Unrealistic, ir-
ritated demands with an addition of demagogy may bring im-

20
a

mediate popularity, but if they are not met they cannot
establish the trust without which we cannot understand each
other. And we do need mutual trust if we are to factually
assess and bring together the multitude of interests.

We would be short-sighted were we not to see a further
feature of the post-January development - a revival of certain non-socialist moods, even of some angry cries demanding revenge. We drew attention to these in the presidiums
published statement of February 21. Our standpoint is, that
the Party will not be caught unprepared, not even by possible attempts at a legalization of these moods under the
disguise of democracy or rehabilitation, and that it will
refute any attempts at a weakening and atomization of progressive socialist tendencies. I am reiterating that the
democracy we have in mind is and must be, even in future,
of a definitely socialist character, and that no anti-socialist tendencies will have a chance to take advantage of this.
The decisive feature is that the general character of the
revitalizing process in our society is by far not determined by certain extreme tendencies and excesses which try to
express these moods. But wherever they may crop up, we must
oppose them on basic ideological grounds so as not to be retarded on our way. The main and decisive factor of our development is the unfolding of socialist democracy, the road
to which was opened by the October, December, and January
plenary meetings of the Central Committee of the Communist
Party of Czechoslovakia.

This must remain the basis of our policy even in the
future. On this basis, and that has been confirmed by the
past three months, an immense energy of our Party and of our
nations was put into motion. This is the basis on which the
efforts of workers, agricultural workers, and intelligentsia
are consolidating. We have, therefore, to go on looking ahead,
to develop all that is new and all the positive features of
our socialist construction.

[83]

a

21

Comrades,

allow me to say a few words about our work as members
of the Central Committee and the Presidium. I think that we
must regularly and self-critically ponder over it, especially
in such a fermenting political period as this, in order to
improve our work in practice too, in the way we resolved at
the January Plenary Session, in order to strengthen leading
Party work and rid it of outdated, unsuccessful and incorrect
methods.

A state has originated in the Party following the January Plenary Session of the CC of the Czechoslovak Communist
Party in which discussion about the problem dealt with by the
Central Committee has continued for quite a long time. As you
all know well, this was an extremely serious discussion on
the position of the Party in the society. The complexity of
the discussion, the contradiction of the process of unification marked the conclusions of the Central Committee's January
Plenary Session with incomplete and diverse, and particularly
non-analytical information - including that provided by members of the Central Committee about the reasons, which led
to the decisions at the January Plenary session. This contributed considerably to the fact that many Party organisations
did not grasp well enough or sufficiently appraise the resolutions and especially the importance of the content of the
Plenary Session's debate. A different situation arose where
correct understanding and verbal report of the conclusions
and content of the Plenary Session's debate, helped it to

22

a

be grasped fully. This led to an unbalanced state, which
really made the situation difficult for functionaries. We
take this for a fact resulting from the state of our Party
before the January Plenary Session and it is impossible to
arrive at any conclusion but that in future we should pay
greater respect to the importance of a more unified approach
to the basic questions by members of the Central Committee
before the Party public. This is not a matter of uniformity.
That would harm the cause. The point at issue is that the
Party – if it is to be a Party of action of revolutionary
practice – must adhere to the principles of democratic
centralism so that in its activity, in action it can proceed
as united as possible.

We assumed that we should first manage to present to
the Party the draft Action Programme, which might function
as an outstanding unifying factor, a factor of unity on the
basic problems of progress and development of our socialist
society. However, the succession of events was more rapid.
This was promoted by increasingly comprehensive information
about the essence of the conclusions to the active Party
group and the course of the latest Plenary Sessions imparted
from a different angle, I should say, "the Šejna case" dis-
turbing the public, as well as other circumstances.

We were aware that the decision of the January Plenary Session would influence the growth of the political activity of citizens, that it would bring about a new political atmosphere, speed up the raising of demands – including
social demands – which are frequently justified and which
will have to be solved gradually and systematically, though
not all at once. The government will have to seek ways of
solving them setting a course and give reasons for it so
that the solution is realistic. Under the pressure of time
we were faced with other new problems, for the solution of
which the Central Committee had not been sufficiently pre-

a

pared in advance. This relates to certain problems of the
work of the Czechoslovak Union of Youth, the tasks and position of the National front and the political parties, the
activities of cultural and art unions and many other problems.

Many questions and problems have accumulated for solution over the past period. The January Plenary Session brought
them to the surface. It is possible to say today, even more
then in January, that the Central Committee has assumed its.
task, but that it was already high time.

At the beginning, the Presidium of the Central Committee of the Czechoslovak C.P. was meeting once a fortnight.
We believed that, contrary to the past, it should not deal
with details, but with really fundamental political problems
of the society. But they are many today. Therefore we had to
meet much more frequently lately. However, it is difficult
in this respect to make up what was neglected in the period
after the 13th Congress. In this period of just over two
months it was beyond our strength to adopt an attitude without proper analysis towards the large quantity of problems
posed by this development.

It proved to be correct that the Presidium of the
Central Committee took a stand on many important principal
problems, for instance, at the Congress of agricultural cooperatives, at the February session of the Presidium of the
Central Committee of the Czechoslovak C.P. at the enterprise
conference at Kladno, where the present position and tasks
of the working class were discussed, and at the district
conference in Brno.

But we must also ponder over how to achieve that the
attitudes being published from the session of the CC Presidium of the Communist Party of Czechoslovakia should reflect the situation more profoundly, more emphatically point
out the reasons of the given phenomena to the entire Party,
serve more as instruction for activity and thus stimulate

even greater activity of communists, and their zest and will
to solve serious social problems.

In this respect, we shall have to rely more effectively on, while channelling the work of the Party apparatus, which we cannot do without. The apparatus itself, its
workers, particularly through the active Party group, must
help more efficiently towards better, really analytical work
of Party bodies. The work of the apparatus must be increasingly orientated, improved and made more efficient in this
direction. It must have the position which is really its
due - no more, no less. It is impossible not to see its important position in the system of our Party work. Therefore
it is also out of place to negate indiscriminately the work
of the Party apparatus. Its overwhelming majority is made up
of brave and honest communists whose aim is to serve devotedly the Party and our people.

There were proposals during the first conferences that
we should call a Plenary Session of the Central Committee of
the CP of Czechoslovakia. The Presidium of the CC of the Communist Party of Czechoslovakia adhered to the set course in
preparations for the first Plenary Session after January.
This was mainly because it was too much to work out a course
for the future work of the Central Committee, which would
proceed from the principles of the Action Programme in this
short time. The Presidium thought it decisive for the future
course of work to concentrate on the content of Party work
in the next period and carry out personnel changes only on
this basis, and not vice versa. Without knowing the conclusions of the response to the January Plenary Session and the
intensity of Party activity, which became evident at the
district conferences, the CC Plenary Session would be unable
to advance. The district Party conferences attested to the
Party´s maturity and to the ability of communists to make
a correct estimation of the situation.

Although we do not want to, and must not, fall into giving directives for particular processes, we could give positive replies to certain questions only in the spirit of the prepared Action Programme. I have in mind for example the problem of youth organisation. In the coming period the youth organisation should respect the differentiation of the interests of young people, while preserving the unity of the Czechoslovak Union of Youth in what unites all the different groups of young people, so that the strength and importance of youth are not split in this fundamental issue. I believe that young people will not only state their demands, but also what they want to do. What is common to, and what unites young people will become evident on the basis of these interests. I think that the unity of a differentiated youth organisation should be as natural as the unity of other important social organisations. In this we must not ignore the fact that the struggle for the unity of youth organisations has been fought for decades so that youth as a whole could apply their political influence more efficiently. This is also why the youth movement should not give up its unity.

I spoke here about certain problems in achieving a more coherent functioning of the Party in society. I should also like to say that by no means can we, nor do we want to, return to some sort of authoritative relationship towards society, towards individual social groups. We should demonstrate this also by subjecting the decisions and conclusions of the Central Committee from the past period to a really profound analysis that would be as objective as possible. We should annul and practically outpace those which proved to be erroneous. I want to inform the Central Committee in this connection that we have also thought of including a political assessment of the Party attitudes towards the 4th Congress of the Union of Czechoslovak Writers of last September on the agenda of this session. As a result of the pressure of time and the insufficient ideological analysis of various aspects of this Congress we have arrived at the conclusion that it is correct to concentrate first on solving the basic political problems of this time and tackling others without haste afterwards.

At the same time we think it inevitable in the interests of normalizing relations between the Party Central Committee and the writers' organisation to cancel immediately the validity of those conclucions of the Central Committee which administratively interfered from a position of power in the ideological conflict which needed to be settled by ideological means. Therefore we recommend that the September 1967 decision of the Central Committee on the transfer of Literární noviny into the sphere of the Ministry of Culture and Information be rescinded and that the proposal of the Central Control and Auditing Commission of the Communist Party of Czechoslovakia revoke the resolution on the expulsion of comrades Klíma, Liehm and Vaculík from the Party, on the punishment by reprimand with caution of comrade Kohout and on the introduction of Party disciplinary measures against comrade Milan Kundera.

Dear comrades,

Allow me now to pass to a brief explanation of the materials submitted to you. In them we stress the political aspect of work, above all the deepening of the content and methods of Party work.

We must purposefully create preconditions already today to be ahead of schedule in our future work. This means to work out with the help of solidly based scientific analyses the key problems of the new policy which is now being formed and which will continue being formed with the advance of preparations for the 14th Party Congress, and to accumulate prerequisites for the formation of a prospective programme. In this respect, we must activate and coordinate the work in all spheres of scientific research, not give way to rashness, and reject the insincerity of cheap slogans and promises. On the other hand though, we must not be afraid to set ourselves the boldest aims the feasibility of which can be scientifically anticipated.

The importance of the choice and leadership of communists, who work in State and non-State institutions and organisations, and especially the importance of Party branches in which they are grouped must be stressed in connection with the new concept of the relationship of the Party to these organisations. Communists in non-Party organisations must be able to work out their policy independently and create scope for its implementation by winning the confidence and support of non-communists through the correct statement of their interests. The growing importance of the mission of communists should become and will be more clearly evident also in the fact that new members will be joining the Party mostly from the ranks of those who have best proved their worth and have grown into respected public officials.

It will be necessary to build up an objective Party system based on the system of democratic relations between all the components of the Party structure on an entirely new foundation. Consistent struggle against undesirable and undemocratic tendencies, lively and permanent confrontation of practical measures with the Party's Action Programme and with the democratic process of policy-making, of protection of rights and interests of communists, will be the main purpose of this system.

It will be necessary now to concentrate the best forces of the Party for practical action and at the same time for working out the general line of the next Party Congress, which would fully correspond to the new stage of the development of our society. In view of the situation and demands of

28

a

many district conferences we believe that it is necessary
not to take a decision on the convocation of the 14th Congress, but to analyse the possibility of speeding up and
intensifying its preparation while starting to work out a
long-term programme of the CP of Czechoslovakia.

The reasons stimulating the speeding up of preparation for the Congress will certainly be intelligible to
our comrades. For if we really want to take the lead in the
current, and especially future, social changes we cannot do
so predominantly through propaganda nor by personnel changes
only. We can lead and inspire mainly by a realistic and
clear policy. Its basis for the next period is the Action
Programme. However, we should not forget that development
is very dynamic. What is good today will be no longer sufficient tomorrow. Our nations rightly expect that, at the
future Party Congress, we shall be able to state a clear
programmatic standpoint, in its entirety. This means inclu-
sive of the problems of the growth of the standard of living, basic objectives of the fifth five-year plan, prognoses
of long-term economic development, etc. Otherwise, the proceedings of the Congress will bring nothing and would only
result in wasting the initiative and activity to which we
have stimulated the Party and masses.

The Party Congress presupposes the completion of the
Action Programme, its extension into the guideline of the
14th Congress, though in unity with the economic programme.
Otherwise, the workers will not understand us. The Congress
will certainly take up everything that was viable and really
progressive in our past policy and in the history of the
Party, that stood the test of historical proof of values.
And this guide-line will also clearly disengage from everything that was unrealistic and wrong.

There will certainly be an opportunity in the process
of the implementation of the Action Programme and preparation

a

[91]

29

for the next Congress – i.e. on the basis of an active and
matter-of-fact attitude, in everyday work – for the Party
public to decide responsibly who should be given the mandate
of member of the Central Committee of the CP of Czechoslovakia at the Congress.

In order to succeed fully in what we shall energeti-
cally strive for we must create the necessary preconditions
in Central Committee bodies and in the central apparatus of
the Party already at this Plenary Session. To reorganise the
Presidium and the Secretariat of the Central Committee is
the first task. We must logically proceed in this from the
results of the past Plenary Sessions. The new Presidium and
the new Secretariat must then prepare proposals for a complete adaptation of the structure of the central apparatus.
Suggestions – although they cannot be regarded as complete –
have been submitted to you. We are submitting them to you
for study and for comment as working material, which has not
yet been approved by the Presidium of the Central Committee
of the CP of Czechoslovakia. We shall take a decision on
them after they are completed and debated by the presidium
of the Central Committee of the CPC, probably at our next
Plenary Session.

All-round rationalization of the state administration
in accordance with the spirit of the proceedings and conclusions of the December and January plenary sessions of the
Central Committee is part of the policy of strengthening our
socialist system. We have taken the first step in this direction by the election of the new president. We are fully
confident that the election of comrade Ludvík Svoboda will
contribute to the unification of progressive forces, to the

30
a

consolidation of political conditions in the state, and
that all our efforts will benefit from it.

A very important task is to intensify the work of
the government. The government must work, from the beginning,
at a level in keeping with its constitutional function and
the requirements of the new era. It must be not only a team
of ministers, but also a collective body actually governing
the republic and ensuring the needs of the society, expressed in the policy of the Communist Party and the National
Front. In its work it must fully respect the will of the
supreme body of state power, the National Assembly, cooperate with it in an active way, and systematically account to
it for its work. Gradually, the government must get rid of
excessive, for the government disproportionate, operative
management of the economy and culture by directives, and be,
above all, a body of conceptual and perspective management
and effective state administration, sufficiently firm and
exact to ensure that desirable order and democratic discipline prevail in our country.

In forming a new government, it will be right to count
with the most urgent changes in the structure of the ministries, as proposed by the presidium of the Communist Party
Central Committee and the government. In the foreseeable future the new government should propose other necessary structural changes and adopt fundamental measures aimed at improving its work.

Mainly, however, we must proceed from the necessity
of substantially changing the composition of the government,
in keeping with the new conditions of its work and function.
The public expects that those people will be appointed to
government posts who will represent guarantees that the spheres assigned to them will be administered well. We must respect and apply the democratic principle that fundamental
changes and turning points in politics are connected with
the changes of political personalities asked to carry out
the changes.

[93]

a

One of the first tasks of our Central Committee, the government and the National Assembly will be to accelerate the consolidation of the situation in the security forces and in the army.

Many critical words have been directed lately against the Ministry of Interior, and security bodies. The public was disquietened by a large number of facts which had come out in connection with the work of some security agencies in the 1950s, and by certain recent events. The measures, including the cadre measures, which are being taken at present will support everything that is sound at the Interior Ministry. Party conferences and meetings of the ministry personnel confirm that the sound forces within the security services represent the overwhelming majority. These forces guarantee that the confidence of the public in security services will be restored.

I am sure you will agree with me that the social need for security services is beyond any doubt. Only recently, Prague was perturbed by the report that another young member of the Public Security had lost his life in a struggle with a criminal. We must show full, sincere understanding for the difficult, responsible work of the security service, and we must extend a helping hand to the comrades in the service.

The Party regards reliable protection of the secure life of the country's peoples as an important political task. The defence of the republic is the concern of all the people, all Party, state, social and economic bodies and organizations. The resolutions and letters addressed to the Central Committee confirm that the communists in the armed forces, and other servicemen, fully and unequivocally support the results of the October, December and January plenary sessions of the Central Committee. They support the progressive trends in the Party and in the society, especially the process of democratization and rectification of errors in the methods

[94]

and work of the Party and state bodies. The communists in the army, security forces and units of the People's Militia have our full confidence, and will be given full support of the Central Committee for their highly responsible, demanding service and work.

The communists in the army realize that the revitalization process in our society and Party applies, to the full extent, to the army. Also we see in that, and in the necessary cadre changes in the army command, the guarantee that not even a shadow of doubt will ever fall on the absolute loyalty of the army to the people and to the progressive development of our society.

We must continue building our army, and improving it on socialist principles, on the basis of full centralism and indivisible authority of command, as a defence bulwark against the external enemy, against the imperialist agressors. The army must be built as a firm link in the alliance of the Warsaw Treaty armies.

The building and operations of the Czechoslovak armed forces, army and security, must proceed under the democratic control of responsible state bodies. It will be right to create appropriate guarantees in this respect. At the same time, to a much greater degree, the problems concerning the army and security must become the subject of interest and democratic supervision of the whole public.

As regards the National Assembly, we must fully ensure the application of the constitutional rights of this supreme state institution, already in its present form and under the conditions of the valid constitution and other laws, with possible necessary partial amendments. It is necessary to recommend inevitable cadre changes in the presidium of the National Assembly. Finally, it will be necessary to draw up new principles for the activities of the communists in the National Assembly. In this connection, the necessity to

a

set up without delay an armed forces and security committee
of the National Assembly is urgent.

The communists in the National Assembly should come
forward with the initiative for the inception, without delay,
of qualified work on the preparations of a new constitution
which will give legal expression to the social transitions
in our society, and which will become a firm legal base of
the democratic structure of our life, as a permanent principle of advancing, modern socialist society. The principles
of the draft constitution should become the subject of broad,
democratic discussion of the public and of experts.

Fundamental changes must also be carried out in the
constitutional expression and protection of the principle
of equal rights of the Czechs and Slovaks. Experience from
development hitherto, and especially following the constitution of 1960, prove convincingly how various aberrations
have affected this sphere of state law, supremely important
for the unity of the two nations, practically annulling the
elementary rights of Slovakia, of the Slovak national bodies.
The existing organization of the Slovak national organs is
the target of justified criticism. It is our task to develop
the relations between the Czech and Slovak nations on sound
foundations, to strengthen the common Czechoslovak statehood.

It is, therefore, necessary, to prepare a new constitutional law in the foreseeable future, even before the elections to the National Assembly and to the Slovak National
Council. This constitutional reform, which should be a continuation of the positive concepts and proposals which have
been born in the periods of the anti-fascist resistance and
of the beginnings of the national and democratic revolutions,
will fundamentally change the status and authority of Slovak
national bodies. The amendment should be based on the wishes
and needs of our nations and nationalities, should fully ensure their national development, and thus contribute to the

34

a

strengthening of Czechoslovak statehood. The development of
our statehood should be directed towards enhancing the equality of our fraternal nations. In this connection, and respecting the will and experience of both nations, it is necessary to analyze constitutional development so far, and
its future direction. On the basis of this analysis, and of
a thorough study of political, cultural and especially economic relations, a federative system should be drafted as
one of the Leninist forms of solving nationality questions
in the constitutional sphere. The "action programme" of the
Party sets this task. The task will require, however, further, very careful work.

The constitutional law should state quite clearly
that the Slovak National Council is to be constituted as a
legislative body, and that the division of legislative authority between the National Assembly and the Slovak National
Council should be consistent with the principles of the Ko-
šice Government Programme. The legislative and executive
powers, vested today in the Slovak National Council and its
presidium, should be separated. In consequence of these changes, the status and structure of the boards of commissioners
and other executive bodies of the Slovak National Council
will change. The constitutional law should also explicitly
state that in constitutional matters in the relations of the
Czechs and Slovaks, the representation of the Slovak nation
cannot be majorized.

With regard to the national committees, we recommend
postponement of the elections to these representative bodies,
in accord with the numerous proposals of the public and of
experts. The presidium of the Communist Party Central Committee and the presidium of the National Assembly have adopted
conclusions in this matter, on which comrade Sádovský will
report. The plenum will have to adopt its position on the
date of the elections during the current session.

The existing and the new national committees should,

a

35

in our opinion, centre without delay their main attention on care for the daily needs of the population.

In the past few months, we have already practically started on the road towards solving a number of questions of socialist democracy. Freedom of speech and criticism, freedom of press - these are no longer demands, but realities. We have begun solving definitely all problems of the rehabilitation of all unjustly persecuted people - communists and non-communists. There is also full-blooded development of initiative in our social organizations, especially in trade unions. The National Assembly and the Slovak National Council are beginning to understand their new role. Changes in certain important state, party and social functions also belong to the realities of the past weeks.

However, these are all only first steps. What will be necessary now? Above all, we must give a legal form to all positive features of the current revitalization process, we must pass laws which will guarantee that the freedoms of speech and criticism, freedom of the press and freedom of assembly will be, in connection with socialism and the inviolability of our statehood and socialist achievements, permanently protected by laws, by the fundamental parts of our political system, by the fundamental rules of our public life.

No democracy - and thus not even our socialist democracy - can live for long only on the fact that opinions can be freely expressed, that criticism is permitted. That in itself is only decisive, if free and sound criticism removes old obstacles from the road of social progress. In order to live and to rule democratically in our society even then, when the obstacles have been eliminated everywhere and for good, we must have a well-thought out and well functioning system of institutions, bodies and organizations, which will work in a new and effective way, where new policy will be pursued, and these bodies will be permanently under democra-

tic supervision of citizens. Therefore, we are faced with
the very urgent task of consolidating political conditions,
developing the whole existing system of political management
in our society so as to make it into a system fully combining
socialism and democracy, a system capable of factually and
in a qualified way solving all problems arising from the
needs of the life of our society, a system in which the relationships of responsibility and control will be determined,
in which it will be clearly stated who is responsible for
what and to whom, in which independent authority and independent responsibility of everyone for his tasks will be
exactly fixed.

This will require systematic work on the part of government bodies and elected state bodies, social organizations and of the Party in the next few months.

All these problems will be dealt with in an atmosphere of genuine socialist democracy. This means the beginning
of a situation - which will now be of a permanent character
- when we, the communists, will have to defend and argue in
public, our views and standpoints in discussion with all the
others. The communists will stand in the vanguard of the development, and will have the status of leadership to the extent to which they will be able to win and keep it by ideological and political means, under democratic conditions.
Authority is not given once and for all - neither to the individual, nor to a party organization, nor to a party. Authority must be unceasingly renewed, on the basis of the results
of work. The Party and its members must be at the head of the
progressive development,must lead and sweep the other masses
of the working people into the vortex of the tasks.

The relationship of the communists and non-communists,
the relationship of the Party and the rest of the society is
thus becoming the key question of today. Quite naturally,
this is being discussed both within and outside the Party.
In doing so, we must proceed from the reality of contemporary processes. The process of revitalization has put into

a 37

motion the whole mechanism of social life. The purpose and
aim of the democratization process is clear: to create an
improved type of socialist democracy, in keeping with Czechoslovak conditions. It is in the interest of the Party and
to the benefit of the whole society that the process should
be completed in a relatively quiet way, without any major
oscillations. Any other transition might seriously endanger
the aims we are following, might thwart the historical opportunity which is offered to us today for our socialist development.

The present process, taking place on a socialist basis, must give a truly democratic scope to the interest of
all social groups, must guarantee the permanence of our international ties. These vital demands cannot be met without
the leading role of the Communist Party. No other organized
force exists in our society which could guarantee the socialist character of the current social process and its even
democratic development.

In solving the problems of relations of the Party to
state and social institutions, we proceed from this realistic position. The past situation in this sphere, especially
as regards the National Front, was not entirely satisfactory.
It has been negatively affecting the authority and activity
of these bodies, as well as the authority of the Party. We
welcome and appreciate that the social organizations are beginning to assert themselves as independent, autonomous parts
of the political system. We especially welcome and wish to
develop the revitalization process in the trade unions, because it enhances their status in the National Front.

The whole National Front, the political parties which
form it, and the social organizations, participate in the
formulation of state policy. The political parties of the
National Front are partners, their political activities proceed from the common political programme of the National

38 a

Front, proceed fully from the socialist character of social relations in our republic. The Communist Party regards the National Front as a political platform which does not divide the political parties into government and opposition parties in the sense that opposition would be formed against the line of state policy as the policy of the whole National Front, and that a political fight for power in the state would be waged.

The formation of political forces striving to deny this concept of the National Front, to exclude the National Front from political power, was on the whole overcome already in 1945 after the tragic experience of both our nations with the prewar political development of ČSR.

In the National Front and in the whole political system, we shall apply the Marxist-Leninist concept as a concept of leading policy so that we shall use all means of political work - in all parts of our system and directly among the masses of the workers and all working people - to win for it such support which will ensure its leading position by democratic political means.

All this contributes, and will contribute even more, to the realization that the responsibility for the development of our society and our state will be a common one, fully and really shared by all, communists and non-communists alike.

For many communists, who have become used to the old methods, it will not be easy. The Party as a whole is, however, bound to succeed. We are firmly convinced of it, because there are many creative forces within the Party, and to fear the new process would be to underestimate deeply these creative forces.

Our political system will certainly not revert to the state in which its foundation would be only the relations of the political parties. In the system of socialist democracy, we are concerned with more than a copy of the parliamentarism typical for formal democracies. The aim is to increase the real independence of social and group-interest organizations, to make the representative bodies of the state – up to the National Assembly – into bodies where political decisions of the state are actually made. During the process of further development of our political system, it will be desirable to give consideration especially to the question of how even the whole scale of interests of the people in certain spheres of the social division of labour – in the economy, in the industries and agriculture, in social services, education, science and culture – will directly assert itself in the system of socialist democracy to a more marked degree. Socialist democracy must differ from formal democracy, inter alia, also insofar that it will be the working people who will have the decisive word in the management of the society.

Naturally today, we cannot yet define the future model of a functioning socialist democracy. The democratic forces and phenomena are at the beginning, and not at the end. We must follow their movement, and strengthen and elaborate it further. The first steps we are taking today are sufficient only for what is most urgent in the given situation, and would be insufficient, even one-sided, for further perspectives. In connection with the preparations of the 14th Party Congress, we should consider how to develop the whole political system so that we could use all knowledge and international experience to make of it a much more intensive union of democracy with socialism under specific Czechoslovak conditions.

᠍᠍᠍

a

Another important task of the future period is the consolidation and development of our national economy. In the current discussions, it is increasingly demanded that the present stage of our national economy be quite frankly and critically evaluated, that it be stated clearly and with full responsibility what our situation really is and that it be said quite clearly and responsibly how and by which methods we want to consolidate our economy. I think that an analysis of the present state of our national economy should be given by the new Government when it submits its program. This analysis should precede the report on the ways and methods by which we want to and must ensure a balanced, smooth and effective development of our economy.

We want to consistently introduce the new system of economic management. We must stop talking only about improving the system of management and say clearly that it is to be a profound economic reform designed to create a new system for the functioning of the socialist economy. We know that it will be a system based on a synthesis of the plan and the market, a synthesis which must be first of all elaborated. In this synthesis, the criterion of economic activities will be not only formal indicators of a directively-conceived plan, but economic instruments ensuring the aims of the whole society, objective criteria of the market and of social-political priorities, resulting from objective economic interrelations and which are fully binding on every state which wants to make its economy permanently prosperous. It should be a system which will fully appreciate high-quality and effective work and which will assure that people are remunerated not only according to the physical and mental energy they expended but, above all, according to the real results by which they contributed to the satisfaction of all the needs of the society. A system which will set free the creative initiative of the working people, will enable the growth of capable people and will create a wide scope for natural

a

selection in making appointments to leading positions.

The main condition for the consistent and rapid implementation of the new system of management is today the institutional adjustment of relationships in the economic sphere and the creation of a new organisational structure in the whole sphere of production. In this connection, I want to emphasize - and this also answers many questions and comments from district conferences - that we are putting through, and shall continue to put through, further measures designed to democratize economic management. As regards enterprises, we expect them to gain such a measure of independence as will enable them to fully develop business activity. Within enterprises, democratic managing bodies will operate to which directors and other leading economic executives will be accountable. In addition to this, the trade organisation will also assert itself in putting through the interests of employees and in exercising control over management.

Profound changes in the system of management will be supplemented by extensive changes in the structure of production which, at present, is not in keeping with Czechoslovak conditions and, moreover, has departed from the objective tendencies of the progressive development of the productive forces which are becoming increasingly predominant in all industrially advanced countries. It will be a difficult transformation which will affect many partial interests. But we have no other choice. At the same time, we must take care that those who are not responsible for the present unsatisfactory production structure should not be the worse for the changes.

The government will have to submit to the National Assembly a set of immediate measures by which these important tasks will be consistently ensured. It will be necessary to carry out changes in the structure of investments, i.e. to allocate means especially to agriculture and to the consumer

[104]

and food industry, as well as to the non-productive sphere, particularly to housing construction and the whole field of services. Since our resources are limited, each measure which will make their use more effective can help to reduce the economic imbalance and achieve a faster growth of the national income. The most important reserves of greater effectiveness are, in our view, the viving activity of the people and the application of that which has always been typical of Czechoslovak workers and technicians and which has been rendered inactive by the old system of management, i.e. an independent approach to tasks, the application of know-how, abilities and skill, as well as of initiative, resulting from the restored feeling that the people´s work is their own creative personal contribution to the successful effort of the whole society. This will be stimulated not only by the application of the principles of the new system of management but also by the current process of revitalization in our public and political life.

These measures are closely interrelated with the program concerning the standard of living. Prosperity can be achieved only on the basis of a modern and highly efficient economy which is able to assert its qualities in tough competition on the world market. All other roads towards prosperity are provisional, temporary and full of risk.

At present, we can solve only the most urgent social problems, those we formulated in the document adopted at the plenary meeting in December. In this conection, I want to emphasize that we must seek possibilities of making cuts also in the field of central management and public expenditure; these cuts will be used for improving the social conditions of the population. However, the achievement of a more substantial improvement will depend to a decisive extent on how we shall be able to run our economy in future. The changed system of management should contribute not only towards rationalizing the state and economic apparatus but

a

[105]

also towards making it cheaper and at the same time towards eliminating many abnormalities and bureaucratic anomalies.

In addition to these measures which we shall implement in the next few months, we must intensify the elaboration of the long-range conception of the development of the Czechoslovak national economy which will not only comprise changes in the structure of production and in its more consistent integration in the world division of labour, but also in which we shall proceed from the new structure of the needs of our population.

Today, attention concentrates mainly on the material and social needs of the people. However, we want to, and must, achieve even more. Socialism, and especially socialism based on broad democratic principles, must create a new humanism of the modern era, one which other systems are unable to give to mankind in spite of all their technical progress, it must create better conditions for the development of man than have been so far created by any other society. This means that when we strive for normalizing the economy, we do not regard this task as an end in itself but as an instrument designed to promote the full development of man, of human personality. It must therefore aim at creating, for every individual person, conditions in which everyone will be able to assert himself in all spheres of work and life. An immense role will, in this sense, be played by science and art. We therefore strive not only for a fast development of the individual branches of science, which are interrelated with the growth of the productive forces, and with the scientific and technical revolution, but also for the development of the humanistic scientific branches and all spheres of art which will help people to find a new way of life corresponding with the era of the scientific and technical revolution and with the socialist principles of our society.

In solving present-day economic difficulties, i.e.

44

a

the economic imbalance, we must take into account the factor on which we could not count before the January plenum of the Central Committee, the factor which could not be counted upon by economists but which must be today seen by politicians, i.e. the activity which is setting in motion the creative mind and energy. Economic effectiveness and economic difficulties can, in no case, be solved at the expense of the living standard of the people. Resources and reserves for solving this vitally important task must be found in production. In solving the present tasks, it is therefore necessary to take fully into account the moral factor emerging with new revitalizing and renascent power after the January plenum. People must be infused with faith in themselves, with faith in knowledge, skill and intellect. This faith in the working people is today a moral force but will tomorrow certainly be a material force on which we shall be able to count fully in our drive for the further development of our national economy, for further growth in the living standard.

The period since the January meeting of the Central Committee of the CP CZ has been characterized up to this day by lively foreign political activities of our Party in spite of the fact that the stormy internal political developments have apparently relegated international policy to second place. However, it has again been confirmed that we are implementing and shall implement all the complicated and exacting internal tasks in a certain concrete international situation.

In this relatively short period of time, several multilateral meetings have taken place which are important for strengthening the cooperation of the socialist countries and for further efforts to achieve unity of the internal Communist movement. In terms of time, first place among them is held by the Budapest consultative meeting of Communist and workers'parties. I do not intend to give a more detailed evaluation of its results but, in this connection, we want to emphasize two aspects of this meeting. It is important

a

45

that the delegations which participated in the Budapest meeting, under complicated conditions reached unity on a number of points which are of decisive importance for convening and preparing a world conference of the Communist parties. This is an encouraging success. Secondly: the Budapest meeting was a step forward in seeking new forms of unity while preserving the independence of the fraternal parties and their mutual international collaboration.

The delegation of the Communist Party of Czechoslovakia undoubtedly made a positive contribution to the talks. It tried to assert a sober and realistic view of the contradictory problems of the present world as well as of complicated questions of the cooperation of the Communist parties. Our delegation strongly supported demands for a substantial extension of ties with all the anti-imperialist forces. It adopted a clear attitude to past incorrect evaluations of the League of Communists of Yugoslavia and it raised its voice in support of sensible efforts to develop relations with those fraternal parties which hold different views on a number of questions.

The recent meeting of the Political Consultative Committee of the Warsaw Treaty in Sofia and the meeting of the highest representatives of certain socialist states in Dresden were also important. The first meant much for political cooperation, the second, I believe, will become an impulse for a more thorough and open discussion on the problems of economic cooperation, both within the framework of the Council of Mutual Economic Assistance and on a bilateral basis.

It is natural that we have taken advantage of all these meetings to supply information on developments in our country and to explain correctly the positive sense of the process of democratization. As you know, I myself met earlier Comrade Brezhnev, Comrade Kádár and Comrade Gomulka. Such meetings will take place in future with representati-

[108]

ves of other fraternal parties also. Comrades Koucký and
Kriegel held talks in this sense with delegations of many
fraternal parties in Budapest as well as on other occasions.
A broad exchange of views took also place during the visit
of the delegations of fraternal parties and states at the
time of the celebrations of the 20.th anniversary of the
February events.

Our last discussion to date took place at the recent meeting in Dresden. It must be stated that the representatives of the socialist countries and the central committees of their parties at this meeting showed understanding for the present views of the Central Committee of the
Communist Party of Czechoslovakia on developments in our Republic and on questions of mutual cooperation. The discussion and the exchange of opinions must be understood in the
sense that the principle of non-interference in the internal affairs of other parties will continue to be valid.

I am sure that I express the identical view of the
entire Central Committee if I once more emphasize that in
the same way as the socialist character of our future road
is inviolable, so are equally inviolable the basic values
of the Czechoslovak foreign political orientation: firm alliance and all-round cooperation with the Soviet Union and
the socialist states, based on the principles of equality,
mutual benefit, non-interference and international solidarity. This basic orientation of our policy is in harmony
with the most vital needs of the security of our nations
and with the development of our national economy. No one
will ever succeed in casting any doubt on the unserving
Czechoslovak-Soviet friendship. This friendship is not only
a matter of historical experience of the people of our country but, above all, the outcome of a realistic appraisal of
the present situation of the Republic in the surrounding
world. If our country is now, at the present time, not exposed to any acute threat from outside, which sometimes

a

gives rise to not exactly profound conclusions as regards
the existence or non-existence of danger, it must be seen
that this is precisely the consequence of our alliance with
the Soviet Union, the consequence of the safeguard we have
in the Soviet Union.

The idea that in today's antagonistically divided
world we could stand somewhere in the background appearing
and behaving neutralistically and speculating that if things
should go badly for our nations we should invite others to
bleed for us, is impossible not only from the political but
also from the ethical point of view.

Proletarian internationalism, its practical application in relations to other socialist countries as well as
towards the whole international Communist movement, respect
for our essential common interests, our assistance to everything representing social progress in the world, constitutes
today, and also for the future, the basis of the foreign policy of our socialist country.

This is also the aspect in which we view our intention to activate generally the foreign political activity
of our state. We must require this activity to have an elaborated conception and to assert with greater initiative our
standpoints on important international problem, our active
contribution to the common, scientifically substantiated,
international political activity of the socialist states.
This will, in particular, mean pursuance of a more effective
European, and primarily Central European, policy contributing to the consolidation of peaceful relations in Europe and
to the expansion of cooperation among countries with different social systems.

Our interest concentrates especially on a peaceful
solution of the German problem which is of cardinal importance for European security and in which an important role
is played by the existence and the policy of the German De-

mocratic Republic. Positive efforts for the creation of a peaceful atmosphere and good relations among the nations of Europe and in the world in general represent the chief line of our international policy.

At the same time, however, the activities of world imperialism and particularly the activization of revenge-seeking forces in the German Federal Republic forces us to continue strengthening and maintaining our armed forces, our Czechoslovak People's Army on a high level. The American aggression against the Vietnamese people is too strong a warning for us to be able to underestimate it. This is also why- and certainly in harmony with the evaluation by members of the Party Central Committee - we are for taking the necessary measures for extending the mechanism of the Warsaw Treaty so that it corresponds to present-day conditions. Concretely, this means to improve the activities of the joint command, which was recently discussed at the Sofia and Dresden meetings. As was shown at the Dresden conference, especially in Comrade Kosygin's speech on the economic sphere, we have still many untapped reserves in this respect. The State Planning Commission has been therefore charged with preparing an initiative proposal for intensifying cooperation with the Soviet Union where we are bound by the raw material basis, but also with other socialist states, especially with our neighbours - with Poland, Hungary and the German Democratic Republic.

The action program could outline only very briefly certain foreign political tasks. It will depend on initiative efforts especially of the Ministry of Foreign Affairs and naturally also of the whole Government the National Assembly, the Central Committee and its Presidium smaller to no extent that these principles are concretized as soon and as well as possible in order that Czechoslovak foreign policy may ensure all the indispensable external conditions for the successful internal socialist development of our country.

[III]

Comrades,

The action program which has been submitted has a double purpose: first of all, to create unity in action for the implementation of the main tasks of our development, to give sufficient impetus for the development of the socialist initiative of the people, to show the road by which it is possible to eliminate the obstacles which have until now been standing in the way of further development corresponding to present-day conditions, obstacles consisting first of all in excessive centralism, in administrative-directive methods rooted in the field of political management.

The second and deeper sense of the program lies in the fact that it opens up scope for basic structural changes in our society and for the creation of a new dynamic of socialism which would be in harmony with the changed social, economic and cultural conditions as well as with specific national conditions. The implementation of this program can, and must, open up the road towards the solution of other more complicated and more important questions concerning the organisation and the dynamic development of our socialist society in directions which could now be only indicated. Greater activity of socialist development can be created only by setting into motion new powerful forces of social life, and - relying on creative Marxist thinking - carrying out bold, but at the same time well-considered, experiments. In the course of this process, it is necessary to deepen and perfect the new general line of the Party.

This is why the program has been drafted as a fundamental political view of the present stage and its needs. It cannot be understood as a directive enumeration of concrete tasks but as a political platform which must be creatively developed. It is an open document which will be further perfected in the course of its implementation. The program does not want to, and cannot in advance, determine the

50   a

detailed course to be adopted by individual organisations
and institutions but it opens up sufficiently wide scope to
enable them to determine and concretize these tasks themselves
in the spirit of the basic lines. Any other approach would
be at variance with the spirit of the program. If people
are to indentify themselves with the aims of the program,
they must participate in their formulation.

I should like to say a few words about work with the
action program, especially about its role in the current general process of democratization. We must be aware of the
character of this process, its rate and its rapid acceleration. Things which, a fortnight ago, appeared as something
basically different from the general view are today becoming
generally accepted and may already tomorrow be out-of-date.
In connection with the action program we may also hear that
people already know its content. It is an actual fact that
certain ideas of this program have already been published,
some of them have even been discussed. However, knowledge,
acceptance or non-acceptance of its ideas are one thing.This
can be achieved in a short time. But the main thing - implementation, elaboration and concretization – is something different. This activity is more difficult, frequently also little effective, ordinary and routine work, it requires perseverance but is indispensable if the program is to serve any
purpose.

The current of democratization, the social mechanism
which began to operate, will indubitably develop even further. Only if the Party submits in its program demands which,
from the present point of view, are sufficiently bold, if it
regards the program as the basis and a starting-point, shall
we be able to be constantly at the head of the creative process and enforce its socialist character. We must endeavour
to master the social interests operating in society. It is
therefore desirable to orientate ourselves to progressive

a

51

II

THE ACTION PROGRAMME

THE document which follows is undoubtedly the most significant of the collection. Its significance attaches to the fact that here, in the Action Programme of the Communist Party of Czechoslovakia, the reader will find spelled out in considerable detail the foundations for a new political, social and economic order. This is not an order based either on the principles of liberal democracy or the free private enterprise system, but rather on the principles of Marxism and an economy oriented toward socialism.

In reading the Action Programme it is important to recognize that the proposals made here originated with the Czechoslovak Communist Party (CCP). Accordingly, they represent the thinking of men who, although profoundly disturbed by conditions around them, are nevertheless undoubtedly convinced of the capacity of their system to meet the challenge of renewal. It would be a mistake, therefore, to read this Programme either as a confession of weakness or an admission of failure, although, as the reader will discover, it contains elements of both. It would also be a mistake to interpret this Programme as a total repudiation of the past. The measures outlined here appear to attest to an awareness of the fact that conditions within Czechoslovakia have changed and that if the system is to survive it too must change. Moreover, they appear to attest to a belief in the ability of the CCP to oversee the innovation.

If this is so, then the message of this Programme is that when confronted with the spectre of irrelevance, Communist political systems must respond, and must respond creatively; they must, moreover, do so without destroying themselves in the process; finally, and by implication, unless they can demonstrate this capacity they are, like any other political system, doomed to extinction.

The Internal Audience

The message is conveyed to the internal audience on three different levels. Speaking, as it were, to the Party, the Programme underscores both the urgency of the challenge confronting the CCP and the necessity for meeting this challenge in a way that will jeopardize neither its own survival nor the survival of the system. In this connection, the Programme gives considerable space to the errors of the past as well as to the problems of the present. The theme throughout appears to be less one of recrimination than of reconciliation. As articulated in the Programme, this theme finds expression in the emphasis on the need to recognize past errors so as to ensure that these mistakes will never be repeated. The call to introspection is thus presented in a way that will inspire confidence rather than demoralize. For those who, because of their close association with the policies of the past, might find this exposition of previous abuses a rather painful exercise, the Programme offers the promise of "salvation" through "repentance." For those who might be inspired to carry this process of self-criticism too far, the Programme stands as a pointed reminder that it was the CCP which recognized the need for reform, and it is the CCP which will lead the way to the future. Finally, for those who opposed the policies of the past, the Action Programme represents both a vindication and a victory.

Although this review of the distortions of the past may serve to intimidate the few, it can hardly be expected to inspire the many. To accomplish the latter, the Programme combines an enumeration of the problems that lie ahead with a projection of what life will be like once these problems are resolved. Such an approach can be considered doubly useful. First, it inspires by holding out the promise of rewards to members of the Party who demonstrate a willingness to accept the challenge of renovation. Secondly, for those in the Party who might be somewhat reluctant to accept this challenge, it offers inspiration of a negative nature—namely, the dire consequences that await a Party which is no longer relevant.

The Programme seeks to motivate in yet another way. In offering a plan of attack which reflects the initiative of the CCP, it implies that the steps to be taken will not lead to the destruction either of the system or of the Party. Thus the prospect of change is made more palatable, while the prospect of resisting change is made unattractive. Since the future of the Party is secure, and since these measures will serve to strengthen rather than weaken that position, there is little to be gained by obstructing implementation of the Programme. But there is much to be gained by wholehearted acceptance of the measures set forth therein.

The same theme is employed in conveying the message to the "masses."

Again, the need for change is keyed to both a frank acknowledgement of past errors and an equally frank acknowledgement of the willingness of the CCP to adapt to the changing conditions within Czechoslovakia. In each instance, however, the acknowledgement is a qualified one. The past is viewed as a period of both significant shortcomings and significant accomplishments. The crisis during these years centred around the reconstruction of a war-ravaged nation and the building of socialism. In the period immediately after World War II, there was a threat to the very existence of the Party. This, however, was successfully overcome and the work of reconstruction was begun. The years that followed are treated as a period of sacrifice, hardship and rapid change; they are also treated as a period in which an inexperienced Party confronted with new and demanding tasks was required to adopt policies which—while suitable for this particular stage of the country's development—were nevertheless retained long after they were needed.

The treatment of the past here, as elsewhere in the documents, is marked by an emphasis on individual and institutional shortcomings rather than Party error. The "masses" are told that while the CCP recognized the need to change with the times, "leading *bodies* and *institutes* of the Party and the State" found it difficult to accept the necessity of adjusting their behaviour in accordance with the requirements of each succeeding stage of development (italics mine). Abuses such as "sectarianism, suppression of the democratic rights and freedoms of the people, violation of laws, signs of licentiousness and misuse of power" are ascribed to the short-comings of individuals and institutional deviation from the Party line.

Again, as in the case of Party members, although a confession of errors may serve to placate the "masses," it hardly constitutes a suitable foundation from which to proceed to the building of a better future. In apparent recognition of that fact, the Action Programme—in addition to rescuing the reputation of the CCP—attempts to salvage as much as possible of the legacy of the past. The "masses" are told that many gains were made during these early years—gains which provide a solid basis for tackling the problems that lie ahead.

By the way of providing further inspiration, the Programme takes the position that while much remains to be done the worst is, in effect, over. In line with this position, there is the assertion that "*at the end of the fifties our society entered another stage of development.*" This assertion, preceded as it is by an exposition of past errors and followed by references to the need for a major renovation of the entire system, in effect constitutes a pledge by the CCP that there will be no turning back. The development theme is thus employed to demonstrate that neither the Party nor existing conditions will permit a return to the economic stagnation, political repression and popular alienation which characterized the earlier period.

The theme has an even more important function, however. In tying past, present and future together, it conveys to the "masses" the idea of progress or forward movement within the context of the existing system. The Action Programme, when viewed in this context, assumes the character of simply another instalment in an ongoing process of continuity and change—a process which, it should be noted, supposes an enduring future under socialism.

The major source of inspiration is, of course, the Programme itself, and more particularly the specific reforms outlined therein. For the most part these reforms speak for themselves. Considered at one level, they constitute a pledge on the part of the CCP to not only eliminate the accumulated shortcomings of past years but to work for the development of a society that is united, socialist, and humane—a society in which the CCP is truly responsive to the needs of the people—needs which are expressed freely and without fear of reprisal—a society wherein the Government becomes more than a hallow instrument of repression; a society moreover, in which the active participation of the "masses" in the process of renovation is supported by the establishment of legal safeguards against an arbitrary and capricious government; in which youth is allowed to partake of a rich cultural heritage in a system of education that encourages individual thought and personal development, and the nationality question is resolved so that Czechs and Slovaks live together in equality and harmony. Finally, a society in which the economy, once freed from the stifling control of a bureaucracy that is top-heavy and unimaginative, develops the capacity to provide the material basis for a full and happy life.

Considered at another level, however, these reforms represent an admission on the part of the CCP that a system which is dedicated primarily to the maintenance of internal security is not a system which is likely to foster internal development. As such, the system, if it is to survive, must change. That change cannot be piecemeal or superficial. It must be fundamental in character and far-reaching in its impact. It must, moreover, be presided over by a Party that is both competent and flexible; a Party that rewards imagination, expertise, and competence rather than unquestioning obedience to higher authority; a Party which tolerates legitimate dissent as the price for remaining relevant to the needs of society; a Party that is capable of demonstrating its right to control the destinies of the people by providing leadership which is conducive to the fulfilment of popular aspirations.

This is not a Party, it should be added, which presides over its own annihilation. Nor is it a Party that permits its will to be thwarted by those "right-wing anti-socialist elements" within Czechoslovakia who would reject the promise of socialism for the corruption of bourgeois democracy. It is instead a Party of strength—strength which is derived not from the forceable repression of opposition, but from opposition to forceable repression. A Party which is capable of distinguishing between legitimate dissent and subversion.

This, then, is the message delivered at the third level. It is a message of resolution and strength, calculated to serve as a reminder to those who would interpret this Programme as a repudiation of the system, that the CCP recognizes the need for renovation and is willing to accept the uncertainties which accompany change. It is not, however, willing to accept an end to its primacy as the leading force in the construction of a socialist society. Development there will be. Liberalization there will be. Revolution there will not be. As this Programme indicates, the CCP is prepared to deal with the challenge of development. It is, as the Programme makes absolutely clear, also prepared to deal with the challenge of denial.

The External Audience
To the external audience the message is presented with equal clarity. To the Soviet Union, members of the bloc, and other "fraternal parties" it is less a gesture of defiance than a statement of intent. The Programme follows the established pattern of first providing a requirement for change and then outlining the methods to be employed in meeting that requirement. In the case of the former, there are references scattered throughout the text covering not only the need for change but the role of the CCP as the initiator of change in Czechoslovakia. The impression conveyed is not one of a Party being dragged along by irresistible forces of change but of a Party which has acted, albeit belatedly, to curb a growing threat to its own survival. The Action Programme is in this way depicted as a product of necessity as well as choice. It is also, and more importantly

from the standpoint of the bloc, depicted as a Czech response to a Czech problem and thus is not presented as a model to be followed by anyone else.

The process of outlining methods to be employed in meeting the needs of the present as well as of the future combines an attempt to establish the fact that the changes will be beneficial with an attempt to establish the equally important fact that the primary beneficiary of the Action Programme will be the CCP itself. To that end, references to specific changes are generally coupled with statements concerning either the source of the change, i.e., the CCP, or comments dealing with the abuses of the past which, in one way or another, have made the changes necessary. Here, too, understandable care is taken to avoid giving the impression that the Action Programme is intended for external consumption. By linking the reforms to internal conditions, the CCP is able to minimize its references to ideology. In a system where, theoretically at least, there is a shared legitimacy of experience, this is understandably an important consideration.

The references to foreign relations which appear at the end of the Programme serve to underscore in a literal sense the message to the "socialist camp." Utilizing a theme of continuity and change, these comments alternately stress a desire to assume a more active international role and assurances that such a desire in no way constitutes a danger to the Soviet Bloc. In the Programme as in the other documents, special reference is made to the question of Czechoslovakia's relations with the German Democratic Republic and the German Federal Republic. The references reflect both the sensitive nature of the question and the fact that the CCP fully understands the political-military implications of its strategic position within the bloc.

The message as presented to the "socialist camp" is thus stated in such a way as to minimize possible objections either to the specific reforms or to the adoption of the entire Programme by the CCP. The clarity with which the message is stated, the moderate tone of the arguments advocated, the reliance on internal necessity as the justification for the changes to be initiated, and the numerous indications of the primacy of the CCP, its awareness of the internal dangers and its commitment to strengthening the instruments of State security, add up to a Programme which should have been palatable to the Soviet Union, if not to the other members of the bloc. Whatever the reasons behind the intervention, it would not appear that the Action Programme was a primary or even decisive factor. On the contrary, it would not be surprising at all if, in the months that follow, this Programme is implemented as stated.

To the non-Communist world the message of the Action Programme is stated in a somewhat obscure fashion. On the surface the Programme would appear to be a break with the past, a break occasioned by disillusionment with the old order and a desire to create a better way of life for the people of Czechoslovakia. Upon closer scrutiny, however, the Programme appears to constitute not a break with, but an extension of, the past—an extension prompted both by disillusionment with the old order and by confidence in the ability of that order to withstand the ordeal of change.

It is for this reason that the Programme deserves careful study—study conducted in an atmosphere which is free of polemics and maudlin sentimentality. For if the reforms proposed here say anything at all, it is that Communist political systems—or at least this Communist political system—have a capacity for self-regeneration which is considerable indeed. This is not to suggest that this, or for that matter any other, political system is indestructible. Nor is it to imply that the system has an unlimited capacity to absorb change. It is instead to suggest that the same system which produced the pressures for change also produced this Programme. That in itself would seem to be a significant accomplishment.

The accomplishment becomes even more significant, however, when one realizes that the Action Programme seeks not to destroy but to modify the system in the light of changing conditions within Czechoslovakia. It may be argued, of course, that in time such modification would have brought about the end of Communist rule in that country. The point is that the individuals who formulated this Programme appear to have been willing to take that chance. In the final analysis, this may well be the most significant aspect of the Action Programme—significant not only for the non-Communist world but for the Communist world as well.

Conclusion

The Action Programme reflects both an awareness of the need for change and a commitment to meet that need within the framework of the existing system. The reforms contemplated by the Programme suggest not a rejection of the system but its renovation. That renovation, involving as it does a series of far-reaching reforms, further suggests a belief in the capacity of the system to absorb change. Finally, that belief, coupled as it were with the desire to provide a better future under socialism for the people of Czechoslovakia, would seem to indicate, at least in this case, that Communist Party State systems are capable of meeting the challenge of political development.

THE ACTION PROGRAMME OF THE COMMUNIST PARTY OF CZECHOSLOVAKIA

adopted at the plenary session of the
Central Committee of the Communist Party
of Czechoslovakia on April 5th 1968

Prague, April 1968

THE CZECHOSLOVAK ROAD TO SOCIALISM

The social movement in the Czech lands and in Slovakia during the 20th century was carried along by two great currents - the national liberation movement and socialism.

The national liberation struggle of both nations culminated in the emergence of an independent state in which, for the first time in history, the political unity of the Czechs and Slovaks in a single state was realized. The founding of the Czechoslovak Republic marked important progress in the national and social development of both nations. The democratic order eliminated the old monarchist remnants and created favourable conditions for fast progress in all spheres of national life.

The pre-war bourgeois order, however, did not solve the onerous class antagonisms and was not able to lay reliable foundations for the lasting prosperity of the new economic entity and to guarantee the workers and employees full employment and a secure existence. Its nationalist regime, though liberal towards the minorities, ignored the individuality of the Slovak nation and did not succeed in eliminating the influence of extreme nationalism and in introducing the harmony desirable among all nationalities of the Republic. Under the conditions prevailing at that time in capitalist

a

3

Europe, not even the independence of the Czechoslovak Republic could be permanently safeguarded.

The progressive forces tried to give an answer to these shortcomings. Their most energetic component was the Communist Party of Czechoslovakia which was striving for a socialist conception of the Czechoslovak society.

In the broad wave of the anti-fascist movement which was born in connexion with the breaking up of Czechoslovakia as it existed between the wars, and especially in the course of the national liberation struggle, the integration of socialism with the national and democratic movement began to take shape.

During the national and democratic revolution of 1944-45 the national and democratic values of socialism were united for the first time. The democratic and national movement began to be socialized and socialism became a really national and democratic affair. The road to socialism taken by Czechoslovakia, at the beginning of which, in 1944-45, stood the Slovak National Uprising and the Prague Uprising is the source of the most progressive traditions of modern Czech and Slovak history.

The Republic, whose liberation was the result of the heroic fighting of the Soviet Army and the national liberation struggle of the Czechoslovak people, was restored on new foundations. These facilitated the solving of the most acute national problems in the country; the existence of the Republic as a State was ensured by close alliance with the Soviet Union; by nationalization the Republic gained an economic system providing conditions not only for rapid restoration but also for further development of the economy towards socialism. The considerable expansion of informal political freedoms was the true culmination of the whole democratic tradition of Czechoslovakia's development. Socialism became the embodiment of the modern national programme of the Czechs and Slovaks.

4   a

Czechoslovakia was the first industrial country to realize socialist reconstruction. The policy of Czechoslovakia's road to socialism, as pursued from 1945 to 1948, was an expression of the endeavours to respect the complexity of the specific internal and international conditions of Czechoslovakia. It contained many elements the understanding of which could contribute towards achieving our present aim of democratizing the socialist order.

We identify ourselves with traditions of the liberation struggle in which patriots participated at home and in various parts of Europe and the world, 375,000 of whom gave their lives for these ideals. We will support a scientific examination of the history of both nations, the conclusions of which cannot be decreed by anyone, but can only be the result of the study of history itself. The February victory of the working people was an important milestone in the socialist development of post-war Czechoslovakia, which created preconditions for accelerating the advance to socialism. After February 1948 the Party took a new road of socialist construction with a fund of great confidence and support of the broadest strata of the population.

This was a difficult road. In a divided world in the grips of cold war, our nations had to increase their efforts to safeguard their hardly won national existence and had to concentrate on reinforcing their own defence and that of all the other socialist states. The building up of the new Republic, which was far from having the internal resources essential for developing the economy, was closely connected with the progress and problems of the whole socialist camp. The inclusion of the Republic in the system of socialist states brought substantial changes in the direction of development of the national economy and also in its internal structure, in the character of the state and the social order. This was a matter of respecting the joint tasks of these countries in which the combating of economic and cultural retardation interwoven with the creation of new forms of ownership, played a leading role.

These connexions and tasks influenced the speed, form and content of the profound economic, social and political reconstruction which the Republic was going through during the building of socialism. They impelled an exceptional exertion of energy of the working class and the whole people, great sacrifice of communists and the dedicated work of tens of thousands of functionaries.

With the size, exceptionality and challenge of the changes, however, correspond the contradictions of development, the grave shortcomings, unsolved problems and deformations of socialist principles which are known as the personality cult.

The construction of the new social system was marked by insufficient experience, lack of knowledge, by dogmatism and subjectivism. Many signs of the times, conditioned by the sharpened international situation and compulsory acceleration in building up industry, were understood as the generally valid forms of the life and development of a socialist society. The stage of development of the socialist states at the beginning of the fifties and the arrest of the creative development of knowledge concomitant with the personality cult, conditioned also a mechanical acceptance and spreading of ideas, customs and political conceptions which were at variance with Czechoslovak conditions and traditions. The leading bodies and institutes of the Party and the State of that time are fully responsible for that acceptance. The centralist and directive-administrative methods used during the fight against the remnants of the bourgeoisie and during the consolidation of power under conditions of heightening international tension after February 1948 were, in this situation, unjustifiably carried over into the next stage of development and gradually grew into a bureaucratic system. Sectarianism,

6

a

suppression of the democratic rights and freedom of the people, violation of laws, signs of licentiousness and misuse
of power appeared in the internal life of the Republic, which
led to undermining the initiative of the people and, what is
more, gravely and unjustly afflicted many citizens - communists and non-communists. The irreparable losses suffered by
our movement at that time will remain for ever a warning
against similar methods.

The extraordinary exertion of the energy of our people
brought great historic successes. Basic socialist social
changes have been accomplished and the socialist order has
sunk its roots deeply and firmly into our land. Our society,
in which the means of production are mainly in the hands of
the socialist state or of workers' cooperatives, has got rid
of capitalist exploitation and the social wrongs connected
with it. Every citizen of the Czechoslovak Socialist Republic
has the right to work and enjoys basic social security. Our
society has gone through a period of industrialization and
now disposes of an extensive industrial base. We have achieved noteworthy successes in the advancement of science and
culture; the possibilities of the broadest strata of the
people gaining appropriate education have increased to an
unheard of extent. The international status of the Republic
among the socialist countries is firmly secured.

At the end of the fifties our society entered another
stage of development. On this fact was gradually formed the
political line which we want to apply in a creative way and
to develop. Characteristic of the present stage are:

● antagonistic classes no longer exist and the main feature of internal development is becoming the process of bringing all socialist groupings in the society closer together.

● methods of direction and organization hitherto used in
the national economy are outdated and urgently demand changes, i.e. an economic system of management able to enforce

a turn towards intensive growth;

⬤ it will be necessary to prepare the country for joining in the scientific-technical revolution in the world, which calls for especially intensive cooperation of workers and agricultural workers with the technical and specialized intelligentsia, and which will place high demands upon the knowledge and qualifications of people, on the application of science.

⬤ a broad scope for social initiative, frank exchange of views and democratization of the whole social and political system – becomes virtually the condition for the dynamics of socialist society – the condition for us being able to hold our own in competition with the world, and to honourably fulfil our obligations towards the international workers movement.

Surmounting the causes of profound social crisis

Already at the time when this Party line was being formed and starting to be applied, it ran up against lack of understanding for the new tasks, with recidivism of redundant methods of work which arose at the time of sharp class struggle in Czechoslovakia, with the opposition of those who in one way or another found the deformations of the socialist reality convenient.

We want to disclose frankly what these mistakes and deformations were and what were their causes so as to be able to remedy them as soon as possible and to concentrate all forces on the fundamental structural changes in our lives which we are facing at the present time.

Already after the 20th Congress of the Communist Party of the USSR, which was an impulse for revival of the development of socialist democracy, the Party adopted several mea-

sures which were intended to overcome bureaucratic-central-
ist sectarian methods of management or its remnants, to
prevent the means of class struggle being reversed against
the working people. Many communists and whole working collectives tried to open the way to progressive development
of the economy, the living standard, science and culture.
The more definitely was the class antagonism overcome and
the foundations for socialism laid, the more urgent was the
stress placed upon promotion of cooperation of all working
people, of all social strata, groups and nationalities in
Czechoslovakia and on fundamental changes in methods employed during the time of sharp class struggle. At the same time,
there was rightly seen in the development of socialist
democracy the main social conditions for realization of the
humanistic aims which are characteristic of socialism. However, they met with lack of understanding, inhibitions and,
in some cases, even with direct suppression. The survival
of methods from the time of the class struggle evoked an ar-
tificial tension among the social groups, nations and nationalities, different generations, communists and non-party
people in this society. Dogmatic approaches impeded a full
and timely re-evaluation of conceptions of the character of
socialist construction.

The measures adopted did not therefore bring the anticipated results. On the contrary, over the years, difficulties piled up until they closed in a vicious circle. Subjective conceptions were not overridden in time, as if construction of the new society were dependent only upon accelerated extensive development of production. This led to a
precipitated expansion of heavy industry, to a disproper-
tionate demand on labour power, raw materials and to costly
investments. Such an economic policy, enforced through directive administrative methods, no longer corresponded to
the economic requirements and possibilities of the country
and led to exhaustion of its material and human resources.

a
9

Unrealistic tasks were placed upon the economy, illusory promises were made to the workers. This orientation served to intensify the unfavourable structure of production which did not correspond with the national conditions in which local skilled labour could be not sufficiently applied, caused considerable technical retardation in Czechoslovak production, put a brake on development of public services, upset the equilibrium of the market, worsened the international status of the Czechoslovak economy, especially of the exchange of Czechoslovak products of labour abroad and finally, had to end in stagnation and, in certain cases, even in the reduction of the living standard of the people.

These shortcomings were directly caused by the maintainence and constant restoration primarily of the old directive system of management: Economic means, forms of supply and demand, and marketing ties were replaced by directives from the centre. Socialist enterprise did not expand. In economic life, independence, diligence, expertize and the initiative of the people were not appreciated, but, rather the contrary, subservience, obedience and even kowtowing to higher ups were.

A more profound reason for keeping up the outlived methods of economic management were the deformations in the political system. Socialist democracy was not expanded in time, methods of revolutionary dictatorship deteriorated into bureaucracy and became an impediment to progress in all spheres of life in Czechoslovakia. And so, political mistakes were added to economic difficulties and mechanism was created which resulted in helplessness, conflict between theory and practice. Much endeavour, activity and energy of workers of the Party, the State, the economy, science and culture was squandered away. When to this was added the adverse external circumstances of the early sixties, serious economic crisis followed. It is from there that the diffi-

culties with which the workers are still confronted daily,
emanate: the slow increase in wages of many-years standing,
stagnation of the living standard and especially the constantly increasing retardation of the infrastructure in com-
parison with advanced industrial countries, the catastrophic
state of housing and insufficient building of houses and
apartments, the precarious state of the transport system,
poor quality goods and public services, lack of cultural
standard in living environment and conditions in general
which tangibly affect just the human factor, possibilities
of developing human energy and the activity of man, all of
which are decisive for a socialist society. Embitterness grew
among the people and a feeling that despite all successes
which had been achieved and despite all efforts exerted, the
socialist society was making headway with great difficulty,
with fateful delay and with moral political defects in human
relations. Quite naturally, apprehensions arose about socialism, about its human mission, about its human features.Some
people became demoralized others lost perspective.

The main link in this circle was that of remnants or
reappearance of the bureaucratic, sectarian approach in the
Party itself. The insufficient development of socialist democracy within the Party, the unfavourable atmosphere for
the promotion of activity, the silencing or even suppression
of criticism - all of this thwarted a fast, timely and thorough rectification. Party bodies took over tasks of State
and economic bodies and social organizations. This led to an
incorrect merging of the Party and State management, to a
monopolized power-position of some sections, unqualified interference as well as the undermining of initiative at all
levels, indifference, the cult of mediocrity and to unhealthy
anonymity. A consequence of this was the spreading of irresponsibility and lack of discipline. Many correct resolutions
were never fulfilled. This adversely affected theoretic thinking, making it impossible to recognize in time the short-

a 11

comings and the danger connected with the outdated system
of management. Amendments in the economy and politics were
held up.

All of these questions became a focus for clashing
of those forces which were insisting upon fundamental changes with the bearers of the old conception. At the same time,
this led to a clarification of the position, and essential social progress was pushed ahead. At the December sessions of the Central Committee, thorough and factual criticism was made of the main causes of the aforementioned shortcomings, and their bearers, and corrective measures were
instigated in the leading bodies of the Party themselves.
One of the immediate causes was said to be that inside the
Party there was too great a concentration of decision, that
there arose an extraordinary status of individuals, in the
first place of A. Novotný. This criticism allowed the whole
Party and the society to start overcoming the old approach
and sectarian bureaucratic practice on the basis of self-
critical evaluation of the work to date, from top to bottom,
so as to create real unity of the society on the same basis
of social democratism, thoroughly to put into practice the
principles of the new system of economic management, to mo-
dernize and rationalize life in Czechoslovakia, to open up
long-term perspectives of gradually including Czechoslovakia
in the process of the scientific-technological revolution -
so that in all spheres of this society the power of socialism will be revived and will start out along a new road of
socialist development.

A policy of unity and confidence

Decisive for the socialist development of this country was the creation of the broad reliance of progressive
forces of the town and country headed by the working class

12

a

and the unity of the Czech and Slovak nations.

The resolution of the 13th Congress of the Communist Party of Czechoslovakia set the task: "In the internal life of the country to continue strengthening the union of the working class which is the leading force in the society, with the agricultural cooperative workers and the socialist intelligentsia as the political base of the State, to help the mutual rapprochement of classes and strata of the nations and nationalities in Czechoslovakia and to consolidate their unity." The sense of the present policy is to stimulate continuously democratic relations of cooperation and confidence among the various social groups without differentiation, to harmonize their efforts, to unite their forces on the basis of the development of the whole society.

All social classes, strata, groups, both nations and all nationalities of the society agree with the fundamental interests and aims of socialism. One of the big advantages of socialist development to date is, that a decisive factor in assessing the standing and activity of the people in this society is their working merits and progressive social activity and not their membership of this class or that stratum. The Party resolutely condemns attempts to put the various classes, strata and groups of the socialist society in opposition to each other and will eliminate everything that creates tension among them.

On behalf of unity and the interests of the whole society, there can be no overlooking the various needs and interests of individual people and social groups according to their work, qualification, age, sex, nationality and so on. In the past we have often made such mistakes.

Socialism can only flourish if scope is given for the assertion of the various interests of the people and on this basis the unity of all workers will be brought about democratically. This is the main source of free social acti-

a

13

vity and development of the socialist system.

The Party is backed, and will continue to be backed, by the <u>working class</u> which has shown that it is able to carry the main weight of socialist endeavour. Under prevailing conditions, we rely especially upon those, who, with their awareness i.e. profound understanding of the real interests and tasks of the working class in the revolutionary reconstruction of the whole society, with their qualifications, and their cohesion with modern technology, the high effectivity of their work, their social activity, contribute markedly to the further progress of Czechoslovak production and to the whole society as such. The working class began the revolutionary struggle so as to abolish every sort of exploitation, to erase all class barriers, to facilitate the liberation of people and with them to transform the conditions of human life, the character of human labour, to make way for the full self-realization of man, and by all this to change even itself. These long-term interests of the working class have not yet been fully realized. The workers, however, now have in their hands new technical, social and cultural means, which allow them to continue changing their working and living conditions, to expand the elements of purposeful creative endeavour in their activity. We are determined to open up wide the road to the assertion of all creative and by far not fully utilized energy which the working class has for these tasks.

In the past, the workers did not always have the possibility of asserting their immediate and specific interests. Therefore the Party will strive to activize the social life of the workers, to provide scope for making use of all their political and social rights through political organizations, and trade unions and to strengthen the democratic influence of collective teams of workers in the management of production. It will strive for the alleviation

14

a

of exhausting labour, for the humanization of work and for improving the labour conditions of workers.

One of the most significant results of the transformation of the social structure was the creation of social groups, organically cohering with the workers - <u>agricultural cooperative workers</u>. This fact must be appreciated politically. The Party will strive for the absolute economic equalization of agriculture with industry and for appraising the social importance of agricultural work. In accordance with the conclusions of the 7th Congress of Agricultural Cooperatives we shall support the setting up of all-state agricultural cooperative organizations and raise their political authority; we want to abolish all administrative, bureaucratic obstructions which impede the independent initiative of agricultural enterprises, everything that endangers the security of cooperative venture and that emanates from lack of confidence in the ability of the agricultural cooperative workers to act independently and in a socialist way.

Likewise it will be necessary to understand that the character of our <u>intelligentsia</u> has gradually changed, it has become an intelligentsia of the people, a socialist intelligentsia. It represents a force, which takes part, in a creative way, in the development of the society and makes the wealth of science and culture available to all people. Today, the workers will find in the intelligentsia their integral component part and their own inner force. The constantly closer collaboration of the technical intelligentsia with the workers in productive collectives simultaneously records the process of surmounting former class barriers. The Party will support the growing unity between the intelligentsia and the other working people, it will combat underestimation of the role of the intelligentsia in this society, which was the case of late, it will combat everything that upsets relations between the intelligentsia and the workers.

a

15

It vill strive for just remuneration of complex and creative mental labour.

Just as with the working class, so with the agricultural workers and the intelligentsia, the Party will rely mainly upon those who best understand and most actively assert social interests and who, by effective work, most markedly contribute to social progress. Cooperation of all groups of the socialist society will be effective and possible only providing everyone becomes aware of his responsibility to the other, and does not give preference to narrow professional interests.

The fundament of Czechoslovak statehood is the voluntary and equal co-existence of <u>Czechs and Slovaks</u>. By the forming of socialist relations, pre-conditions will be given for the strengthening of the fraternal co-existence of our nations. Our Republic can only be strong providing, there will be no sparks of tension, or signs of nervosity and suspicion in the relations of the Czech and the Slovak nations and all nationalities. We must therefore resolutely condemn all expressions which would undermine the principles of the equality and sovereignty of both socialist nations and which occured in the past. The unity of the Czechs and Slovaks can be strengthened only on the basis of an unhampered development of their national individuality in harmony with progress made in economy, with objective changes in the social structure of both nations and on the basis of absolute equality and voluntariness. Our Republic will be that much stronger, the more developed will be the two nations, the greater will be the use made of the enormous economic and cultural resources in Slovakia, in the interest of the progress of the whole Republic. Indifference to national interests or even endeavours to suppress them, is considered by the Party to be a gross distortion of its programme, of its political course. The Party will consistently defend the Leninist prin-

16

a

ciple that the overlooking of the interests of a smaller nation by the larger is incompatable with socialist relations
between nations. It will oppose any kind of endeavour to
place the continuous searching for the best methods of development in the constitutional relations of our nations,
established on equal rights and voluntariness, in the light
of weakening of the Republic. Communists of both nations
and all nationalities in this country defend the principles
of internationalism; the communists of every nation and nationality are themselves surmounting nationalistic relics
in their own surroundings.

Under socialist conditions, each of the national minorities - Hungarian, Polish, Ukrainian, German and so on -
have the right to their own national life and consistent
fulfilling of all other constitutional rights.

The Party stresses it will oppose all expressions of
antisemitism, racism and any anti-humanistic ideology,which
would set the people against each other.

Various generations of our society have grown up under different conditions and naturally vary in their outlook
on many questions of our life. The Party strongly rejects
endeavours to put into contradiction the interests of these
generations, it will devote special care to harmonizing and
satisfying the needs of the different age groups.

It is true that our system, on the basis of the dedicated work of the older generation, as compared with the pre-
Munich Republic has provided better conditions for the young
people. Nevertheless, we have still remained greatly indebted to the youth. Shortcomings and mistakes in political,
economic and cultural life, just as in human relations, affect the young person especially strongly, contradictions
between words and deeds, lack of frankness, phrasemongering
bureaucracy, attempts to settle everything from a position
of power - these deformations of socialist life must pain-

a

17

fully affect students, young workers and agricultural workers, arousing in them the feeling that it is not they, their
work, their efforts which are decisive for their own future
life. An urgent task is that of restoring contact with young
people everywhere and of making them responsible which pertains to them for their independent work under socialism.

This especially applies to improving working conditions, and possibilities of young people being active in social and cultural life and of consistently erasing everything that evokes non-confidence towards socialism in young
people. We are all glad about the enthusiasm of the youth,
their positive and critical initiative, which is a condition for them finding their cause and future in socialism
and communism.

Neither should we overlook the material conditions,
the social necessity, respect for and social assertion of
the old people, which makes possible for them a dignified
and well-merited retirement. This society should give great
attention to ensuring the active participation of members
of the resistance movement to whom the respect of everyone
is due.

The deformations of the Party and State policy also
include the fact that in the past the problem of women,
especially those in employment was not considered a serious
political matter. In State, economic and cultural policy,
women should have access to such positions which comply
with principles of socialist democracy and the significant
role taken by women in creating material and spiritual values of the society.

In the further development of our society we must
reckon with the activity of all strata of the population
in public life and constructive endeavour. We can say quite
openly that we are calculating with believers too, who, on
the basis of their faith wish, as equals, as builders of a

18
a

socialist society, to take their part in helping to fulfil all our exacting tasks.

To develop democracy and eliminate equalitarianism

The assertion of the manifold interests of the social groups and individuals, and their unification, calls for the elaboration and implementation of a new political system in our lives, a new model of socialist democracy. The Party will strive for such a development of the State and social order as will correspond to the actual lay-out of interests of the various strata and groups of this society, as will give them the possibility of expressing their interests in their organizations and of voicing their views in public life. We expect that in an atmosphere of mutual confidence between people and their institutions civic responsibility will grow at the same time and that norms of human relations will be respected.

Meanwhile, the Party will strive to link the democratic principles of the social system with expert and scientific management and decision. In order to be able to judge responsibly what is in the interest of the whole society,we must always have before us other alternatives for appraisal, expertly justified proposals for solving all disputable matters, and we must ensure that the people get much more information, more candidly.

Today, when class differences are being erased, the main criterion for evaluating the status of people in society is how the person contributes towards social progress. The Party has often criticized equalitarian views, but in practice levelling has spread to an unheard of extent and this became one of the impediments to an intensive development of the economy and to raising the living standard. The harmful-

a

19

ness of equalitarianism lies in the living standard. The
harmfulness of equalitarianism lies in the fact that it puts
careless workers, idlers and irresponsible people to advantage as compared with the dedicated and diligent workers,
the unqualified compared with the qualified, the technical-
ly and expertly backward people as compared with the talented and those with initiative.

When attempting today to do away with equalitarianism,
to apply the principle of actual achievements in the appraisal of employees we have no intention of forming a new privileged stratum. We want in all spheres of social life, the
remuneration of people to depend upon the social importance
and effectivity of their work, upon the development of workers initiative, upon the degree of responsibility and risk.
This is in the interest of the development of the whole society. The principle of actual achievements raises the technical standard, profitability and productivity of labour,
respect and authority of the managers responsible, the principle of material incentive, it stresses the growing importance of qualification of all workers.

One of the key conditions of the present and future
scientific, technical and social development is to substantially increase the qualifications of managers and experts
at all levels of economic and social life. If the leading
posts are not be filled by capable, educated socialist expert cadres, socialism will be unable to hold its own in competition with capitalism.

This fact will require great changes in the existing
cadre policy in which for years the aspects of education,
qualification and ability have been underrated.

Application of the principle of remuneration according to the quantity, quality and social usefulness of work
calls for a de-levelling of incomes. It does not however
mean neglecting the interests of citizens in the lowest in-

come group, the interests of families with many children, citizens with reduced working ability, pensioners and certain categories of women and youth. On the contrary, consistent application of the principle of differentiated remuneration according to actual work achievement, is the only effective means for such a development of resources which would enable a raising of the standard of living and, according to the spirit of socialist humanism, determine and ensure good living conditions for all strata of the society. We want to make it quite clear that honest work for the society and efforts to improve qualification are not only duly remunerated but they must also enjoy due respect. The socialist society respects those who achieve exceptional results, who are active and show initiative in advancing production, technical, cultural and social progress; it respects the talented people and creates favourable conditions for their assertion.

The leading role of the Party - a guarantee of socialist progress

At present it is most important that the Party practices a policy fully justifying its leading role in society. We believe that at present this is a condition for the socialist development of the country.

The Communist Party, as a party of the working class, won the struggle with capitalism and the struggle to carry out revolutionary class changes; with the victory of socialism it becomes the vanguard of the entire socialist society. Especially during the present time has the Party proved its ability to lead this society, when from its own initiative it launched the process of democratization and ensured its socialist character. In its political activity the Party intends to depend particularly on those who have understanding for the requirements of the society as a whole, who do not

a

21

see their own personal and group interests against those of socialism, those who use and improve their abilities for the benefit of all, who have a sense for everything new and progressive and are willing to help advance it.

The Communist Party enjoys the voluntary support of the people; it does not practice its leading role by ruling the society but by most devotedly serving its free, progressive socialist development. The Party cannot enforce its authority but this must be won again and again by Party activity. It cannot force its line through directives but by the work of its members, by the veracity of its ideals.

In the past, the leading role of the Party was often conceived as a monopolistic concentration of power in the hands of Party bodies. This corresponded to the false thesis that the Party is the instrument of the dictatorship of the proletariat. This harmful conception weakened the initiative and responsibility of the State, economic and social institutions and damaged the Party's authority, and prevented it from carrying out its real functions. The Party's goal is not to become a universal "caretaker" of the society, to bind all organizations and every step taken in life by its directives. Its mission lies primarily in arousing socialist initiative, in showing the ways and actual possibilities of communist perspectives, and in winning over all workers for them through systematic persuasion, as well as by the personal examples of communists. This is determined by the conceptional character of Party activity; Party bodies do not deal with all problems but should encourage activity and suggest the solution to the most important ones. At the same time the Party cannot turn into an organization which would influence the society only by its ideas and programme. Through its members and bodies it must develop the practical organization functions of a political force in society. The political and organizational Party activity coordinates the practical ef-

22   a

forts of the people to turn the Party line and programme into reality in all respects - in the social, economic and cultural life of the society.

As a representative of the interests of the most progressive part of all the State - and thus also representative of the perspective aims of the society - the Party cannot represent the entire scale of social interests. The political expression of the many-sided interests of the society is the whole National Front, as an expression of the unity of the social strata, groups of interests and of the nations and nationalities of this society. The Party does not want to, and will not take the place of social organizations, but, on the contrary, it must take care that their initiative and political responsibility for the unity of the society is revived and flourishes. The role of the Party is to seek such a way of satisfying the various interests which would not jeopardize the perspective interests of the society as a whole, but which would promote them and create new progressive interests. The Party policy must not lead to non-communists getting the impression that their rights and freedom are limited by the role of the Party. On the contrary, they must see in the activity of the Party a guarantee of their rights, freedom and interests. We want, and shall achieve, a state of affairs when the Party right at basic organization level, will have informal, natural authority based upon its working and managing ability and the moral qualities of communist functionaries.

Within the framework of democratic rules of a socialist state, communists must over and again strive for the voluntary support of the majority of the people for the Party line. It is necessary to alter Party resolutions and directives if they fail to express correctly the needs and possibilities of the whole society. The Party must endeavour for its members - as the most active workers in their spheres of

a

23

work - to have corresponding weight and influence in the whole society,to hold functions in State,economic and social bodies. This, however, must not lead to the practice of appointing party members to functions, without regard to the principle that leading representatives of institutions of the whole society are chosen by the society itself and by its various components and that functionaries of these components are responsible to all citizens or to all members of social organizations. It is necessary to abolish the discriminating practice and the creation of a "Cadre ceiling" for people not members of the party.

The basis for the Party s action ability is its ideological and organizational unity based upon broad intra-Party democracy. The most effective weapon against introducing methods of bureaucratic centralism in the Party is the strengthening of the influence of Party members, of forming the political line, reinforcing the role of really democratically elected bodies. Elected bodies of the Party must first of all guarantee the application of all rights of its members, the making of decisions collectively, and, that all power will not be concentrated in a single pair of hands.

Only down-to-earth discussion and exchange of views can be the pre-condition for responsible deciding of collective bodies. Confrontation of views is an essential expression of a multilateral responsible attempt to find the best solution, to advance the new against the obsolete. Each member of the Party and Party bodies has not only the right,but the duty to act according to his conscience, with initiative, criticism, with different views on the matter in question, to oppose any functionary. This practice must become deeply rooted if the Party is to avoid subjectivism in its activity. It is impermissible to restrict communists in these rights, to create an atmosphere of distrust and suspicion of those around who voice different opinions, to persecute the minority under any pretext - as has happened in the past. The

24

a

Party, however, cannot abandon the principle of requiring the fulfilling of resolutions once they are approved.Within the Party, all its members are equal regardless of whether they hold any function in Party bodies or in bodies of State and economic organizations. Nevertheless, he who occupies a higher position, also carries greater responsibility. The Party is aware of the fact that there will be no more profound democracy in this society if democratic principles will not be consistently applied in the internal life and work in the Party itself, among communists. Decisions on all important questions and on the filling of posts by cadres must be ensured by democratic rules of negotiation and by secret ballot. The democratization of Party life also means the strengthening of work contacts between the Party and science. In this line we shall make use of consultations, exchange of opposing and contrary views since the role of science does not end by preparing analyses and documents. It should continue on Party grounds, by observing the processes evolved by the various resolutions and by contributing to their materialization and to the control of the correctness of the resolutions in practice.

The Central Committee of the Communist Party of Czechoslovakia set out on this road at its December and January sessions and it will make sure that in the months to come the questions of content and democratic methods of Party life, of relations between elected bodies and the Party apparatus are clarified throughout the Party and that rules will be elaborated defining the authority and responsibility of the individual bodies and links of the Party mechanism, as well as the principles of the Party's cadre policy which, among other things, will ensure an effective, regular change of leading officials, guarantees of the standard of information of members and relations of Party bodies to Party members in general. In preparing the 14th Party Congress the Party will make sure that the Party statutes correspond with the present state of its development.

FOR THE DEVELOPMENT OF SOCIALIST DEMOCRACY, FOR A NEW SYSTEM OF THE POLITICAL MANAGEMENT OF SOCIETY

In the past decade, the Party has many times put forward the demand for a development of socialist democracy. Measures taken by the Party were aimed at enhancing the role of elected representative bodies in the state. They emphasized the importance of voluntary social organizations and of all forms of popular activities. The Party policy initiated a number of laws which increased the protection of rights of every citizen. It was clearly stated in the theses of the Central Committee of the Communist Party of Czechoslovakia prepared for the 13th Party Congress that "the state of working class dictatorship had fulfilled its main historical mission in our country" and the guide line for further development of our democracy was given no less clearly - "the system of socialist democracy - the state, social organizations, and the Party as the leading force - purposefully endeavours to bring out the differing interests and attitudes of working people to social problems in a democratic way and to settle them inside the socialist society organizations correctly and with regard to nationwide needs and goals. The development of democracy must proceed hand in hand with strengthening of a scientific and professional approach to social management."

Nevertheless, <u>harmful characteristics of centralized directive decision-making and management have survived up to the present day</u>. In relations among the Party, the state, and social organizations, in internal relations and methods within these individual partners, in the relations of state

and other institutions to individuals, in the interpretation
of the importance of public opinion and of people being informed, in the practical effect of personnel policy - in all
these fields there are too many things souring the life of
the people, while obstructing a professionally competent and
scientific decision-making, and encouraging highhandedness.
The reason may be sought, first and foremost, in that these
relations in our political system have been built up for
years as the instrument for carrying out the orders of the
centre, and hardly ever made it at all possible for the decision itself to be the outcome of a democratic procedure.

The different interests and needs of people not fore
seen by the system of directive decision-making were taken
as an undesirable obstacle and not as new needs of the life
of people which have to be respected by politics. That was
why the often well-meant words of "an increase in the people's participation in management" could not help as in time
this "participation of the people" came to mean chiefly
help in carrying out orders and not in settling the correctness of the decisions. Thus it was possible that views, measures and interventions were enforced that were highhanded
and did not comply either with scientific cognition, or with
the interests of the various strata of the people and of individuals. Centralized decision-making put into effect in
this way could not then be effective either and, on the contrary, led to a number of resolutions not being fulfilled
and weakening of the purposeful management of social development. This, in turn, has in many cases kept such people in
functions that are not capable of any other way of "management", who consistently revive the old methods and habits,
who surround themselves with people who humour them and not
with people whose capacities and character would be a guarantee of the successful carrying out of the functions. In
spite of consistently condemning the "personality cult" we
are still not able, therefore, to eradicate some character-

a

27

istics of our society typical for that period. This under-
mines the people s confidence in the Party being, in fact,
able to change this situation, and old tensions and political nervous strain are again raised and revived.

The Central Committee is firmly determined to overcome such a state of affairs. As said above, it is necessary
to prepare,for the 14th Congress, the fundamental issues of
the development of the political system into a concept meeting the demands of life, just as we have elaborated the fundamental concept of the new economic system.

The main thing is to reform the whole political system
so that it will permit the dynamic development of socialist
social relations, combine broad democracy with a scientific,
highly qualified management, strengthen the social order,
stabilize socialist relations and maintain social discipline.
The basic structure of the political system must, at the same time, provide firm guarantees against a return to the old
methods of subjectivism and highhandedness from a position
of power. Party activity has, so far, not been turned systematically to that end, in fact, obstacles have frequently
been put in the way of such efforts. All these changes necessarily call for commencement of work on a new Czechoslovak
constitution so that the draft of the new constitution may
be thoroughly discussed among professionals and in public in
all important points and submitted to the National Assembly
shortly after the Party Congress.

But we consider it indispensable to change the present state of things right now, even before the 14th Congress,
so that the development of socialism and its inner dynamics
are not hampered by the outdated factors in the political
system. Our democracy must provide more room for the activity of every individual, every collective, every link in the
management, both at lower and higher levels, and in the centre, too. People must have more opportunity to think for

28

a

themselves and express their opinions. We must radically change the practices that turn the people's initiative and critical comments and suggestions from below into words that meet with the proverbial deaf ear. We must see to it that the incompetent but adaptive /to anything/ people are really replaced by those who strive for socialism, who are concerned with its fate and progress, with the interests and needs of others, and not with their own power or advantages. This will affect people both "above" and "below". It is going to be a complicated process taking some time. It is necessary to make clear everywhere - at all levels of management, in the Party, in state and economic bodies and in social organizations - which body or which official or which worker is really responsible, for what, where to look for guarantees of improvement, where to change institutions, where the working methods, and where to replace individuals. The attitude of individual Party officials to new tasks and methods, their capability of carrying the new policy into practice, must be the basic political criterion.

No responsibility without right

Who, which body and which official is responsible for what, what are his rights and duties, must be perfectly clear in all our system of management for the future, and we consider this to be the basic prerequisite for correct development. To this end, each component part should have its own independent position. Substitution and interchanging of state bodies, agencies of economic and social organizations by Party bodies must be completely stopped. Party resolutions are binding for the communists working in these bodies, but the policy, directing activities, and responsibility of the state, economic, and social organizations are independent. The communists active in these bodies and organizations must take

a

29

the initiative and see that the state and economic bodies as well as social organizations /notably the Trade Unions, the Czechoslovak Union of Youth, etc./ take the problem of their activities and responsibilities into their own hands.

The whole <u>National Front</u>, the political parties which form it, and the social organizations, will take part in the creation of state policy. <u>The political parties</u> of the National Front are partners whose political work is based on the joint political programme of the National Front and is naturally bound by the Constitution of the Czechoslovak Socialist Republic, is fully based on the socialist character of social relations in our country. The Communist Party of Czechoslovakia considers the National Front to be a political platform which does not separate the political parties into the government and the opposition in the sense that opposition would be created to the state policy as the policy of the whole National Front and a struggle for political power in the state were to exist. Possible differences in the viewpoints of individual component parts of the National Front, or divergency of views as to the policy of the state, are all to be settled on the basis of the common socialist conception of the National Front policy by way of political agreement and unification of all component parts of the National Front. Formation of political forces striving to negate this concept of the National Front, to remove the National Front as a whole from political power, was ruled out as long ago as 1945 after the tragic experience of both our nations with the prewar political development of the then Czechoslovak Republic; it is naturally unacceptable for our present republic.

The Communist Party of Czechoslovakia considers the <u>political management</u> of the Marxist-Leninist concept of the development of socialism as a precondition for the right development of our socialist society. It will assert the Mar-

30   a

xist-Leninist concept as the leading political principle in
the National Front and in all our political system by seeking, through the means of political work, such support in all
the component parts of our system and <u>directly among the masses of workers and all working people</u> that will ensure its
leading role in a democratic way.

Voluntary social organizations of the working people
cannot replace political parties, <u>but the contrary is also
true: political parties in our country cannot exclude common-
interest organizations of workers and other working people
from directly influencing state policy</u>, its creation and application. Socialist state power cannot be monopolized either
by a single party, or by a coalition of parties. It must be
open to all political organizations of the people. <u>The Communist Party of Czechoslovakia will use every means to develop such forms of political life that will ensure the expression of the direct say and will of the working class and all
working people in political decision-taking in our country</u>.

The whole existing organization, forms of activities,
and incorporation of the various organizations in the National Front must be revised in principle under the new conditions and built up so that the National Front may carry out
the qualitatively new tasks. <u>The National Front as a whole
and all its component parts must be allowed independent rights
and their own responsibility for the management of our country
and society</u>.

<u>Voluntary social organizations</u> must be based on real-
ly voluntary membership and activity. People join these organizations because they express their interests, therefore
they have the right to choose their own officials and representatives who cannot be appointed from outside. These principles should be the foundation of our unified mass organizations the activities of which are still indispensable but
which should meet, by their structure, their working methods,

a
31

and their ties with their members, the new social conditions.

The implementation of <u>constitutional freedoms of assembly and association</u> must be ensured this year so that the possibility of setting up voluntary organizations, special-interest associations, societies, etc. is guaranteed by law to meet the actual interests and needs of various strata and categories of our citizens, without bureaucratic interference and without monopoly of any individual organization. Any restrictions in this respect can be imposed only by law and only the law can stipulate what is anti-social, forbidden, or punishable. Freedoms guaranteed by law are applicable in this sense, in compliance with the constitution, also to citizens of individual creeds and religious denominations.

The effective influence of views and opinions of the working people on all our policy, opposition to all tendencies to suppress the criticism and initiative of the people, cannot be guaranteed if we do not ensure constitution-based freedom of speech and all political and personal rights of all citizens, systematically and consistently, by all legal means available. <u>Socialism cannot mean only liberation of the working people from the domination of exploiting class relations, but must make more provisions for a fuller life of the personality than any bourgeois democracy</u>. The working people, who are no longer ordered about by any class of exploiters, can no longer be prescribed by any arbitrary interpretation from a position of power, what information they may or may not be given, which of their opinions can or cannot be expressed publicly, where public opinion may play a role and where not. Public opinion polls must be systematically used in preparing important decisions and the main results of the research are to be published. Any restriction may be imposed only on the basis of a law stipulating what is anti-social - which in our country is mainly the criminal law. The Central Committee of the Communist Party of Czechoslovakia considers it necessary to define more exactly than hitherto in the shortest possible time by a press law,when a state body can forbid the propagation of certain information /in the press, radio, television, etc./ and exclude the possibility of preliminary factual censorship. It is necessary to overcome the holding up, distortion, and incomple teness of information, to remove any unwarranted secrecy of political and economic facts, to publish the annual balance sheets of enterprises, to publish even alternatives to various suggestions and measures, to extend the import and sale of foreign press. Leading representatives of state, social and cultural organizations are obliged to organize regular press conference and give their views on topical issues on television, radio, and in the press. In the press, it is necessary to make a distinction between official standpoints of state, Party and journalist bodies; the Party press especially must express the Party's own life, development and criticisms of various opinions among the communists, etc., and cannot be made fully identical with the official viewpoints of the state.

The Party realizes that ideological antagonists of socialism may try to abuse the process of democratization. At the present stage of development and under the conditions of our country, we insist on the principle that bourgeois ideology can be challenged only in open ideological struggle before all of the people. It is possible to win over people for the ideas and policy of the Party only by struggle based on the practical activity of communists for the benefit of the people, on truthful and complete information, and on scientific analysis. We trust that in such a struggle, all sections of our society will contribute actively towards the victory of truth, which is on the side of socialism.

At present the activity and responsibility of publishing houses, chief editors, of all Party members and progressive staff of mass communication media, must grow to

a

33

push through socialist ideals and to put into effect the policy of the Party, of the National Front, and of the State.

Legal norms must guarantee more exactly <u>the freedom</u>
<u>of speech of minority interests and opinions</u> also /again
within the framework of socialist laws and in harmony with
the principle that decisions are taken in accordance with the
will of the majority/. The <u>constitutional freedom of movement</u>
particularly the travelling of our citizens abroad, <u>must be</u>
<u>precisely guaranteed by law</u>; in particular, this means that
a citizen should have the legal right to long-term or permanent sojourn abroad and that people should not be ground-
lessly placed in the position of emigrants; at the same time
it is necessary to protect by law the interests of the state,
for example, as regards the drain of some categories of spe-
cialists, etc.

We must gradually solve in the whole legal code the
task of how <u>to protect in a better and more consistent way</u>
<u>the personal rights and property of citizens</u>, we must espe-
cially remove those stipulations that virtually put individual citizens at a disadvantage against the state and other
institutions. We must in future prevent various institutions
from disregarding personal rights and the interests of individual citizens as far as personal ownership of family houses, gardens, etc. is concerned. It will be necessary to
adopt, in the shortest possible time, the long-prepared law
on compensation for any damage caused to any individual or
to an organization by an unlawful decision of a state organ.

It is a serious fact <u>that hitherto the rehabilitation</u>
<u>of people</u> - both communists and non-communists - who were
the victims of legal violations in the past years, <u>has not</u>
<u>been always carried out in all its political and civic con-</u>
<u>sequences.</u> On the initiative of the Communist Party Central
Committee bodies, an investigation is under way as to why the
respective Party resolutions have not been fully carried out,

and measures are being taken to ensure that the wrongs of
the past are made good wherever it has not been done yet. No
one having the slightest personal reason from his own past
activity for slowing down the rectification may be either in
the political bodies, or prosecutor's and court offices that
are to rectify the past unlawful deeds

The Party realizes that people unlawfully condemned
and persecuted cannot regain the lost years of their life;
it will, however, do its best to remove any shadow of the
mistrust and humiliation to which the families and relatives
of those affected were often subjected, and will resolutely
ensure that such persecuted people have every opportunity of
showing their worth in work, in public life, and in political activities. It goes without saying that even in carrying
out full rehabilitation of people, we cannot change the consequences of revolutionary measures made in the past years
in accordance with the spirit of class law aimed against the
bourgeoisie, its property, economic, and social supports.The
whole problem of a rectification of past repressions must be
approached with the full responsibility of the state bodies
concerned, and based on legal regulations; the Central Committee of the Communist Party of Czechoslovakia supports the
proposal that the procedure in these questions and the problems of legal consequences be incorporated in a <u>special law.</u>

A wide democratic concept of the <u>political and person-</u>
<u>al rights of citizens,</u> their legal and political safeguards,
are considered by the Party to be a prerequisite for the necessary strengthening of social discipline and order, for a
stabilization of socialist social relations. A selfish com-
prehension of civil rights, an attitude to social property
according to the principle "it's not my concern", a preferring
of particular interests over those of the whole society - all
these are features which communists will oppose with all
their might.

a

35

The real purpose of democracy must be the achievement of better results of practical work based on wider possibilities of purposeful activity, in order to carry out the interests and needs of the people. Democracy cannot be identified with general speechmaking, cannot be understood in opposition to discipline, professionalism, and effectiveness of management. But arbitrariness and obscure stipulation of rights and duties makes such a development impossible. It leads to irresponsibility, to a feeling of uncertainty, and hence also to indifference towards public interests and needs. On the other hand, it is a more profound democracy and its measure of civic freedom that will help socialism to prove its superiority over the limited bourgeois democracy and will make it an attractive example for progressive movements even in industrially advanced countries with democratic traditions.

Equality of the Czechs and Slovaks – the basis for the strength of the public

Our republic, as a joint state of two equal nations – Czechs and Slovaks – must consistently ensure that the constitutional arrangement of relations between our fraternal nations and the status of all other nationalities of Czechoslovakia develops as required to strengthen the unity of the state, the development of the nations and nationalities themselves, and in keeping with the needs of socialism. It cannot be denied than even in socialist Czechoslovakia, in spite of outstanding progress in solving the problem of nationalities, there are serious faults and fundamental deformations in the constitutional arrangement of relations between the Czechs and Slovaks.

Let it be stressed that the assymetrical arrangement alone was not suitable, by its very character, to express and ensure the relations between two independent nations, as

the respective standings of the two nations were necessarily expressed in different ways. The difference was mainly
in the fact that the Czech national bodies were identical
with the central ones which, having jurisdiction over all
the state, were superior to the Slovak national bodies;this
prevented the Slovak nation, to all means and purposes, in
taking an equal share in the creation and realization of a
country-wide policy. The objective shortcomings of such a
solution were underlined by the existing political atmosphere and practice, adversely affecting the standing and activity of Slovak national bodies.

Under such conditions, the activities of Slovak national bodies were weakened, both in the fifties and in the
fundamental ideas of the 1960 Constitution of the Czechoslovak Socialist Republic. Thus the Slovak national bodies got
into a position from which their influence on the state machinery could be only of peripheral importance. These shortcomings, especially in view of the unsound elements of the
political atmosphere of recent past could not be overcome
even by the joint document of the Central Committee of the
Communist Party of Czechoslovakia and the Central Committee
of the Communist Party of Slovakia of 1964 on a strengthening of the role of the Slovak National Council.

This development necessarily caused misunderstanding
to arise between our two nations. In the Czech lands the non-
existence of their own national bodies gave an impression
of superfluity of Slovak national bodies. In Slovakia the
people were convinced that it is not the Slovaks who govern
their own house but that everything is decided in Prague.

In the interest of the development of our socialist
society it is therefore absolutely necessary to strengthen
the unity of the Czechoslovak people and their confidence
in the policy of the Communist Party of Czechoslovakia, <u>to
effect a crucial turn in the constitutional arrangement of</u>

the relations between the Czechs and Slovaks and to carry
out the necessary constitutional changes. It is now essential to respect the advantage of the socialist federal arrangement as a recognized and tried state form of the co-
existence of two equal nations in a common socialist state.

For reasons of organization, the final federative
arrangement must be preceded by the removal of the most
pressing shortcomings in the existing unsatisfactory state
of things in the legal relations between the Czech and Slovak nations as its integral part and development stage. It
is therefore necessary to draw up and pass a constitutional
law which will embody the principle of a symetrical arrangement as the goal to which our development after the 14th
Congress will aim in the new constitution and which in a
new way, on the basis of full equality, will solve the status of Slovak national bodies in our constitutional system
in the nearest future - before the elections to the National
Assembly and the Slovak National Council. It will have to

● constitute the Slovak National Council as a legislative
body and the Slovak Council of Ministers as a collective
executive body, and ministries as individual executive organs of the Slovak National Council, extending the real powers of all these organs so that the division of legislative and executive powers between the state and the Slovak
bodies may basically comply with the principles of the Ko-
šice government programme;

● entrust the directing of national committees in Slovakia to Slovak national bodies and, in connection with an efficient arrangement between the state centre and the Slovak
national bodies, set up a Slovak ministerial office for internal affairs and public security covering the full extent
of responsibilities;

● adjust the competence of Slovak national bodies so that
they may draw up and approve the economic plan and budget

for <u>Slovakia</u> in all its items including the relevant economic tools. Set up a suitable structure of ministerial economic and executive bodies of the Slovak National Council and
adapt the organizational pattern of the material and manu-
facturing basis in Slovakia accordingly;

● renew state <u>secretaryship</u> in central ministries, especially in the ministries of foreign affairs, foreign trade and
national defence, the secretaries being members of the government;

● <u>exclude</u>, politically and constitutionally, <u>the possibi-
lity</u> of outvoting the Slovak nation as far as the state relations between the Czechs and Slovaks and the constitutional
status of Slovakia are concerned;

● in addition, outside the scope of the constitutional law,
<u>to effect</u> in real political practice <u>the principle of equal
rights of both nations in appointments to central bodies,
diplomatic service, etc.</u>

　　　In preparing the 14th Congress of the Party and the
new constitution it is necessary to submit, on the basis of
all-round professional and political preparation, a proposal
for a constitutional arrangement of relations between our
two nations that will fully express and guarantee their equality and right of self-determination. The same principles
shall be applied to the pattern of the Party and social organizations.

　　　In the interests of strengthening the unity, coherence and <u>national individuality of all nationalities</u> in Czechoslovakia - of <u>Hungarians, Poles, Ukrainians, and Germans</u> -
it is indispensable to work out a statute stipulating the
status and rights of the various nationalities, guaranteeing
the possibilities of their national life and the development
of their national individuality. The Central Committee of
the Communist Party of Czechoslovakia realizes that, in spite

a

of indisputable achievements in solving the problems of nationalities, serious shortcomings exist. We deem it necessary to stress that the principles of our programme in respect of our two nations extend also to other nationalities. To that end, it is necessary to stipulate constitutional and legal guarantees of a complete and real political, economic, and cultural equality. The interests of the nationalities will have to be safeguarded also from the point of view of the pattern of state, regional, district, municipal, and local state power and administration. It is necessary to see that the nationalities are represented, in proportion to their numbers, in our political, economic, cultural, and public life, in elected and executive bodies. It is necessary to ensure an active participation of the nationalities in public life in the spirit of equality of rights and according to the principle that the nationalities have the right to independence and self-administration in provinces that concern them.

The power of elected bodies emanates from the will of the voters

The coming elections are to be the onset of implementation of the principles of this Action Programme in the work of the elected bodies of the state.

Although efforts were made in the past few months to improve the preparation of elections, it proved that it is not possible to effect the elections in the originally proposed term while meeting the requirements of the principles of advanced socialist democracy. It is therefore necessary to work out such an electoral system that will be in harmony with the changes in our political life. By means of the electoral law it is necessary to lay down exactly and clearly the democratic principles for the preparation of the elections, the proposal of candidates and the method of their

election. The changes in the electoral system must be based,
in particular, on the new political status of the National
Front and the elected bodies themselves.

It is the national committees that make the backbone
of the whole network of representative bodies in our country
as democratic organs of state power. It must be in the national committees that state policy is formed, especially in
districts and regions. In their work the principle of socialist democracy is to be fully applied: to bring out various
interests and requirements of the people and to mould them
into the general, public interest of communities, townships,
districts, and regions.

The Party regards the national committees as bodies
that have to carry on the progressive traditions of local
government and people's self-administration. They must not
be taken for local bureaucratic offices supervising local
enterprises. The essential political mission of national
committees is to protect the rights and needs of the people,
to simplify the process of settling all matters with which
the people turn to the national committee, to pursue public
interest and oppose efforts of some institutions to dupe the
people and ignore their requirements.

The Party regards the National Assembly as a socialist parliament with all the scope of activities the parliament of a democratic republic must have. The communists-
deputies must see to it that the National Assembly works
out a number of concrete measures before the new electoral
period that will put into actual practice the constitutional status of the National Assembly as the supreme organ of
state power in the Czechoslovak Socialist Republic. It is
necessary to overcome formalism in dealings, the unconvin-
cing unanimity concealing factual differences in opinions
and attitudes of the deputies. From this point of view it
is necessary to solve, in the nearest future, the relations

a

between the National Assembly and Party bodies, and also a
number of problems of internal activities of the National
Assembly, particularly those concerning organization and
competence. The result must be a National Assembly which
actually decides on laws and important political issues,and
not only approves proposals submitted. The Party supports a
strengthening of the controlling function of the National
Assembly in our entire public life and, more concretely, in
respect of the government; from that point of view, it is
necessary to subject the controlling machinery fully to the
National Assembly, to establish it as its own body. Together
with closer bonds between the National Assembly and our public opinion , all of this may, in a short time, increase the
role and the prestige of the National Assembly in our society.

Division and supervision of power - guarantees against highhandedness

The communists in the government, too, must ensure as
soon as possible that the principle of responsibility of the
government towards the National Assembly covering all its
activities is worked out in detail. Even under the existing
practice of political management, the opportunity afforded
for independent activity of the government and of individual
ministers was not sufficiently made use of, there was a tendency to shift responsibility on to the Party bodies and to
evade   independence in decision-taking. The government is
not only an organ of economic policy. As the supreme executive organ of the state it must, as a whole, deal systematically with the whole scope of political and administrative problems of the state. It is also up to the government to take
care of the rational development of the whole state machinery.
The state administration machinery was often underrated in
the past; this machinery must consist of highly qualified people, professionally competent and rationally organized, it
must be subject to a systematic supervision in a democratic way
42
a

it must be effective.Simplified ideas as if such goals could be attained by underrating and decrying the administrative machinery in general, were rather detrimental in the past.

In the whole state and political system it is necessary to create, purposefully, such relations and rules that would, on the one hand, provide the necessary safeguards to professional officials in their functions and, on the other hand, enable the necessary replacement of officials who can no longer cope with their work by professionally and politically more competent people. This means to establish legal conditions for the recall of responsible officials and to provide legal guarantees of decent conditions for those who are leaving their posts through the normal way of replacement, so that their departure should not amount to a "drop" in their material and moral-political standing.

The Party policy is based on the principle that no undue concentration of power must occur, throughout the state machinery, in one sector, one body, or in a single individual. It is necessary to provide for such a division of power and such a system of mutual supervision that any faults, or encroachments of any of its links are rectified in time, by the activities of another link.This principle must be applied not only to relations between the elected and executive bodies, but also to the inner relations of the state administration machinery and to the standing and activities of courts of law..

This principle is infringed mainly by undue concentration of duties in the existing ministry of the interior. The Party thinks it necessary to make of it a ministry for internal state administration including the administration of public security. The schedule that in our state was traditionally within the jurisdiction of other bodies and with the passage of time has being incorporated into the ministry of the interior, must be withdrawn from it. It is necessary

a

to elaborate proposals as soon as possible passing on the
main responsibility for investigation to the courts of law,
separating prison administration from the security force, and
handing over of press law administration, of archives, etc.
to other state bodies.

The Party considers the problem of a correct incorporation of the security force in the state as politically
very important. The security of our lives will only benefit,
if everything is eliminated that helps to maintain a public
view of the security force marred by the past period of law
violations and by the privileged position of the security
force in the political system. That past period impaired the
progressive traditions of our security force as a force advancing side by side with our people. These traditions must
be renewed. The Central Committee of the Communist Party of
Czechoslovakia deems it necessary <u>to change the organization
of the security force</u> and to split the joint organization into two mutually independent parts - State Security and Public
Security. <u>The State Security</u> service must have such a status,
organizational structure, numerical state, equipment, methods
of work, and qualifications which are in keeping with its
work of defending the state from the activities of enemy centres abroad. Every citizen who has not been culpable in this
respect must know with certainty that his political convictions and opinions, his personal beliefs and activities, cannot be the object of attention of the bodies of the State
Security service. The Party declares clearly that this apparatus <u>should not be directed and used to solve internal political questions</u> and controversies in socialist society.

<u>The Public Security service</u> will fulfil tasks in com-
batting crime and in the protection of public order; for
this its organization, numerical state, and methods of work
must be adapted. The Public Security force must be better
equipped and strengthened; its functions in the defence of
public order must be exactly laid down by law and, in their

44   a

fulfilment, the service will be directed by the national committees. Legal norms must create clearer relations of control over the security force by the government as a whole and by the National Assembly.

It is necessary to devote the appropriate care to carrying out the defence policy in our state. In this connection it is necessary to work for our active share in the conception of the military doctrine of the Warsaw Treaty countries, the strengthening of the defence potential of our country in harmony with its needs and possibilities, a uniform complex understanding of the questions of defence with all problems of the building of socialism in the whole of our policy, including defence training.

The legal policy of the Party is based on the principle that in a dispute over right /including administrative decisions of state bodies/ the basic guarantee of legality is proceedings in court which are independent of political factors and are bound only by law. The application of this principle requires a strengthening of the whole social and political role and importance of courts of law in our society. The Central Committee of the Communist Party of Czechoslovakia will see to it that work on the complex of the required proposals and measures proceeds so as to find the answer to all the necessary problems before the next election of judges. In harmony with and parallel to that, it is also necessary to solve the status and duties of the public prosecutor's office so that it may not be put above the courts of law, and to guarantee full independence of barristers and solicitors from state bodies.

Youth and its organization

We regard young people as those who are to continue in the socialist transformation of the society. The present

a
45

political activity and the part young people take in the social process of revitalization proves the reproaches often addressed against them to be without any foundation. The decisive part of the working and student youth is, by its energy, critical approach, matter-of-factness, and initiation a natural ally and important factor in the creation and implementation of the programmed aims of the Party. For this reason, it is indispensable to open wide and confidently the doors of our Party to young people.

At the same time it is necessary to give young people of all social categories, in proportion to their age and abilities, full possibility of co-deciding on all their own and public matters in elected bodies; their organizations should be recognized as partners of Party and social organizations, economic bodies, national committees, and administration of schools in solving social, working, study, and other urgent problems of youth and children. Young people must be given the opportunity of timely application of their knowledge, qualifications, and talents in appropriate places including leading positions. Cultural, sporting and recreation facilities must be built with their cooperation for them to spend their leisure in a healthy and effective way. The work of voluntary and professional trainers, coaches, instructors, and other workers who sacrifice their time and devote their abilities to children and youth as socially highly beneficial and praiseworthy must be appreciated.

In this connection, let us say a few words of self-criticism on the relations of the Party and the Czechoslovak Union of Youth. Until recently, we expected the latter or its representatives to pass on to the young people more or less ready-made instructions, often the result of subjective opinions, which tactlessly interfered with the internal affairs of the youth organization. We did not sufficiently influence young communists to take part in the creation of Party policies by making them consistently defend, develop,

46
a

and express the interests, needs, requirements, and viewpoints of the youth as a whole and of its individual categories. Thus the initiative of the youth and the role of
its organization was impaired in public and political life.
This tendency was strengthened by the incorrect principle of
direct Party control of the Czechoslovak Union of Youth.

However, the independence of the youth and children´s
movement does not eliminate, but in fact presupposes ideological guiding, a systematic interest of the whole Party in
the problems of youth and of children´s education, the practical help of communists to children´s and youth collectives
and tactful attention to young people in everyday life.

The multiformity of needs, interests and frequently
changing inclinations of young people, which itself is internally differentiated as regards age, social strata, qualifications, etc., requires also a diversified and differentiated organization of children and young people. Apart from
partial interests and inclinations of the moment of individual categories of young people, there are the pressing immediate and prospective needs and interests affecting the
whole younger generation, which can be expressed and pushed
through only by joint action of all the important youth categories; this calls for a suitable form of organization and
social representation of young people. We are of the opinion,
without, of course, wanting to prescribe any pattern of youth
organization, that a form of federation would be most fitting
for the present needs and situation of youth and children´s
movements.

It will depend, to a great extent, on the present
officials of the Czechoslovak Union of Youth and of other social organizations to assist this process, to prevent both a
suppressing and an unnecessary diversification of the sound
initiative of young people, to make use, purposefully, of all
experience and opportunities in the search for the best formed development of our socialist youth and children´s movement.

a

[169]

47

THE NATIONAL ECONOMY AND
THE STANDARD OF LIVING

The 13th Congress approved conclusions stating that the improvement of our economy and the transition to intensive economic development cannot be achieved by traditional approaches or partial improvements of the directive system of management and planning, but by a basic change of the mechanism of socialist economy. The idea which prevailed was the idea of an economic reform based on a new economic system, the revival of the positive functions of the socialist market, necessary structural changes of the economy and a profound change in the role of the economic plan which would cease to be an instrument for issuing orders and would become an instrument enabling society to find the most suitable long-range trends of its development by scientific methods; a change from an instrument designed to enforce subjectively determined material proportions into a programme of economic policy, ensuring an effective development of economy and the growth of the standard of living. The implementation of the first important steps of the economic reform has met with the active support of the working people, experts and the broad public.

Certain features of the economic development over the past two years, better utilization of production factors, the drop of the share of material costs in the social product, the growing demands placed by consumers on the technical level and the quality of products etc., fully confirm the correctness of the conclusions adopted by the 13th Congress. These positive features of the economic development have not so far resulted in a better satisfaction of the needs of society and have not led to reducing

48

the tension on the internal market. This is objectively
caused by the fact that the former tendencies are still
strongly apparent, that the old structure of production and
foreign trade still survives and that production is being
only slowly adapted to the changes and the growing demand
of the market. This is connected with many inconsistencies
and gaps in implementing the programme of economic reform.

Instead of a consistent effort to establish more objective market criteria which would expose the economic
backwardness and old deformations of the economic structure
and gradually eliminate their existence, there are still considerable efforts to deform these criteria, to adapt them
to the given conditions and thus create an easy situation
in which the backwardness and the deformations would remain
concealed, could survive and thrive at the expense of us all.

The system of protectionism applied will regard to
economic backwardness, connected with the policy of prices,
subsidies and grants and mainly with the system of surcharges
in foreign trade continues to prevail in the economic policy.
The confused system of protectionism is creating conditions
under which ineffective backward enterprises, managed in an
unqualified way, may exist and are often given preferences.
It is not possible to blunt for ever the economic policy by
taking from those who work well and giving those who work
badly. It is therefore necessary to objectivize value relations that the differences in the income situation between
enterprises should really reflect actual differences in the
level of their economic activities. Nor is it politically
correct for the consumer to pay indefinitely for inefficiency
by means of prices, taxes and indirectly by different forms
of siphoning off means of effective enterprises.

Enterprises facing a demanding market must be given
a free hand in making decisions on all questions concerning
directly the management of the enterprise and its economy

a

and must be allowed to react in a creative way to the needs
of the market. A demanding market, together with the economic policy, will thus put pressure on production to become
more effective and to introduce healthy structural changes.
Economic competition, especially with advanced foreign firms,
must be the basic stimulus for improving production and reducing costs. This competition cannot be replaced by subjective adjustments of economic conditions and by directive
orders of superior bodies.

Socialism cannot do without enterprising

The programme of democratization in economy links the
economic reform more closely with the processes facing us in
the sphere of politics and the general management of society,
and stimulates the determination and application of new elements which would develop the economic reform even further.
The programme of democratization of the economy includes particularly the provision of ensuring the independence of enterprises and enterprise groupings and their relative independence from state bodies, a full and real implementation of
the right of the consumer to determine his consumption and
his style of life, the right of a free choice of working activity, the right and real possibility of different groups of
the working people and different social groups to formulate
and defend their economic interests in shaping the economic
policy.

In developing democratic relations in the economy we
at present consider as the most important task the final
formulation of the economic position of enterprises, their
authority and responsibility.

The economic reform will increasingly push whole working teams of socialist enterprises into positions in which
they will feel directly the consequences of both the good

50

a

and bad management of enterprises. The Party therefore deems
it necessary that the whole working team which bears the consequences should also be able to influence the management of
the enterprise. There arises the need of democratic bodies
in enterprises with determined rights towards the management
of the enterprise. Managers and head executives of the enter-
prises.which would also appoint them to their functions would
be accountable to these bodies for the overall results of
their work. These bodies must become a direct part of the
managing mechanism of enterprises, and not a social organization /they cannot therefore be identified with trade unions/.
These bodies would be formed by elected representatives of
the working team and by representatives of certain components
outside the enterprise ensuring the influence of the interests of the entire society and an expert and qualified level
of decision-making; the representation of these components
must also be subordinated to democratic forms of control.At
the same time it is necessary to define the degree of responsibility of these bodies for the results of the management of
socialist property. In the spirit of these principles it is
important to solve many concrete questions; at the same time
it will be necessary to propose a statute of these bodies and
to use certain traditions of our works councils from the years
1945-48 and experiences in modern enterprising.

This naturally in no way reduces the indivisible authority and responsibility of the leading executives in managing the enterprise which, together with their qualifications and managing abilities, is the basic pre-condition of
successful enterprising.

In this connection it is also necessary to reassess
the present role of trade unions. In the centralized system,
their function of supporting directive management blended
with defending the interests of the working people. Moreover,
they performed also certain state functions /labour legislation etc./. The resulting situation was that on the one side

a

they took inadequate care of the interests of the working
people and on the other they were accused of "protectionism".
Even socialist economy places working people into a position in which it is necessary to defend human, social and
other interests in an organized way. The central function
of trade unions should be to defend with increasing emphasis
employment and working interests of the workers and the working people, to appear from this aspect as an important partner in solving all questions of economic management; on
this platform, the trade unions would develop more effectively also their function of organizing workers and employees
for a positive solution of the problems of socialist construction and their educational function connected therewith. Communists in trade unions will proceed from these principles
and ensure in an initiative way that the trade unions themselves analyze their position, the functions and activities
of the central and union bodies on the basis of the whole
Action Programme of the Party, that they evaluate the internal life of trade unions as an independent democratic organization and work out their own political line in solving these
questions.

The enterprise must have the right of choosing its
organizational integration. Supra-enterprise bodies /of the
type of the present general and branch managements/ cannot
be imbued with State administrative power. The individual
branches must, with due regard to their conditions, be in
future enabled to transform into voluntary associations, on
the basis of the economic interest and requirements of enterprises. Enterprises must have the right to decide about
the content of the activity of these associations, the right
to leave them and become independent and to join such associations which will ensure in a better way the functions
following from the concentration and specialization of production and from integration processes.

52

a

The withdrawal of enterprises from the existing supra-enterprise agglomerations and their free association cannot begin before the rules for this process are outlined by the government; during the transition period it will be necessary to ensure that even after becoming independent the enterprises should fulfill the precisely termed financial and cooperation obligations set to them before, and resulting from their previous membership in the supra-enterprise body.

It is necessary to put an end to the previous simplified, schematic approach to formulating the organizational structure of production and trade. The structure of enterprises must be varied, just as are the demands of our market. It is therefore necessary to count also with the development of small and medium-sized socialist enterprises, whose importance lies in the first place in the completization of production, in a fast supply of new items to the market and in a flexible reaction to the different demands of customers. In the development of the organizational structure of production and trade it is necessary to open up scope for economic competition among enterprises of all sorts and forms of enterprising, in the first place in the sphere of production and supply of consumer goods and foodstuffs.

Agricultural production contributes to a great extent towards the consolidation of our national economy. The latest period and particularly the future needs of the economy clearly emphasize this positive role of consolidation of agriculture whose composition should develop in a way which would gradually ensure a rational structure of nutrition to the population. This is why the Party considers it necessary to raise and concentrate the aid of the State and of all branches, especially the chemical and engineering industry, in ensuring the growth of crop and animal production. This is and continues to be the fore-

a

53

most taks of our economic policy.

Cooperative enterprising in agricultural production
is of exceptional importance for the development of our
economy. The Party supports the conclusions of the Seventh
Congress of the Unified Agricultural Cooperatives, particularly the creation of a national organization of cooperative farmers, the right of the unified agricultural cooperatives to do business also in other branches and the possibility of selling part of farm products directly to the population and to retailers. The State bodies will help to ensure all-year employment for the farming population.

The Party considers the development of agricultural
production in cooperatives and in State farms to be the decisive line of large-scale production in agriculture. It
would be expedient for Communists to prepare proposals which
will develop new forms of closer contacts of agricultural
producers with supply and sales organizations of agricultural products so that these new forms may ensure direct contact of agricultural production with suppliers and the market and would be to a certain extent similar to the former
farm cooperatives.

We shall support the development of different forms
of credit in farming and recommend to examine the whole
credit system in agricultural economy. At the same time,
the Central Committee recommends that agricultural and other
State managing bodies should seek and support also other
forms of business in utilizing land in mountainous, hilly
and border regions. In the border regions it is necessary
to strive for the creation of further suitable conditions
designed to intensify economic activities, i.e. to make better use of existing small workshops, to extend recreation
possibilities and engage in further capital construction.
This should help stabilize the settlement of the border regions and normalize their life. Even though the production

54

a

of individual farmers constitutes a relatively small part of overall production, it is important to facilitate their work, to improve their conditions of economy and to enable their cooperation with cooperative and State enterprises.

In keeping with the proposals made at the 13th Congress of the Communist Party of Czechoslovakia, it is also necessary to create possibilities for cooperative enterprising wherever cooperatives earn the money for their activity. It will be expedient to make individual cooperatives independent economic and social organizations with full rights, to abolish inexpedient administrative centralization of cooperatives and to create only such bodies superior to cooperative enterprises whose economic activity is advantageous for them. In connection with the development of cooperative enterprizing, it appears to be expedient to elaborate more thoroughly the co-ownership relations of cooperative farmers towards cooperative property.

A serious shortcoming existing in economic life over a long period of time is the low standard and shortage of services of all sorts which reduces the standard of living and arouses justified discontent among the population. The improvement of communal services /water, gas, sewerage, municipal transport, road cleaning etc./ will require considerable investments and can be achieved only gradually while ensuring their profitability. The unsatisfactory state existing in other services is caused by the way of their organization and their exacting administration, by ' low interest of the workers in their economic results, by the fact that certain services are unprofitable, by bad supply of material and low and wrong investments.

Neither the standard of productive forces, nor the character of work in services, repairs and artisan production correspond to the present high centralization in their management and organization which involves quite unnecessary

a

administration and burdens the services with inexpedient costs. This is why it is necessary to take immediate measures for improving and extending all existing forms of services /cooperatives, communal enterprises/, to simplify their management and organization in the spirit of the principles of the new system. In the sphere of services it is particularly justified to make individual shops independent and to remove unnecessary administrative links of management. Small-scale individual enterprising is also justified in the sphere of services. In this respect it is necessary to work out legal provisions concerning small-scale enterprising, which would help fill the existing gap in our market.

The role of the State in economy

The expansion of social wealth is the concern of our entire society. The actual tasks and responsibility fall both on enterprises and on managing bodies, particularly on the Government. It is therefore their common interest and task to make use of the growing political activity of the working people, which has been taking place since the December and January plenums of the Central Committee, and to win them over for the road which means the consolidation of the national economy.

To achieve this it is necessary to adjust the whole organism of the implementation of the economic policy of the State. The appropriate organizational questions must be solved by State and economic bodies. At the same time the Party considers it desirable that the final set up should correspond to the following principles:

Decision-making about the plan and the economic policy of the State must be both a process of mutual confrontation and harmonization of different interests - i.e. the interests of enterprising, consumers, employees, different

56 a

social groups of the population, nations etc. - and a process
of a suitable combination of view of the long-term development of the economy and its immediate prosperity. Effective
measures protecting the consumer against the abuse of the
monopoly position and economic power of production and trading enterprises must be considered as a necessary part of
the economic activity of the State.

The drafting of the national economic plan and the
national economy policy must be subject to democratic control
of the National Assembly and specialized control of scientific institutions. The supreme body implementing the economic policy of the State is the Government. This presupposes
such an institutional set-up of central management which
would make it possible in the process of decision-making to
express and unify special interests and views and to harmonize, in the implementation of the economic policy, the operation of individual economic instruments and measures of
the State. At the same time, the institutional set-up of the
bodies of economic management must not offer opportunities
for the assertion of departmental and monopoly interests and
must ensure a marked superiority of the interests of citizens
as consumers and sovereign bearers of the economic movement.
In all central economic bodies it is indispensable to ensure
a high level of specialization, rationalization and modernization of managing work, to which the necessary changes in
cadres must be also subordinated. All this must be the concern of a group of government bodies which analyze the national economy, work on alternative solutions of this development and the national economic plan, compare the planned
development with the real development in the market, and
proceeding from these findings, take effective economic measures etc., and thus consistently and purposefully influence
the real movement in the economic sphere (i.e. the activity
of enterprise and their associations)in the direction outlined by the economic policy of the State.State bodies approach
enterprises and their associations and integrated groups

in the same way as they approach other independent legal
subjects. The means which are at the disposal of the State,
are the result of the work of all the people and must be
used for satisfying the needs of the entire society in a
way which society recognizes to be reasonable and useful.
An important part of economic management must be a well
conceived technical policy based on the analysis of technical
progress in the whole world and on own conceptions of economic development. The purpose of this policy will be to
regulate the technical level of the production base and to
create economic conditions which would arouse strong interest in seeking and using the most up-to-date technology.

In this connection it would be useful for the State
bodies concerned to examine all kinds of public expenditure
and for the Government to work out a programme of State and
public measures designed to reduce expenditure. The State
budget must become an instrument for restoring the equilibrium and not for its weakening. The Central Committee considers it necessary and possible to reveal and reasonably
utilize extraordinary internal and external resources for
achieving a speedy restoration of the economic equilibrium.

At the same time, the Central Committee appeals to
all enterprises, their associations, plants and workshops
to work out and implement, in connection with their enhanced
economic authority, a programme of rationalization of all
managing, productive and business activity, in order to
achieve a concerted harmonization of work and to reduce production costs. The programme of rationalization is the pre-
condition for an economic evaluation of existing capacities
and for technical modernization of production.

We are putting great hope into reviving the positive
functions of the market as a necessary mechanism of the
functioning of socialist economy and for checking whether
the work in enterprises has been expended in a socially use-

full way. However, we have in mind not the capitalist, but the socialist market, and not its uncontrolled but its regulated utilization. The plan and the national economic policy must appear as a positive force contributing to the normalization of the market and directed against tendencies of economic imbalance and against monopolistic control of the market. The society must do the planning with due insight and perspective, it must scientifically discover the possibilities of its future development and choose its most reasonable orientation. This, however, cannot be achieved by suppressing the independence of other subjects of the market /enterprises and the population/, since this would on the one hand undermine the interest ensuring economic rationality, on the other hand it would deform information and decision-making processes which are indispensably necessary for the functioning of the economy.

The economic structure of Czechoslovakia, its technical standard, concentration and specialization must be developed in a way enabling it to react quickly to economic changes at home and in the world.

The level of the adaptibility and flexibility of the national economy is also the result of the skill and the technical and cultural standard of the working people, their ability to adapt themselves quickly to the changing technical and economic conditions of production. From the point of view of the resources of economic growth in Czechoslovakia, manpower, their abilities and quality, technical and cultural standard as well as their adaptibility and mobility are of quite exceptional importance. Even from the point of view of future economic growth, the Czechoslovak economy does not possess more promising resources than are its great human resources. Czech and Slovak workers and farmers have always been known for their know-how, their skill and creative approach to work. As a result of the directive method of management, the new generation has only partly taken over

a

these qualities from the older generation. Instead of the
feeling of satisfaction from well done work, there frequently developed indifference, mechanical fulfilment of tasks,
and resignation to situations caused by incompetent and un-
initiative management. The Party believes that the prime
condition for eliminating these losses is to put to leading
positions people who are really capable and who are able to
secure natural authority in working teams by their professional and human level.

Effective inclusion in international division of labour

Experience resulting from the many years' isolation
of economic units from the competitive pressure of the world
market, has clearly shown that this creates exceptional conditions for the activity of economic units, conditions resulting especially in relative lagging behind the rate of technical progress and of structural economic changes this progress conditions, in the loss of competitiveness of our products on the world markets and in the creation of undue tension in external trade and payment relations. The limited
raw material base of our economy and the limited size of
the home market make it impossible to implement the changes
in the material base of production carried along by the scientific and technical revolution without widely integrating
our economy into the developing international division of
labour.

The development of international economic relations
will continue to be based on economic cooperation with the
Soviet Union and the other socialist countries, particularly those aligned in the Council of Mutual Economic Assistance.
At the same time, however, it should be seen that the success
of this cooperation will increasingly depend on the competitiveness of our products. The position of our country in

the development of international division of labour will
strengthen with the more general convertibility of our products. In our relations with the CMEA countries we shall
strive for the fuller application of criteria of economic
calculations and mutual advantage of exchange.

We shall also actively support the development of
economic relations with all other countries in the world,
which show interest in them on the basis of equality, mutual
advantages and without discrimination. We support the development of progressive forms of international collaboration, especially cooperation in production and in the
pre-production stage, the exchange of scientific and technical know-how, business in licences and suitable forms of
credit and capital cooperation with interested countries.

The opening up of our economy to the pressure of the
world market makes it necessary to consistently rid the
foreign trade monopoly of the administrative conception and
methods and to eliminate directive management in foreign
trade transactions. In this sphere, the Central Committee
considers it necessary to carry out an effective State com-
mercial and currency policy, based particularly on economic
rules and instruments of indirect management.

The Central Committee considers it indispensable
to raise the authority and responsibility of enterprises
for the concrete implementation of international economic
relations. Production and trading enterprises must have the
right to choose their export and import organizations. At
the same time it is necessary to formulate conditions under
which, if they are fulfilled, enterprises would be entitled
to act independently on foreign markets.

The many years' isolation of our economy from the
world markets has divorced home trade price relations from
price relations in the world market. Under this situation,
we consider it necessary to enforce the line of bringing

a

the home and world market prices gradually closer together.
This practically means a more energetic elimination of vario
surcharges and subsidies to prices of the foreign market.
Enterprises must be aware that this is only a temporary protection, they are receiving from the State and on which they
cannot count indefinitely, and must therefore work out a
programme of such changes in production which will enable
them already in the next few years to do without subsidies
and surcharges. Another side of this policy of eliminating
price surcharges and subsidies must be a more broad-minded
approach to those branches and enterprises in the national
economy, which are from the point of view of the national
economy capable of selling effectively their products in
foreign markets. The Party considers it expedient to speed
up the necessary changes in the present system of price relations and put them gradually in order both by the pressure
of the market forces and by creating a proper rational price
system through purposive economic policy of the State. This
policy must be accompanied by energetic measures designed
to ensure internal stability of the currency. This presupposes the development of the production of effective and good-
quality funds of products marketable on foreign markets, the
achievement of equilibrium in the internal market of commo-
dities, money and labour, an effective restrictive investment policy, the achievement of equilibrium in the balance
of payment and the creation of necessary currency reserves.

The phased opening up of our economy to the world
market, whose final aim is to create conditions for the convertibility of our currency must be carried out in an extent
that would not pile up too many social problems and would
not endanger the growth of the standard of living. However ,
it must be realized that we are living in conditions of sharp
competition and that every concession today will worsen the
prerequisites of effective economic development and of the
growth of the standard of living in the future.

Problems of the standard of living - an urgent task of the economic policy

The basic aim of the Party in developing the economic policy is the steady growth of the standard of living. However, the development of the economy was in the past one-sidedly focussed on the growth of heavy industry with long-term returnability of investments. This was done to a considerable extent at the expense of the development of agriculture and the consumer goods industry, the development of the production of building materials, trade, services and non-productive basic assets, particularly in housing construction. This one-sided character of the former economic development cannot be changed overnight. If, however, we take advantage of the great reserve existing in the organization of production and work, as well as in the technical and economic standard of production and products, if we consider the possibilities offered by a skillful utilization of the new system of management, we can substantially speed up the creation of resources and on this basis to raise the growth of nominal wages and the general standard of living.

Greater stress in the growth of the standard of living must be laid on the growth of wages and salaries. However, the growth of average wages and salaries cannot be speeded up in the way that enterprises will raise wages regardless of the real economic results. It will be necessary to consistently apply the principle that the development of wages depends on really achieved production which will find its social utilization. The methods of influencing the development of wages will have to be in this sense elaborated. In keeping with the growth of wages in production, it is at the same time necessary to ensure the growth

a

of wages in education, health services and other non-productive branches.

The present system of retail prices is markedly divorced from the costs of production, gives an incorrect
orientation to the structure of personal consumption of the
population including the consumption of food and in its consequences reduces the possible degree of satisfying their
requirements. Under these conditions it is indispensable to
be more energetic in removing existing disproportions in
prices so as to create prerequisites for a faster growth of
the standard of living. The solution of these questions will
require opposite movements of prices of individual products
and their groups - the prices of some articles will have to
be raised and others will have to be reduced. Rational price
relations cannot be fixed and proclaimed by a State authority, it is necessary to enable market forces to influence
their creation. This naturally involves a certain risk that
the changes of price relations will take place along with a
certain growth of the level of prices; this risk results
from the fact that in the situation we have taken over from
the directive system of management overall demand is greater
than supply. While opening up the required scope to internal
price movements, the central bodies must therefore regulate
general economic relations in a way preventing an excessive
growth of the price level and ensuring the growth of real
wages by at least 2.5 - 3 per cent per year.

It is not possible in the nearest future to substantially raise claims for appropriations from social funds,
since this could not be done without substantially weakening remunerations for work. However, in the spirit of the
resolution adopted by the plenary meeting of the Central Committee of the Communist Party of Czechoslovakia in December
1967, it is possible to solve the most urgent problems of
social policy,such as the raising of low pensions,the extension of paid maternity leave and aid to families with children. It is also possible to outline the principle that social

pensions will grow in keeping with the growth of the cost-of living. The Central Committee demands from State bodies to ensure the removal of obstacles which weaken the interest of citizens to permanently continue active work after qualifying for old age pensions. We also want to examine the justification of certain measures carried out in connection with the reorganization of the social security system in 1964 /for example the taxation of pensions and the possibility of its gradual removal, the introduction of a higher basic qualifying for students' scholarships etc./. We consider it necessary to raise the social security allowances of those who participated in the national struggle for the liberation. We shall also elaborate the conception and the further course of improving the wage tax system so that it might be possible after 1970 to solve more justly the taxation of women, mothers and persons who have brought up children, and to further strengthen measures promoting a more favourable population development.

An important component determining the standard of living and the style of life is the care for the health of the people. In our society, we have introduced a number of measures in health care which capitalism was unable to solve. However, there are still many untopped possibilities in this sphere, both in the organization of health care and of spa services as well as in the working conditions of doctors and health personnel. The Central Committee appeals to Communists in the health service and to other health workers to submit their initiative proposals designed to solve the problems which unnecessarily embitter citizens and health workers and which are the result of bureaucratic methods in medical care.

From the point of view of preventive care designed to strengthen the health of the people, particularly children and youth, and of effective use of spare time, we con-

a

sider it indispensable to duly appreciate the social importance of all forms of physical and para-military training and recreation; we are in this respect expecting a
principled stand from the government and the educational administration as well as initiative from social organizations.

An important qualitative aspect of the standard of
living will be the general introduction of a five-day working week for which it is necessary to create technological,
organizational, economic and political conditions in order
to enable its operation already at the end of 1968.

It is a serious shortcoming that the programme of
housing construction was not carried out in the past years.
We at present regard the solution of housing construction
as the altogether decisive question of the standard of living. We consider it necessary to concentrate forces in this
sphere and to secure also the necessary support of the Government and of State bodies for substantially raising, the
annual number of flats built by building organizations and
for utilizing the initiative of the population in building
family houses. At the same time, it is necessary to work
out a conception of a long-term housing policy corresponding with the changing social conditions, which would gain
the confidence and support of the population, promote the
interest of citizens in building and modernizing flats and
which would also influence the development of the material
basis of the building industry and its capacity. For a
transitional period it will be also expedient to endeavour
to employ building organizations and manpower of other
countries and concentrate construction to places where the
need is most urgent.

It is characteristic of the bureaucratic and centralist tendencies, applied over and over again in our life
in the past that one of the places most affected by insen-
sibility towards people is the centre of our Republic,Prague.

[188]

a

The capital city, with its experienced and highly qualified cadres of workers, technicians, scientists, artists, organizers of our construction and which comprises an immense wealth of monuments and cultural values, has paid dearly for sectarianism in economy and politics, for the low standard of responsible officials. Its facilities and amenities are not in keeping with its social functions, growing tourism and the requirements of the life of its inhabitants. It is indisputably necessary to speed up housing construction in the capital and, in addition, to concentrate efforts on at least some of the other problems which annoy the people in Prague most: municipal and suburban transport, as well as cleanliness in the city. It is necessary to solve similarly the problems of the capital city of Slovakia-Bratislava. To see to it that as many children as possible from these cities may be able to spend their holidays outside the capital in view of the present inadequate possibilities of recreation in Prague.

The Central Committee is of the opinion that despite the faster growth of the standard of living, the present results and these measures do not by far meet existing needs. Nor do they correspond to our real economic possibilities; however, the low effectiveness of our economy is creating barriers which in the process of the further satisfaction of personal and social needs can be overcome only by efforts to mobilize the reserves and to develop resources in production. The elimination of the shortcomings in economy will require time. But we are convinced that the consistent implementation of the economic reform and the activation of all Communists and non-party members will enable our country to embark upon the road of a fast, modern development of the economy.

By rational utilization of the resources in Slovakia to the prosperity of the Republic

The economy of the Czechoslovak Socialist Republic is the integration of two national economies which makes it possible to multiply the economic potential of our entire society. This is conditioned by rational utilization of the resources and reserves of the growth of both our national political regions in the interest of an effective development of the Czechoslovak national economy as well as by the creation of a social and economic balance between the various regions. The new constitutional set up must definitely rely on the integration basis and further integration tendencies in the economy of the entire State.

The past development of Slovakia within the unified Czechoslovak economy was marked by major changes in the economic and living standard. Slovakia has become an advanced industrially developed agricultural part of the Republic. For the further development of the integrated Czechoslovak economy it is not decisive to make partial individual adjustments but to fundamentally elaborate the rational integration of the national political regions in the economic complex of the entire State.

However, the undeniable achievements were accompanied by the emergence of serious problems. Slovakia's share in the creation of the national income increased from 14.2 per cent in 1948 to 24.4 per cent in 1965, it is not adequate to the possibilities of growth which exist in Slovakia. /Favourable geographic position, qualitative changes in the fund of manpower, possibilities of space concentration, new basis of chemistry, metallurgy, fuels and power, agriculture, natural resources./

68   a

The processes of creating a balanced social and economic level between Slovakia and the Czech lands are characterized by their internal contradictions. An undeniable success of the Party policy is the elimination of social and economic backwardness and the decrease of relative per capita differences. However, the faster rate of growth was not sufficient for reducing absolute differences. The process of creating a balanced level was not based on the conception of national economic effectiveness of the development of the Czechoslovak economy.

The existing problems are caused mainly by the fact that the extensive economic growth of the Czechoslovak Socialist Republic was markedly enforced also in the economic development of Slovakia. The potential source of growth was not used rationally, both in industry and in agriculture. The tertiary sphere, particularly the build-up of the scientific, research and development bases, has lagged greatly behind. Slovakia's development was not sufficiently coordinated, it proceeded along departmental lines, without internal integration relations of modern economic entities.

The intensive development of Slovakia's economy is conditioned by a complex of measures connected with the solution of short-term factual problems, with the clarification of conceptual questions of long-term development, with the effective operation of the new system of management and with the definition of the competence and authority of the Slovak national bodies.

The measures designed to speed up Slovakia's econmic development up to 1970 constitute the starting-point for a fundamental change in Slovakia's integration into the process of transition of the Czechoslovak economy to the road of intensive growth. At the same time it is necessary to seek possibilities of solving acute problems: employment, the lagging behind of micro-regions with special re-

a

gard to those which are inhabited by Hungarian and Ukrainian fellow-citizens, specific problems of the standard of living, particularly the housing problem etc.

It is of decisive importance for Slovakia's long term economic development to raise substantially Slovakia's participation in the creation and the utilization of the national income and to solve the task of creating a balanced economic level essentially by 1980.

This necessitates faster economic development in Slovakia than is the national average. The prerequisite of this is to give strong support to progressive structural changes, to intensify agricultural production and the interconnected processing industry; to develop the tertiary sector in all spheres; to purposefully concentrate production and the infra-structure.

The development of Slovakia is taking place within the new system of management. However, this system in its present form has not created scope for the development policy of national political regions. Past adjustments of the plan and of economic instruments are not sufficient. It is therefore necessary to elaborate the system of management in such a way as to ensure that also territorial and national aspects of development become an equal organic component of the system of management of the entire national economy.

THE DEVELOPMENT OF SCIENCE, EDUCATION AND CULTURE

At the present stage we must base the development of our society to a much greater extent on the progress and application of science, education and culture, It will be necessary that their wealth is used fully and completely to the benefit of socialism and that our people should understand the complicated claims connected with creative work in these spheres.

The importance of Science in our Society is Growing

Socialism originates, lasts and wins by the connection of the working movement with science. There is no relationship of subordination and compromise between these forces. The more resolute and impartial is the advancement of science, the more is it in harmony ith the interests of socialism; the greater are the achievements of the working people, the bigger is the scope opened up to science. In the relationship to the development and application of science in the life of socialist society is reflected how much the working people are aware of their historical tasks, to what extent they really enforce them. Socialism stands and falls with science, just as it stands and falls with the power of the working people.

Just now, at the beginning of the scientific-technological revolution in the world, the social position of science is changing considerably. Its application in the entire life of society is becoming the basic condition for the intensive development of the economy, care for man and

a

his living environment, culture of the society and growth of the personality, modern methods of management and administration, the development of relations between people and the solving of various problems raised by the current period. It is in the field of science and technology where the victory of socialism over capitalism is decided in long-term perspective.

Therefore the Party regards it as one of its primary tasks to provide an ever greater scope for the promotion of creative scientific work and for a timely and more efficient application of its results in social practice.

Relatively complete foundations of basic, applied research and development unprecedented in extent and importance, have been built up in this country together with the construction of socialism. A number of qualified scientific workers have grown up, who made an important contribution by their achievements to building up this country and whose qualification is recognized all over the world. In spite of this the opportunities offered by socialism for the development of science and especially for the application of its results to the benefit of society are, for the time being, far from being fully used which is also because of the still existing branch barriers between science, technological development and production. The inflexibility of the system of management by directives, connected with the low-level qualification of managing personnel is the reason for this; in the sphere of research the reasons are mainly differences in the level of applied research institutes, caused by lack of scientifically trained staff.

To solve the existing state we shall continue making substantial improvements particularly in the material conditions of our basic research so that in the decisive branches it could remain permanently at a world level. The development of science must at the same time proceed from the real possibilities of Czechoslovakia as a middle-size country, which can ensure top-level scientific research only by efficient specialization and concentration of energy in connection with extensive international cooperation and exploitation of the results of world science as such. Therefore it is also necessary to develop the system of the evaluation of scientific workers in such a way that selected progressive, scientific and socially important directions of research be supported more fully by a system of moral and material incentives.

If the social sciences are really to become an official instrument of scientific self-cognition of socialist society, it is necessary to respect the principles of their internal life and to ensure such a position and conditions for them as would enable them to achieve high scientific standards. By means of its bodies the Party will take the initiative in encouraging the development of social sciences and contributing towards their orientation to important social problems; but it does not interfere with the very process of creative scientific work and in this respect relies on the initiative and social responsibility of scientists themselves.

In addition to creating favourable conditions for the very development of science it is an urgent task <u>to strive for surmounting all the obstacles between science on the one hand and social practice on the other.</u> Even though the full and more consistent application of the new system of management is expected to bring the fundamental solution, we shall help this process also by new measures at the level of central management. The Party will especially support the development of feasible stimuli for the application of the results of science in production and other social practice and for a rapid improvement of the qualification structure of slowly developing applied research institutes. At the same time we shall also support a more profound exami-

[195]

nation of the social function of science, especially the problem of its effectiveness and the relationship between science and economy in Czechoslovak conditions.

The development of socialist society is at the same time a process of constant increase of the social involvement and responsibility of science and its application in the management and shaping of the entire life of society. We shall strive on a broader scale than hitherto for scientific staff to take part in the work of representative bodies and in the activities of other bodies of social management; we shall intensify the active participation of scientific institutions and scientific workers in drawing up proposals for political and economic measures. We shall encourage the application of scientific workers in social management and the system of education on the broadest possible scale and create favourable social and economic conditions for their activity in these fields. We shall prepare without delay the introduction of a binding system of scientific expertise and opponency on important proposals. This will contribute towards qualified decisions at all levels of management.

Quality of education -

the aim of our educational system

The progress of the socialist society is conditioned by the growth in education of the people. This is a precondition for solving initial tasks of the scientific-technological revolution, promoting the relations and institutions of socialist democracy and further asserting the cultural and humanistic character of socialism and the development and employment of every man in it.

Therefore we regard further progress of education as a primary task. In this respect we proceed from the traditions of the education of our nations and from the good

74

a

results by which the socialist stage of development has improved our school system, especially by its broad democratization and materialization of the principles of co-education. It is still necessary to surmount the consequences of past shortcomings, when the quantitative development of education was frequently achieved at the expense of the quality of teaching. Neither was sufficient care given to the qualitative training of teachers. The frequent reorganization in the past did not contribute to the desirable improvement of the standard of education. On the contrary, this was the reason why, in many respects, it was lagging behind the existing needs and future demands. Therefore it is a foremost task today to concentrate the main attention and strength towards a purposeful improvement of the standard, exaction and value of education and especially towards improving and raising the standard of general education of people, towards expanding the base for a more efficient choice and education of talents, and towards modernizing the content, forms and means of education.

The dynamic development of our economy and of the whole society requires an end of the underevaluation of education and of the needs of schools and teachers; it requires that a much bigger proportion be set aside from social resources for the development of education. We shall ensure that educational bodies in cooperation with the broad masses prudently materialize projects which will enable our economy to fully keep pace with the dynamics of the development of science and technology and with the needs of the time. We consider the following tasks as the most urgent ones:

a/ to work out a draft hypothesis on the long-term development of the educational system, which will make it possible to stabilise the development of the educational system at all levels, to solve its personnel and material

base in advance so as to gradually eliminate the uneven-
ness in the development of education in individual regions
of the country.

To prepare a new concept in harmony with the long-
term project of basic polytechnic education, which would be
based on the logical grasping of the subject, to take advantage of the independence and initiative of students and make
it   possible to fully apply the principle of differentiation according to interests and talents; to solve the urgent problems of secondary general education schools by extending the base and time of secondary general education,
thus to improve preparations for later university studies
while providing conditions for those secondary school students who will not study at universities to take up practical jobs.

To form and to gradually introduce a system of ad-
ditional education of young people who start working at 15
years. To increase the thoroughness of the preparation of
young skilled workers in harmony with the technological and
structural changes in our economy by improving the theoretical, specialised and general education of young apprenti-
ces. To take advantage to a greater extent of the resources
of plants and enterprises for the construction and equipment of apprentice centres in the sense of the new system
of management of the national economy and in justified cases also to grant state subsidies. Not to allow a further
decrease of material investments in these establishments.
The same criteria should also be applied by National Committees in the construction and equipment of apprentice
schools.

b/ To create material and personnel conditions at secondary schools and universities for all young people, who
fulfil the necessary requirements and proved it by their
results during preceding education, to be enrolled for stu-

[198]

a

dies. Therefore the system of enrollment at secondary schools and universities should be made more flexible. Administrative methods should be replaced by economic and moral stimuli, a sufficient amount of information and improvement of educational advice, which will help regulate sensitively the influx of students to particular branches and bring closer the abilities and interests of individuals and the needs of society. Meanwhile secondary and university education should not be understood only as training for a certain profession, but as a means of improving the extent of education, the cultural level of man and his ability to solve new situations in the production process as well as in the economic, social and qualification structure of society. This requires simultaneously an increase in the social responsibility of economic, cultural and political institutions and of every individual for the application of education in practice.

c/ At universities, democratic principles and methods should be consistently applied in their management. The prerequisites of scientific work, unity of teaching and research should be continually strengthened, the authority and autonomy of university scientific councils should be increased. Universities should be given preference regarding modern equipment, the possibilities of scientific work should be improved, all-round cooperation between research, universities and secondary schools should be intensified, expensive equipment should be taken advantage of jointly by research institutes and universities. Universities should be given broader access to foreign literature and more opportunities of study and training visits abroad in view of their pedagogical and scientific work, while understanding correctly the importance of acquiring knowledge for the development of science and flexibly applying the principles of profitability of foreign currency resources.

d/ The structural changes in the national economy will

also require re-training and complementing of the general
or specialised education of adults. Therefore it will be
necessary that schools, enterprises, social organisations
and mass information media /press, radio, television/ cooperate in order to improve and intensify the system of
education for adults.

e/ The complexity of education management should be safeguarded by legal arrangements so as to raise the role of
school administration. In this connection it will be desirable to ascertain the effectiveness of university law so
as to strengthen the democratic relations in the internal
and external management and the social position of universities. The authority of Slovak National Council bodies in
education in Slovakia should be applied fully in view of
the importance of education as a basic element of national
culture.

f/ Equal study and development conditions should be
consistently ensured for young people of all nationalities.
An end should be put to the belittling approach towards solving problems of nationality education, and legal and institutional preconditions should be created to allow the nationalities to have something to say on the specific issues
of nationality education.

The Party appreciates the work of our teachers in
educating the young generation. Teachers belong above all
to school and young people and their work must not be disturbed by anything. Educational work is of nation- and so-
ciety- wide importance. Therefore the social position of
teachers must be safeguarded in the first place by the respective state bodies and National Committees. Efforts to
provide conditions essential for their work must also correspond to this. This means to ensure a high standard of
the training of teachers, development of wage relations of
teachers and other school staff so as to be in harmony with

78

a

th: growth of the real wages of workers in other branches, and also to solve other urgent material needs of teachers so they can perform their responsible profession with full concentration. In projects and the materialization of school capital construction, it is essential to ensure its complex character   including flats for teachers. The Party regards this as part of its policy to increase the prestige, authority and social importance of the educationalists of the young generation.

The Humanistic Mission of Culture

The development of culture in the broadest sense is one of the basic conditions of dynamic and harmonious development of socialist society. The culture of socialist Czechoslovakia consists of independent and equal Czech and Slovak cultures, together with the cultures of the other nationalities. The arts and culture are not a mere decoration of economic and political life, but they are vital for the socialist system. If culture lags behind, it retards the progress of policy and economy, democracy and freedom, development of man and human relations. <u>Care for culture, material and spiritual, is not only the concern of the cultural front, but it must become an affair of the entire society.</u>

It was an important tradition of the Communist Party from the start that it was able to unite the best men of culture and art around itself. This is proved not only by the socialist orientation of our pre-war artistic vanguard, but also by the fact that most of the cultural intelligentsia were standing on the left or were in the ranks of the Party after the liberation in 1945. Later, especially in the early fifties, certain representative of culture were discriminated, some were subjected to unjustified political

a

repression and the cultural policy of the Party was also demand.

The documents of the 13th Congress should have been a starting point of a new cultural policy, which would proceed from the best traditions of the past and from much positive experience acquired after 1956 and after the 12th Congress of the Communist Party of Czechoslovakia. However, the surviving bureaucratic attitudes and old methods of management prevented the impetuses of the Congress from developing. The contradictions between the proclaimed and practiced policies were creating a conflict tension and restricting the involvement and development of socialist culture. The Central Committee will investigate all the reasons for these conflicts and will create favourable conditions to normalize the situation.

We reject administrative and bureaucratic methods of implementing cultural policy, we dissociate ourselves from them and we shall oppose them. Artistic work must not be subjected to censorship. We have full confidence in men of culture and we expect their responsibility, understanding and support. We appreciate how the workers in culture helped force through and create the humanistic and democratic character of socialism and how actively they participated in eliminating the retarding factors of its development.

It is necessary to overcome a narrowed understanding of the social and human function of culture and art, overestimation of their ideological and political role and underestimation of their basic general cultural and aesthetic tasks in the transformation of man and his world.

The Party will guard and safeguard both the freedom of artistic work and the right to make works of art accessible.

To socially administer culture means, first of all, to create favourable conditions for its development. Disputes,

[202]

which will naturally arise, will be solved by discussion
and democratic decisions. Independent decisions of cultural
workers in the spheres of their activity must also be an
expression of the necessary autonomy of culture and art.
They must be indispensable partners for state bodies. We
are convinced that communist intellectuals and all other
leading workers in the sphere of culture and art are capable of cooperating in the formation of, and carrying out
responsibly and independently, the policy of the Party in
state, social, cultural and group-interest institutions,
that they are a guarantee of the socialist, humanistic orientation of our culture.

Of course, the social effect of culture does not
occur outside the political context. We shall ensure that
the freedom of different views, guaranteed by the Constitution, is fully respected. However, the Communist Party
cannot give up its inspiring role, its efforts that art,
too, should efficiently help form socialist man in the struggle for the transformation of the world. The Party will apply consistently its political programme, it will stimulate
the development of Marxist thinking.

Socialist culture is one of the primary agents of
the penetration of socialist and humanistic ideas in the
world. It helps unite the humanistic streams of world culture. It has the capacity of bringing closer the socialist
nations and of strengthening the cooperation and fraternal
relations of nations and nationalities. Culture is a traditionally important value for our nations, by the means of
which we have always proved our vitality and individuality
to the world. But the interpretation of the national traditions of the culture of the Czechs and Slovaks was one-sided
in many respects, whole important periods were artificially
omitted from it. We give our full backing to the humanistic
traditions of national cultures and we shall support all

a   [203]   81 efforts to endorse this heritage in the present psychology of Czechs and Slovaks.

We are supporters of both internationalism and national specificity of culture. We think it inevitable to take efficient measures without delay so that culture in Slovakia has the same conditions and possibilities as those in Bohemia, so that disproportions do not grow, but disappear. The equal position of national cultures also requires an equal position of national institutions. The competence of national bodies in Slovakia includes the management of the decisive instruments of national culture, such as radio, television, film, scientific institutes, artists' unions, book publishing, care for historical monuments, etc. It is necessary to secure the representation of Slovak national culture abroad; to increase the exchange of information and cultural values between the Czech and Slovak nations; to ensure the cultural life of the Slovaks in the Czech lands and of the Czechs in Slovakia in their native tongue.

Similar principles must be applied also towards the cultures of all the nationalities in Czechoslovakia, while realising that they are specific cultures and not Czech and Slovak culture translated into another language. The culture of nationalities is an organic part of Czechoslovak socialist culture, but it is also in context with the general culture of its own nation, with which it is inseparably linked. Material conditions and personnel problems of the further development of national cultures must be guaranteed institutionally, scientific and cultural institutions and offices must be established with a view to nationality needs. The decisive role and care for the material base of national cultures pertains to state bodies, National Committees, together with the cultural unions of the various nationalities.

We shall take care not only of cultural work, but also of the system of communication of cultural values, we

[204]

a

shall strive for the active participation of citizens in
the development of socialist culture and in their cultural
education, in the closest possible cooperation and complex
influence of mass and local culture. We consider it urgent
to examine the reasons of the catastrophic shortcomings of
cultural and aesthetic education and to take measures to
rectify them; - to create sufficient material, organisations
and other conditions of cultural activity, to loosen the
organisational forms; - to allow the establishment of various cultural and hobby groups as well as their regional
and national associations; - to complete an efficient network of cultural establishments with an active participation
of National Committees, enterprises, social and group-interest organisations; - to purposefully build up new important
regional cultural centres in addition to the capitals.

The entire sphere of culture must be decently and
responsibly secured economically in view of its importance,
and protected from the uncontrolled nature of the market
and from commercialism. We shall recommend, in the spirit
of the 13th Congress resolution, that the government should
complete without delay the planned solution of the entire
complex of culture economy. The planned expenditure on culture must be stabilised and must increase progressively in
harmony with the trend of the national income. We shall also
support voluntary combination of the means of industrial and
agricultural enterprises, national committees and social
organisations for culture. The means invested in culture can
become an important instrument of its development, if he,
who uses them, becomes a modern socialist customer.

We regard the following problems as the most urgent
ones, dependent upon new distribution of the means for culture on a national scale: to guarantee material care for
the creators of important cultural values; - to eliminate
discrepancies in the royalties, wages, incomes and taxes
system in culture; - to cover the whole territory of the

[205]

Republic with a good-quality radio and television signal as soon as possible, to open the second television programme in 1970; - to overcome without delay the disastrous state of polygraphy; - to secure more polygraphic paper in desirable assortment for the press and publishing houses; - to improve care of historical objects of art and save handicraft among others things by making way for co-operative or private enterprise in this sphere.

The planned expenditure on culture must be concentrated in culture directing bodies which must distribute it to cultural institutions. To increase the economic independence and responsibility of cultural establishments, enterprises and groups is a prerequisite of the functioning economy of culture. Independent control will lead towards a more rational exploitation of means and possibilities, towards increasing the spirit of enterprise.

The International Status and Foreign Policy of the Czechoslovak Socialist Republic

We shall be putting the Action Programme into practice during a complicated international situation and its further development will influence the realisation of certain important principles of the programme. On the other hand, the process of the revival of socialism in Czechoslovakia will make it possible for our Republic to influence this international development more actively. We stand resolutely on the side of progress, democracy and socialism in the struggle of the socialist and democratic forces against the aggressive attempts of world imperialism. It is from this point of view that we determine our attitude to the most acute international problems of the present, and our share in the world-wide struggle against the forces of imperialist reaction.

Proceeding from the real relationship of internatio-

[206]

nal forces and from the awareness that Czechoslovakia is an active component of the revolutionary process in the world, she will formulate her own attitude towards the fundamental problems of world policy.

The basic orientation of Czechoslovak foreign policy was born and verified at the time of the struggle for national liberation and in the process of the socialist reconstruction of this country - it is in alliance and cooperation with the Soviet Union and the other socialist states. We shall strive for friendly relations with our allies - the countries of the world socialist community - to continue, on the basis of mutual respect, to intensify sovereignty and equality, and international solidarity. In this sense we shall contribute more actively and with a more elaborated concept to the joint activities of the Council of Mutual Economic Aid and the Warsaw Treaty.

In the relationship to the developing countries, socialist Czechoslovakia will be contributing to the strengthening of the anti-imperialist front and supporting within its power and possibilities all the nations opposing imperialism, colonialism, neo-colonialism and striving for the strengthening of their sovereignty and national independence and for economic development. Therefore we shall continue supporting the courageous struggle of the Vietnamese people against American aggression. We shall also be enforcing a political settlement of the Middle East crisis.

We shall actively pursue the policy of peaceful coexistence towards advanced capitalist countries. Our geographical position, as well as the needs and capacities of an industrial country require that we should carry out a more active European policy aimed at the promotion of mutually advantageous relations with all states and international organisations and at safeguarding collective security of the European continent. We shall consistently proceed from

a

the existence of two German states, from the fact that the German Democratic Republic, as the first socialist state on German territory, is an important peace element in Europe, from the necessity of giving support to the realistic forces in the German Federal Republic, while resisting neo-nazi and revanchist tendencies in that country. The Czechoslovak people want to live in peace with all nations. They want to develop good relations and cooperate with all states in the interests of strengthening international peace and security as well as mutual confidence in the economic, cultural, scientific and technological fields. We shall also take more active advantage than we have done so far of our Republic's membership in international organisations, especially in the United Nations and its agencies.

Our science, culture and art can strengthen and increase much more the international authority of socialist Czechoslovakia in the world. Czechoslovak foreign policy must provide conditions and extend the scope for the international application of our culture abroad. A broad application of our science and art abroad helps to prove efficiently the advantages of socialism and the possibilities of an active policy of peaceful co-existence.

Our foreign policy did not make use of all the opportunities for active work, it did not take the initiative in advancing its own views on many important international problems. The Central Committee of the Communist Party of Czechoslovakia, the National Assembly, the Government and the respective ministry must overcome these shortcomings without delay and consistently ensure that our foreign policy should express fully both the national and international interests of socialist Czechoslovakia.

A full development of the international role of socialist Czechoslovakia is inseparable from the education of citizens in the spirit of internationalism, which comprises both the grasping of common interests and aims of the world progressive forces and understanding of specific national needs. This is linked with the necessity of making prompt and detailed information on international problems and the course of our foreign policy available to the public and thus creating conditions for an active participation of Czechoslovak citizens in the shaping of foreign political attitudes.

The Communist Party of Czechoslovakia will be more active in the sphere of the international communist and workers' movement. We shall put special emphasis on friendly ties, mutual consultations and exchange of experiences with the Communist Party of the Soviet Union, with the communist and workers' parties of the socialist community, with all the other fraternal communist parties.

The Communist Party of Czechoslovakia will continue taking an active part in the struggle for the unity of the international communist movement, for strengthening the action cooperation of communist parties with all the progressive forces while regarding a resolute struggle against the aggressive policy of American imperialism as the most important task. The Communist Party of Czechoslovakia will take full advantage of its specific possibilities of establishing contacts with the socialist, peaceful and democratic forces in the capitalist and developing countries. It will contribute to expanding the forms of cooperation and coordinating the work of communist parties, while attaching great importance to international party consultative meetings. From this point of view it welcomes and supports the outcomes of the Consultative Meeting of Communist and Workers' Parties in Budapest. With dozens of fraternal parties the Communist Party of Czechoslovakia supports the proposal for convening an international communist consultative meeting in Moscow late in 1968.

Comrades,

We are submitting to you quite frankly all the main
ideas which guided us and which we want to adhere to at the
present time. Everyone will understand that the proposals
comprised in this Action Programme are far-reaching and
their realisation will profoundly influence the life of
this country. We are not changing our fundamental orientation; in the spirit of our traditions and former decisions
we want to develop to the utmost in this country an advanced socialist society, rid of class antagonisms, economically, technologically and culturally highly advanced, socially and nationally just, democratically organized, with
a qualified management, by the wealth of its resources giving the possibility of dignified human life, comradely relations of mutual cooperation among people and free scope
for the development of the human personality. We want to
start building up a new intensely democratic model of a socialist society, which would fully correspond to Czechoslovak conditions. But our own experiences and Marxist scientific cognition lead us jointly to the conclusion that these
aims   cannot be achieved along the old paths while using
means, which have long been obsolete and harsh methods,
which are always dragging us back. We declare with full responsibility that our society has entered a difficult period
when we can no longer rely on traditional schemes. We cannot squeeze life into patterns, no matter how well-intended.
It is now also up to us to make our way through unknown conditions, to experiment, to give the socialist development a
new look, while leaning upon creative Marxist thinking and
the experiences of the international workers movement, relying on the true understanding of the conditions of the
socialist development of Czechoslovakia as a country which
assumes responsibility to the international communist movement for improving and taking advantage of the relatively
advanced material base, unusually high standards of education and culture of the people and undeniable democratic
traditions to the benefit of socialism and communism. No

one could forgive us were we to waste this chance, were we to give up our opportunities.

We are not taking the outlined measures to make any concessions from our ideals - let alone to our opponents. On the contrary: we are convinced that they will help us to get rid of the burden which for years provided many advantages for the opponent by restricting, reducing and paralysing the efficiency of the socialist idea, the attractiveness of the socialist example. We want to set new penetrating forces of socialist life in motion in this country to give them the possibility of a much more efficient confrontation of the social systems and world outlooks and allowing a fuller application of the advantages of socialism.

Our Action Programme comprises tasks, intentions and aims for the immediate future, up to the 14th Party Congress. We are aware that many of the shortcomings and difficulties which have accumulated over recent years cannot be fully overcome in a short time. However, the fulfilment of this programme can open up the way to solving other, more complicated and important problems of the organisation and dynamic development of our socialist society in directions which could be only indicated until now; in the coming years, we want to start working out a long-term programme, which would give form and elaborate in detail the concept of the over-all development of our socialist society in the stage we are entering, make clear the conditions and open up prospects of its communist future. After everything we have lived through over the past years we are obliged to give a reply to all our workers and ourselves as to how the Party imagines its aims can be achieved, how it wants to materialise the expectations and desires which are being invested by workers in their life and in their participation in the communist movement. We believe that our Marxist science has gathered and will gather now and in future such an amount of strength as to enable it to prepare responsibly scientific preconditions for such programme.

a

We are not concealing the fact that difficult moments and extraordinarily exacting and responsible work face us in the coming months and years. For the fulfilment of the forthcoming progressive tasks it will be necessary to unite as many citizens of our Republic as possible, all who are concerned with the welfare of this country, with its peace efforts, with a flourishing socialism. Confidence, mutual understanding and harmonious work of all who really want to devote their energy to this great human experiment will be needed. But the work and initiative of every communist, every worker will be needed above all. We want to responsibly, consistently and without reservations make room for this, remove all the barriers which stood in its way, set the creative capacities of our man, all the physical and moral capacities of society in motion. We want to create conditions so that every honest citizen, who concerns himself with the cause of socialism, the cause of our nations, should feel that he is the very designer of the fate of this country, his homeland, that he is needed, that he is reckoned with. Therefore let the Action Programme become a programme of the revival of socialist efforts in this country. There is no force which could resist the people who know what they want and how to pursue their aim.

**The Central Committee of the
Communist Party of Czechoslovakia**

III

DUBČEK'S REPORT
MAY 29 - JUNE 1, 1968

THE document which follows should be read as a blueprint for the implementation of the Action Programme. As such, it deals less with the decision to initiate change than with the decision to ensure that the process of change is presided over by the Czechoslovak Communist Party.

When read in this context, the message of the document seems fairly obvious. It is, in brief, that the initiation of change carries with it the risk of failure as well as the risk of extinction—that in both cases it is the Party's responsibility to see to it that neither danger ever materializes, that at present the Party is ill-equipped to fulfil this responsibility, and that accordingly it must prepare itself for the difficult days ahead.

The Internal Audience
This message is conveyed to the internal audience in a pattern of challenge and response. Within the framework of that pattern the document considers the internal development of the CCP in terms of its consequences for the past, present and future development of Czechoslovakia in what amounts to an apparent effort to establish the need for, and define the scope of, internal Party reform.

The emphasis throughout is, as might be expected, on individual and institutional shortcomings. As in the documents already discussed, the Party emerges as the repository of "truth," a repository which—although admittedly presided over at times by less than perfect individuals—nevertheless retains the capacity to inspire and lead the people of Czechoslovakia in the development of a society which, if not perfect, will be as close to perfection as is humanly possible.

Just as the Action Programme sought to intimidate and inspire, so too is it with this document. For those who would minimize the need for internal reform, there are the familiar references to the evils of the past coupled with pointed reminders that as far as the present leadership is concerned the responsibility for these errors rests squarely on the shoulders of those who formerly presided over the Party. Thus a distinction is made between the leadership on the one hand and the rank and file members on the other. Although neither escapes the brunt of the criticism, the presumption is that in a Party organized around the principle of democratic centralism, primary responsibility for conditions within that Party as well as for conditions throughout the society belongs to the leadership elements.

In this way the problems of the past are defined as essentially problems of poor leadership. To be sure, the fault is shared by the members and by the constraints of operational necessity. Having already replaced the former leaders, Dubček and his supporters must now deal with their sources of strength within the membership. This, however, poses a difficult problem. A thoroughgoing shake-up of the Party, assuming they were capable of carrying it out, would be, under the circumstances, both internally disruptive and, as viewed by other members of the bloc, externally harmful. The only solution, therefore, is to win these elements over or, if that is not possible, to neutralize their effectiveness. In part, this is accomplished by assigning the blame for past errors to the former leaders of the CCP. In part, it is accomplished by criticism which is directed against the membership itself. Finally, it is accomplished on the one hand, by pointing out the advances of the past and, on the other, by recognizing that some of the difficulties were related to the conditions under which the Party had to operate. In this way, elements who might reject the authority of the new leadership are warned of the dangers which attach to continued opposition and obstructionism. They are at the same time assured of "forgiveness" if they "confess" the errors of their ways.

Such a solution, unless accompanied by organizational changes, is likely to be of only limited utility. As the document suggests, this fact was not lost on the members of the Central Committee or, at least, on those members who supported the changes outlined in the Action Programme. For reasons of internal necessity and external reality, the reorganization of the CCP could not appear to be a direct attack on those elements who probably still supported the policies of Novotny. Internally, these elements undoubtedly cut across Czech-Slovak lines. A purge directed against them would have only served to fragment the Party at a critical period in its history—a period in which unity of effort would be essential to a continued mastery of the process of change. Externally such a move would have only served to further alarm members of the bloc who were already concerned about the course of developments within Czechoslovakia.

An alternative solution to this problem lay in relating the need for internal reform to the capability of the CCP to respond to the challenge of change. In this way dissident elements could be effectively isolated and, perhaps even more importantly, the leadership could at the same time develop an organizational structure which would be responsive both to the demands of Party leaders and to the demands of Party programmes.

As I understand this document, it was precisely this solution which was finally adopted. Thus, for example, the proposed organizational changes are characterized here as a necessary prerequisite for dealing effectively with problems of the present as well as those which are likely to occur in the future. In part, the justifications provided are probably quite valid. Presiding as it were over a Party which had traditionally rewarded loyalty and faithful service and had discouraged individual initiative and competence, the leadership of the CCP undoubtedly felt that internal reform was essential if the proposals outlined in the Action Programme were to be effectively implemented. This would appear to be particularly true with respect to the call for an improvement in the relationships between the Party and other segments of Czech society. After all, institutional arrangements and practices which were created for the purpose of maintaining a rigid imposition of Party rule could not be expected to function as effectively when it came to guiding the development of Czech society. The requisites for presiding over change were, in short, somewhat different from those needed to preside over the status quo.

To an equal, if not greater, extent, however, the call for reform seems to have been guided by the necessities of exercising power in a system where legitimacy resides in a party rather than a government, and where, as a result, the struggle for power is characterized by a minimum of institutional constraints. Again, let me emphasize that I am not suggesting that Dubček and his followers were concerned with nothing more than consolidating their own positions of authority within the CCP. Although this was probably a major consideration, the call for reform outlined in this document was undoubtedly also motivated by the desire to maintain effective control over the process of change and a recognition that this could only be accomplished by eliminating internal weaknesses of the

Party while at the same time improving its capabilities for dealing with other groups in the society.

What I am suggesting is that here, as in other Communist political systems, the two are interrelated. For the Party to effectively control the Action Programme, Dubček would have to effectively control the Party. While the removal of Novotny paved the way for the implementation of the first of these objectives, the reforms proposed in this document were undoubtedly viewed as a contribution to the second.

If this is correct, then the message set forth here should be interpreted both as a gesture of confidence in the ability of the CCP to preside over the process of change and a concession to the realities of gaining and maintaining power in Czechoslovakia. In the first instance, the intended audience is the "masses" as well as those identified as anti-socialist elements. To them, the call for internal reform represents a determination on the part of the CCP to organize and direct the process of change. In the second instance the intended audience is the membership of the CCP. To them, the call for internal reform represents a determination on the part of Dubček and his supporters to organize and direct the activities of the CCP.

The External Audience
The message is presented to the Soviet Union, members of the bloc, and other "fraternal parties" in essentially the same fashion, although there are, of course, the usual assurances of continued solidarity with the "socialist camp." Seen in the light of the subsequent developments, it raises the question of whether the message was actually received and, if so, why the decision was taken to intervene. There are, it seems to me, at least two possible explanations. On the one hand, the message could have been misinterpreted—that is to say, the Soviet Union and other members of the bloc could have taken these documents as simply another indication of what appeared to be a growing tendency on the part of the CCP to further compromise its already shaky position as the dominant force in Czech society. There are certainly suggestions of this view in the statements published by the Soviet Union during the months preceding the intervention. Considered against the background of events then taking place within Czechoslovakia, such a misinterpretation would be understandable.

The second explanation, and one that I find more plausible, is that the message contained in this document came through as intended. I find it difficult to believe, for example, that men accustomed to the manipulation of power in a similar context would not be able to understand the dual meaning of this call to reform. What I do not find difficult to believe is that the Soviet Union and its Allies had strong misgivings about Dubček's ability to manage both the consolidation of internal Party control and the regulation of external change at one and the same time. Recognizing, as I suspect they did, the interrelationship of the one to the other, they must have had even greater misgivings about the future of the CCP. For unless Dubček could maintain effective control over the Party, it was highly unlikely that he could, no matter how well intentioned, maintain effective control over the implementation of the Action Programme. Failing in that, it was almost certain that the initiation of change would become less and less the exclusive prerogative of the CCP, and more and more a responsibility shared with other groups in Czech society. To extend the thesis developed in the introductory comments to the internal arena, so too would the obligation for accommodation. I will return to this question in my concluding remarks. For now let me only suggest that the events which both preceded and followed the release of the statements contained in this document must have confirmed their worst suspicions.

In the non-Communist world, the message appears to have been completely misinterpreted—understandably so, I might add. Unaccustomed as we are to the vagaries of manipulating power in a Communist political system, it is easy to read this document as another indication of Dubček's liberal instincts at work. The confusion is further compounded by the fact that the proposals advanced here do seem to constitute a genuine attempt to transform a party dedicated to the maintenance of authoritarian rule into a party which is capable of initiating and directing change. Bound as most of us have been to certain preconceptions regarding the operations of these parties, it is difficult to separate the search for flexibility from the search for "freedom." It is even more difficult to associate the pursuit of individual power with the pursuit of political, social, and economic development. Thus the tendency is to regard the call for Party reform either as a sign of liberal trends at work or as a propaganda effort designed to hide an intramural struggle for personal power.

As I have suggested above, the message of this document is, or at least appears to be, consistent with neither interpretation. On the contrary, the aim of these reforms seems to have been that the CCP would preside over the initiation of change and that Alexander Dubček and those around him would preside over the CCP. This is not to suggest either the illusion of change or to imply a condition of acute megalomania. It is to argue that Dubček, committed as he seems to have been to the initiation of change and trained as he obviously was in the exercise of power within the context of a Communist political system, undoubtedly recognized that the danger of failure, like the danger of extinction, could only be avoided if those making the decisions also controlled their implementation.

Based on that understanding, he appears to have set out to create a Party that would not only be better able to manage the complexities of change but would be able to do so under the direction of those in the Party who had formulated the Action Programme and who were therefore presumably most interested in its successful implementation.

Conclusion

In the preceding analysis I have tried to indicate what I regard to be the message of this document. If I have interpreted the contents correctly then it would appear that the reforms proposed here were intended to ensure the continued primacy of the CCP as the dominant force in Czechoslovakia. It would also appear that the intention of these proposals was to ensure that the dominance of the Party would be consistent with the successful implementation of the Action Programme and whatever other changes would be introduced in the years to come. Finally, and in a related sense, the intent seems to have been to ensure that the future of the Party and the future of the reforms would be in the hands of those in the CCP who were genuinely committed to both objectives.

FROM THE MEETING OF THE CENTRAL COMMITTEE OF THE COMMUNIST PARTY OF CZECHOSLOVAKIA /May 29 - June 1 1968/

CONTENTS

FROM THE REPORT DELIVERED BY A. DUBČEK

AT THE PLENARY MEETING OF THE CENTRAL COMMITTEE OF THE COMMUNIST PARTY OF CZECHOSLOVAKIA ON MAY 29 1968

Dear Comrades,

In view of the development of the situation, we propose to today's plenary meeting of the Central Committee that it decides about the further tactical course of the Party in the present intense social process, and especially about making arrangements for the next extraordinary Party Congress.

In preparing today's plenum, we proceeded from the results of the regional conferences, from the evaluation of the written reports about the development of the political situation which we demanded from all district Party committees as well as from resolutions and standpoints of basic organisations which are still being received by the Central Committee of the Communist Party of Czechoslovakia (CPCz) in great numbers.

When preparing the plenary meeting, we also arranged a number of nation-wide conferences; a conference of leading secretaries of district and regional Party committees, a meeting of chairmen of Party organisations from the largest industrial enterprises, as well as of village organizations, a conference of Communist journalists, of workers active in the ideological sphere and others. We also proceeded from an independent evaluation of the decisive political questions in the Presidium.

a

3

In the Party Central Committee, we hold the identical view that the most important task facing this meeting of the Central Committee is <u>for the whole Party to move unitedly, in an organized and purposeful way over to the offensive,</u> to more resolutely take the lead in the social process in the forthcoming new stage, by its conclusions and measures and its bold and active work. The time has come to fulfil the expectations and hopes of the people by practical deeds and at the same time to publicly and resolutely react to all attempts to obstruct our road ahead.

This fundamental task of the Party determines our present approach to the whole complex of problems posed by the new stage of the socialist process of regeneration.

The central point of the offensive course will be the preparation of the Party Congress which must become the basis for the unification and the political drive of the Party in the next few months.

In the eight weeks since the April plenum the social process has accelerated. While in the period immediately after January there was an essentially uniform stream, it now begins to become gradually differentiated. Various specific interests are appearing and individual political tendencies are more sharply crystallizing.

The differentiation of society is reflected also within the Party in the diversity of views on the evaluation of the present situation, its causes and the further course of the Party. There are fears - as can be seen from resolutions of Party organs and organizations - as to whether the Party is not giving up its positions, whether it does not resign its leading role and give free scope to rightist, non-socialist forces. On the other hand, there are fears lest the Party should slow down the process of democratization.

4

a

If we want to arrive at a correct view, we must not see only extremes and absolutize partial phenomena.

The fundamental characteristic of the present day is determined by the positive social process initiated in January. Since the April plneum, which in principle characterized the situation existing at that time correctly, it has been possible to strengthen certain elements of political consolidation. The regional conferences created conditions for activating the Party. The ideas of the Action Programme and of the Government statement have met with widespread support even though efforts to make them the basis of the everyday political and organizational activities of Party bodies, organizations and all Communists are still not always successful. We have resolutely started, along Party and State lines, to rectify unlawful acts and deformations. We are also changing the methods and the style of Party work. We have not only worked out clear programme principles of the future course in the main spheres but we have also created the most important organizational and institutional prerequisites for pushing them through.

The most valuable capital for the Party is the fact that after the January plenum it was able to restore confidence in our policy. This is proved by positive socialist activities of even those people who in the past stood aside from political life and to whom the January plenum has given new hope and trust in socialism. We realize that their confidence in the Party is conditioned by the way in which we shall be able to fill it by concrete deeds.

The contradictions and conflicts which quite naturally appear in the present process and which frequently become even dramatically acute are neither the product nor the consequence of the policy we started in January. They are in the first place the fruit of the long social crisis which had been

a

5

growing over many years, which accumulated a whole number of unsatisfied needs and unsolved problems to which the previous policy not only did not react but which, on the contrary, it gradually worsened by its methods although attention had been drawn to this by many voices in the Party since the 12th Congress and, more intensely, since the 13th Party Congress. In January, we opened up scope for their solution. This cannot naturally proceed without contradictions and a certain degree of element-al development. The present difficulties therefore originate in the burden of social contradictions, mistakes and deforma-tions which crystallized especially in the past few years, under conditions of concentrated personal power, in a situa-tion of extreme crisis.

This historical view is necessary in the interest of truth and also in order that we may not only understand the necessity of the January plenum and its conclusions but that we may also see in proper perspective the basic causes of the difficulties in the present political development.

We naturally do not shirk a critical analysis of our work after January. We know about the weaknesses in our work. But it should be recalled that under the former system of work in the Party it was impossible for us to prepare a ready-made programme of the further course in advance, and that there was no other possibility than to shape it on the march. It was even less possible for us to prepare conditions for organiza-tional work in advance. At the same time, developments have made it necessary and continue to make it necessary for us to re-examine and revalue things which had been shaping and ac-cumulating over many years and perhaps decades and which had remained unsolved, and to defend them in public discussion.

The many years of administrative regime and administra-tive methods of work have also paralyzed the action capacity of the Party. The Party as a whole was therefore unable to re-

6   a

act with sufficient speed to the rapid change in the political conditions of work, to the need to wage an open political struggle for confidence. Many Party organizations were pushed into the defensive under the pressure of the exposed deformations of the 'fifties. The wave of elemental criticism and the exposure of past deformations have even shaken certain links of the State and economic apparatus.

Were we not to get this development under control, were we not to give it purposive leadership and a system, it could happen that it might become hardly bearable for the present social and political power structure and that it could lead to a certain conflict.

The past few weeks have also seen the emergence of certain other phenomena we are following with anxiety, since they could hamper the socialist process of regeneration. We drew attention to them already at the plenary meeting in April.

However, since that time the situation has changed insofar that anti-Communist tendencies have intensified and certain elements are trying to go over to more active forms of activity. This danger which today constitutes the main threat to the further development of the process of democratization, has been realized by the decisive part of the Party and is also being realized by ever wider sections of the progressive public.

The activation of right-wing forces leads also to a certain activation of sectarian tendencies which are trying to solve the situation by fundamentally incorrect methods which could also promote the emergence of undesirable tension and conflicts.

Comrades, in what do we see these negative features of development? Firstly in the one-sided onslaught which is constantly developing and intensifying with the aim of discredit-

a   7

ing the Party as a whole. I am referring to the large number of small, sometimes indirect and sometimes also directly and purposively conceived political tendencies and manifestations which in their total represent such a stream of one-sided criticism we had to politically evaluate because, in its consequences, it could have a destructive influence on the Party, it could blunt its action capacity and unity and create an unfavourable atmosphere directed against socialist development.

I am not referring to the justified criticism of various deformations which is being raised by people with honest views. neither to the justified criticism of actual persons, but to efforts to morally discredit the whole Party which objectively tend to create the view that the Party has no right to play a leading role in our society. Even if this is a temporary, one-sided reaction of a certain part of public opinion to certain shortcomings of the past, we cannot ignore the political danger that these tendencies and manifestations could be abused.

If this stream of unobjective criticism were to grow and if it were to remain without our answer, it could lead to a disparagement of the past work of Communists and of all those who honestly ensured postwar reconstruction, socialist revolutionary changes, the establishment of cooperatives, nationalization and eventually also the February events; it could lead to a disparagement of all who contributed to the past achievements of socialist construction.

We must realize that such one-sidedness is in its consequences very harmful.

We have no reason to let ourselves be provoked into changing the political course adopted in January. However, we must not give room to unsocialist or even anti-revolutionary forces. This is why we are focussing the attention of the Party on these questions in time.

8

a

It is extremely important for our course to evaluate the real forces and possibilities of these tendencies.

The socialist Republic has been in existence for only twenty-three years. Among us, there live remnants of the former exploiting classes and their political exponents. Old ideological influences and their bearers still survive. We live in a divided world in which the class struggle has not ceased to exist. These facts do not determine the character of our social development. They do exist however, and we cannot fail to take them into account, especially in the present intense social process.

This is why we must closely follow the political and ideological activation of the remnants of the defeated bourgeois classes, of bankrupt pre-February right-wing politicians and so on. We can see how, here and there, they are trying to create ideological and political preconditions for their activities. Attempts are also being made to create a legal basis for their activities in certain organizations which are now elementally emerging, especially in the K 231, which includes also people rightly sentenced for anti-State activities.

Increased interest is being also displayed by hostile emigré circles. The interest of enemy espionage services in events taking place in Czechoslovakia has been also intensifying recently. Various enemy news agencies are spreading false information, half-truths and conjectures by which they are trying to disrupt mutual relations between the socialist countries, the unity of the Party, and to disorientate Party members and the general public.

It is true that, for the time being, the internal anti-Communist forces are showing restraint. They are even ready to maintain that they support the process of regeneration. In this, they apply the tactics of achieving their aims by de-

a   9

grees. If we consider what a profound contradiction there exist between their aims and the real interests of society, we can rightly say that the extremist, marginal forces cannot of themselves seriously threaten our Party and socialism. The reality of their danger, however, lies in the fact that they are trying to create themselves a basis in an atmosphere of anti-Communism and anti-Sovietism, in supporting various elemental and disintegrating tendencies which would threaten the structure of our society. We must realize that in the present period of the struggle between the two antagonistic class ideologies, anti-Sovieti is the greatest vogue among the various sorts of anti-Communism

We must naturally differentiate, distinguish between individual tendencies, between disorientation and deliberate intention. At the same time, however, it is necessary to demand consistent observance of valid legal regulations, valid law, and ensure that no propaganda be made and support be given to the activities of organizations which do not have legal authorization. We need as quickly as possible the Act on Assembly in order that the present period of activities of various organizations without a legal basis, without duties towards the State and the principles of the National Front may rapidly end.

Through our policy we must endeavour to overcome the doubts and mistrust of people, endeavour to win over the widest sections of socialist and democratically-minded citizens for joint work and we must not permit sectarianism and a commanding attitude in relations with them. At the same time, however, we shall resolutely and publicly expose all anti-Communist tendencies, politically isolate their bearers and intentions which represent the greatest danger for undisturbed socialist development and the process of socialist regeneration. The measures of the Central Committee which are directed against attacks on the Communist Party are not being taken against but in the interests of furthering the process of democratization. Relying

10

a

on the people the Communists have opened scope for the development of socialist democracy. This is why the Party continues
to be the decisive force and the guarantee of this movement.

We shall use the Party's full authority to defend honest
and honorable members and officials of the Party, national committees and the State apparatus who are not unfrequently exposed to unjustified an unjust attacks. I should like to say
that the Party fully supports honest officials, that we consider it our duty to defend the results of their honest work.
This in no way prevents resolute and concrete rectification
wherever necessary, wherever the principles and norms of our
socialist laws were violated.

All this is a natural and inseparable part of the policy we developed in January.

We consider the main road to combatting right-wing
anti-Communist forces to be a positive policy of the Party
which will unite all positive, pro-socialist forces of society
for creative work in developing our society. The basic course
for us is a policy which will be fully supported and recognized as its own by the working people, the working class, cooperative farmers and the intelligentsia. The leadership
of the Party is fully aware that without the working class
the foundations of socialism cannot be successfully defended
in case of an active open stand by anti-Communist right-wing
forces. We shall be guided by this in the policy of the Party.

Besides fears of a right-wing danger there are also
fears of the conservative forces in the Party, of a return to
the state of affairs which existed before January 1968. This
danger lies in the surviving stereotype of past thinking, in
the persistence of bureaucratic methods and ways.

Although their bearers voice recognition of the correctness of the new policy, they have not yet discarded old think-

ing and evaluate social development in such a way that they support nervousness and mistrust in the policy of the leadership of the Party and readily give the worst labels to each deviation from the old routine, to each more original socialist initiative. Some of them even develop purposive activities aimed against the policy of the Party. I recall for example the attempts made to distribute slanderous leaflets in the Party as well as among the public, leaflets which demagogically slander the policy of the Party and try to bring about a split between the workers and the Party, between Party members and the leadership as well as within the leadership itself.

Such views and attitudes naturally threaten the action capacity of the Party and could discredit the Party in the eyes of broad sections of the people who are rightly linking their hope for a new Party policy with the elimination of the old sectarian and dogmatic methods of work. It is therefore necessary to take resolute action also against these activities. Any attempt to revive sectarianism, dogmatism and pre-January conditions in general, even in the name of fighting anti-Communism, would greatly damage the Party and its **policy** and would objectively play into the hands of anti-Communist tendencies.

It is clear, from all I have said, that our present development includes intertwining tendencies of the most varied character. We must therefore have a very well-conceived, bold and prudent policy which must take all these factors into consideration. We cannot give truth to views which do not take into account political facts and the contradictory character of the transitional period, and which one-sidedly absolutize or underestimate the danger of these or those tendencies.

As so frequently happens in politics, both extremes eventually join in their objective effect and prevent progres-

12   a

sive development which is and must continue to be our primary
concern. We must not and shall not stop half-way.

If I were to sum up the results of the development since the January plenum, I would say that its essential feature
is the fact that social progress has entered a new phase.The
present polarization of views in the Party and in society reflects the contradictions arising out of the need to cope with
this transition. While immediately after January it was necessary to form new bodies, to fight against rigidity, to shape
and popularize the new policy, this policy now begins to be
tested in practice. If we are to succeed, we must consolidate
the process of democratization, define clear aims and methods
of their implementation in a way resulting in the development
of socialism, in the consolidation and not in the weakening
of the positions of socialism. An unconstrained process would
give scope for the growth of extremist tendencies, which in
their effect are strengthening each other, and would in its
consequences lead to clashes which in their consequences could
endanger the development of socialism in our country. This
would not be only a defeat for the progressive forces of the
Party but it would also disappoint the hopes of the forces
of the international workers' movement. We have assumed a
responsibility from which we cannot retreat. We must therefore draw the necessary conclusions from the new situation.

The offensive political onset of the Party makes it necessary to lay down a clear tactical and political course for
the immediate future. From what positions do we proceed?

First of all, we must not waste the confidence given
to the policy of the Party after the January plenum by the
broad sections of the people. This makes it necessary to consistently unite the healthy forces of the Party for putting
into practice the Action Programme, to markedly focus the attention of the Party on the social-political problems of the

a

13

working class and the broad masses of the people, to activate the policy of the National Front on a consistently socialist basis, and to speed up preparations for the constitutional arrangement and for the extraordinary Party Congress.

It is just by this active course that we must avert the growth of elemental and disintegrating forces.

In other words, we cannot permit the destruction of the existing political power structure before we gradually and deliberately replace it by a new one. We must gradually change it. Not destruction, but a qualitative transformation and development of the socialist system – this is the main thing at present. We must discriminate between the aims we want to achieve and the transition to these aims through which we are now passing and which must proceed gradually, in stages. We must also very accurately define and frankly explain certain necessary conditions which we must at present respect and without which this transition cannot be made.

This does not mean to abandon the final goal. But it would be threatened if we wanted to anticipate developments, if we wanted to achieve premature solutions to problems which cannot, under existing conditions, be solved, if we were to formulate demands people would not understand. We must clearly and convincingly tell the broadest masses for what we stand, for what we are fighting, for what we are striving, and at the same time make it clear to them what we are defending, what we cannot renounce under any circumstances if we want to preserve and augment the positive values which form the basis of socialist society.

Which, then, are the main tasks we must solve?

First of all, we must consistently dissociate ourselves – the Party as a whole – from past deformations. We must dissociate ourselves especially from the crimes of the 'fif-

14   a

ties for which responsibility rests with certain groups in the leadership of the Party who slipped out of the control of the Party, placing themselves above the Party and Communists, just as above the society and above the laws of the State, groups of people who relinquished and besmirched the programmatic Communist ideals of the Party and the democratic and socialist ideals of the whole society.

Let us ask ourselves: what prevents Communists from actively pushing through the policy of the Party, from reacting in a really polemical and convincing way to various incorrect and untrue accusations, to views they cannot and do not accept because they are frequently clear manifestations of right-wing or anti-Communist tendencies?

To a certain extent, this is because of unpreparedness, a small ability to get adapted to the conditions of real political fight to win the confidence of the people. Other factors are certainly also shortcomings in the political and organizational activities of the Party. But there is also a deeper cause. It is signalized at Party meetings and conferences, in hundreds of resolutions and letters being sent to the Central Committee. Communists demand that the Party should clearly and consistently dissociate itself from all deformations of the past, that it should part with those who are concretely mainly responsible for these deformations. They demand that the Party gives clear and convincing guarantees that there is no going back to the old, bureaucratic methods of management and even less to the deformations which so tragically affected the 'fifties.

Have we actually given such guarantees? In certain things we undoubtedly have. In the past four months, we have clearly dissociated ourselves in the leadership of the Party from the methods which were typical of the state of affairs before January. But I nevertheless believe that the shortage

a

15

of time, the complexity and contradictory character of the
situation under which we are working as well as other circumstances are having the effect that the dividing line between the
things which must be justifiably criticized in the practice
of the Party, and our sincere effort for a new approach to
problems, is not always sufficiently clear to Communists, and
to the working people. We have fundamentally changed the composition of the bodies of the Central Committee and its leadership but Communists and non-Party members draw attention to
the fact that the supreme Party body still includes certain comrades who have lost the confidence of Communists and of the
entire public. This only increases pressure on the Central Committee and serves as a pretext for disparaging its work.

We have adopted the Action Programme in which the new
general line of the policy of the Party began to take shape
but the necessary tempo was not always maintained in implementing many measures which must and can be taken immediately. In
addition, it appears as if we had in this connection forgotten
the rudiments of propaganda: we are even largely unable to
convey and explain things we have already done. This applies
to all links of Party management and media of influencing. Important steps of the Central Committee, the National Assembly,
the Government and other institutions remain sometimes unnotic-
ed and the mood of public opinion is frequently determined by
highly doubtful sensations which are not dictated by a responsible political approach to the interests and needs of society
but rather by efforts to be original at any price. Members of
the Party as well as the public then ask themselves why there
is no harmony in this respect.

For instance, we adopted a clear attitude in the Action
Programme on the abolition of censorship. However, the adoption
of the respective legal measures is proceeding slowly. The same
applies to preparations for the law on assembly and so. This
is giving rise to an atmopshere which makes it possible, by

16   a

the establishment of "clubs in defence of freedom of the press", to create doubts as if the Party were changing its attitude, and the public is thus being disorientated. We believe that such initiative is unjustified.

How can the Party dissociate itself from the faults of the past? How can all people be given guarantees that the way from today's state of affairs leads neither to conditions existing before January nor to those from before February 1948 and even less to those before 1938 but that the road leads only ahead, to a higher stage of socialist development? How can we positively develop the policy on which we decided at the January plenum and by adopting the Action Programme?

The most important task is to adapt the Party so that it may as a whole stand at the head of social development, to be able to fulfil its leading role under the new conditions.

The consistent regeneration of the Party makes it necessary especially in view of certain new circumstances, to speedily convene the extraordinary 14th Party Congress. Without this, no definite guarantee can be created within the Party for the consistent implementation of the new policy. We therefore propose to convene the Party Congress for September 9th, 1968.

We are convinced that the Congress will reaffirm the course which was adopted in January and that it will create the pre-requisites for developing it into a new political line. It is necessary to evaluate the political development since the 13th Party Congress and after the January meeting of the Central Committee of the Communist Party of Czechoslovakia and to lay down the political and tactical course of the Party for the immediate future. We must unite the Party for consistently implementing our policy of further socialist development of the society whose starting-point is the Action Programme and whose basic line must be discussed and approved by the 14th

a

17

extraordinary Congress. In view of urgent demands to speed up the realization of the new constitutional arrangement, the Congress must approve the principles of the Party course in solving this question, and work out the principles of the Party structure under the conditions of a federative arrangement of the State. Another task facing the Congress will be the adoption of new Party Statutes and the election of a new Central Committee which, with full authority, will improve and defend the unity and action capacity of the Party and stand at the head of a uniform and organized course of the Party in implementing the Congress decisions.

The tasks should be relfected in the following programme of the Congress:

1. Report on the activity of the Party and the development of society since the 13th Congress of the Communist Party of Czechoslovakia and the principal tasks of the Party in the immediate future.

2. Report of the Central Control and Auditing Commission.

3. Draft of the political directives for the constitutional arrangement of the Czechoslovak Socialist Republic, for the structure of State bodies and the Party structure under conditions of the federative arrangement of the State.

4. Draft of the new Statutes of the Communist Party of Czechoslovakia.

5. Election of the Central Committee of the Communist Party of Czechoslovakia and of the Central Control and Auditing Commission.

Membership meetings for the election of delegates, as well as district and regional conferences, should be held in the period from June to August. The Presidium of the Central Committee will submit the respective proposals at the next meeting.

18

a

Why did we decide to speed up the convocation of the Congress? Our earlier considerations concerning the date for convening the extraordinary Congress were based upon the need - - on which we placed great emphasis - that we should have as much time as possible for a really good and all-round elaboration of these questions. We also intended to prepare an economic-political directive for the Congress. In view of new circumstances we agreed in the Presidium to drop this idea. We made the fixing of the date of the Congress dependent on the level of the elaboration of the Congress materials. According to preliminary information, it is possible to prepare the materials intended for the Congress within a short time although we shall not have the originally anticipated time for intra-Party and public discussion.

The regional conferences came to the conclusion that the Congress should not solve only measures concerning cadres but also concrete issues appertaining to the Congress. The regional conferences also demanded that the Congress should be held as soon as possible. They substantiated this standpoint especially by the demand that the comrades who have lost confidence should leave the Central Committee without any delay. Clear standpoints were voiced especially with regard to comrade Novotný.

In deciding about the Congress, the Presidium of the Central Committee also took into consideration the fact that the past few weeks were characterized by a considerable acceleration of political movement introducing qualitatively new elements. Demands for convening the extraordinary Congress as soon as possible not only continue but are growing stronger. The tasks facing the Central Committee are constantly increasing. It is necessary to make decisions on vitally important questions concerning the future of our country. It is necessary to take concrete measures to strengthen the unity of the

a

19

Party, to unify its active forces, to strengthen its unity in action. However, in contrast to these tasks the authority of the Central Committee is ever more declining and consequently this also applies to its ability to solve these questions with authority, to lead the Party in this complicated situation.The election of a new Central Committee is therefore the natural and democratic method, corresponding to the Statutes of the Party, for solving these questions.

The conference of chairmen of basic organizations, who in addition to this informed the Central Committee of certain negative tendencies in the development of Party work, has shown that a situation is arising in which the question of speeding up the holding of the Party Congress has become extremely urgent. These voices and all circumstances must be taken into consideration. There are also other questions which are pressing for time. This applies, in particular, to the constitutional arrangement which cannot be implemented without discussing its principles at the Congress.

As can be seen from the whole preceding analysis, the fundamental question which has to be resolved is to strengthen the authority and the influence of the Party in society. Without solving this question, it would be illusory to believe that there will be no further growth of the pressure of extremist tendencies which could lead to attacks on the socialist power in our country. We therefore arrived at the conclusion that without an extraordinary Congress the Party today will not unite quickly enough and be able to fulfil its tasks.This is why even such an extraordinary measure as we propose – to prepare the Congress within three summer months – is a question of fundamental importance for the development of the whole internal political situation.

It must be also taken into account that autumn will see the beginning of a new wave of social activity.

The Congress could be prepared to greater advantage and more thoroughly according to the originally planned time-table but the complex of new circumstances, which we must take into account, forces us even at the cost of reducing the time available for holding pre-Congress membership meetings, district and regional conferences, to convene the Congress at a much earlier date. We therefore propose to the Central Committee that the Congress be held as early as September. Its preparation and proceedings could become instrumental in unifying the Party on the basis of a new policy, in stimulating an offensive onset of Communists.

Preparations of the elections of the Central Committee and of the Central Control and Auditing Commission as regards cadres will make it necessary to consistently democratize the method of selecting delegates for the conferences and new members of the Central Committee in order that it may express the social composition of the Party and enable the choice of the most able representatives of the Party, who enjoy high authority and full confidence among Party members and non-Party people. Despite the shortage of time we shall organize preparations for the Congress so as to enable the participation in it of the whole Party and, as regards problems concerning the society as a whole, the participation of the general public.

An especially important role and consequently also responsibility in preparing the Congress falls to Communists in the press, radio and television which, in modern times, are becoming a very important instrument of exerting political influence. The Central Committee seriously reckons with the work of Communists in this sphere and invites them to responsible work also in the preparations for the 14th extraordinary Party Congress. They should pay special attention to organizational work which is partly suppressed in the entire Party and which should be more strongly supported by these media as well. Com-

a

21

munists from these places of work should prudently respond to
certain critical comments which are being made at present in
connection with their work and should purposefully contribute
towards strengthening the self-confidence, certainty and action unity of Party members, Party bodies and organizations
contribute towards the growth of strength and confidence in
the further successes of the Party.

The Presidium of the Central Committee realizes that the
preparation of the Congress within such a short period will
place extraordinary demands on the whole Party, on all Party
organizations, on district and regional committees, as well
as on Communists active in the theoretical sphere who will
take part in preparations for the Congress. It therefore expresses the conviction that, aware of the importance of the
mission of the Congress, they will devote such care to its
preparation as will enable its successful work and the attain-
ment of the desired results.

The preparation of the Congress, which will become the
central point in the present life of the Party, will enable us
to solve a whole chain of tasks facing us today in the field
of Party work. This applies especially to the consolidation of
the unity of the Party on the basis of the Action Programme.
A uniform voice and united deeds which we now need so urgently
have nothing in common with what we condemned in January and
in April.

I want to emphasize that for the future we are not at
all concerned with false "unity" which is blind obedience in
executing directives from "above". We expect there will be
clashes of views and efforts to find the best solution. However,
the seriousness of the situation and the principles of Party
structure make it necessary that after the adoption of decisions
and conclusions Party members should unite their efforts to
secure their implementation. The role of the Party in society

22

a

makes it necessary for us to unite on the basic principles of the tactical course of the Party and to uniformly apply them in keeping with democratic centralism.

Organizational Party work must be based on the Action Programme. All regional and district committees and committees of basic organizations must elaborate it within the scope of their activities into their own programme of political work and must set themselves concrete political aims for which they will enlist the support of the people and with whom they will jointly strive for its realization.

When we emphasize the political-organizational work of the Party, we have in mind especially the forming of close ties between Communists and non-Communists in order that the whole Party, all Communists, workers, farmers, the intelligentsia, in brief, the absolute majority of the working people may participate in shaping the policy of the Party and in its being put into practice. Our policy will be successful only if it expresses the interests of the people as far as possible, if it is intelligible to them, in brief, if it is their policy.

This makes it urgently necessary to extend and intensify our policy in the outward direction. In this sense we must return in methods and forms of Party work to the period of before February 1948. If our political work is to fulfil a purpose, if our discussions are to fulfil a purpose, we must go out from the secretariats, conferences and Party meetings, out among the working people, to factories and villages, to the press, radio and television. We must over and again publicly explain for what we stand, what is our programme, what are our aims, how they can be achieved and what obstacles stand in the way, what we shall oppose. Under the new conditions, a great deal depends upon the assertion of the leading role of the Party, upon the work of Communists in social and other non-Party bodies and organizations.

a

23

It is from these points of view that we must develop and also "regenerate" a well-conceived ideological education and in a certain sense also a re-education of Party members. Ideological work must be at present stimulating, it must be part of the vigorous struggle for the Party policy.

Preparations for the Congress will also be an opportunity for admitting new Party members.We can say that the influx into the Party has even in this complicated period a rising tendency. The Party has in the post–January period gained great capital among young people who are not indifferent to the future of the Republic and of socialism. This must be taken into account and young people must be given every care on the part of the Party. In admitting new members to the Party, it is necessary to concentrate especially on young people to whom the present Party policy is opening the road.

In order to improve the work of the Party and in the interest of a thorough preparation of the Congress it is necessary to reorganize the forces of the apparatus in keeping with the needs of the present policy. The apparatus of the Central Committee and other Party bodies must be much more closely linked with the work of the members, especially through various commissions,including temporary commissions,in which Communists from the various spheres will take part in managing Party work in these spheres. We say quite unequivocally that indiscriminate attacks on the Party apparatus do not pursue honest aims. We reject them and will counter them. The Party cannot do without good work of the apparatus. In intensifying its work, we shall place emphasis on making the apparatus serve Communists and Party bodies effectively in the implementation of the policy of the Party.

I should like to say once more quite clearly; the purpose of our work - and this must be a distinct feature of the pre-Congress period — is to strengthen the political management of

24

a

society by the Communist Party. This includes the rejection of all attempts to discredit the Party as a whole, attempts to create mistrust in the Party and to deny it the moral and political right to lead our society.

The Party has been leading our society since February 1948 as the leading political force. It therefore assumes responsibility for the successes in socialist construction as well as for shortcomings. It has self-critically drawn attention to past mistakes and is resolutely ridding itself of them.

However, in the interest of truth we must emphasize that responsibility for the deformations is not borne by the Party as a whole. Rank-and-file members and functionaries did not know about the reprisals of the 'fifties. Direct responsibility for them rests with concrete culprits of the Security Force, as well as in judicial, State and Party bodies. Some Communists in this period became victims of the deformations. Most Communists have gradually and increasingly realized their harmful character and have taken up the risk of fighting against them. The Communists were the initiators of the current regeneration of socialism. This gives them the moral and the political right to strive for the leading role in the further development of socialism in this country.

Denial of these facts and efforts to discredit the Party as a whole are considered by the Party as concrete anti-Communist, anti-socialist and essentially anti-popular tendencies. In very many cases the Party has already carried out consistent rehabilitation and continues to rehabilitate all Communists and non-Communists who were in the past unlawfully affected. The Party is determined to purge itself of those who are responsible for past deformations. We resolutely declare that we reject an atmosphere of hysteria, as well as the creation of indiscriminate distrust in Party, judicial, security and State officials. We say quite frankly - and this is also con-

a

25

tained in the Government statement - that the revolutionary measures which affected the bourgeois class, regardless of whether they were economic or political and state power measures after February 1948, will not be the object of any revision.

The Communist Party of Czechoslovakia is today the only political force in this country with a scientific socialist programme. It is the main guarantee of good relations between the Czechoslovak Socialist Republic and other socialist countries and consequently also the guarantee of a stable international position of our Republic. It is the unifying force of both our nations - Czechs and Slovaks. It associates hundreds of thousand of workers, land workers and brainworkers, who enjoy respect and esteem among their fellow-workers. Its ranks include the overwhelming majority of the best creative forces of society - scientists, technicians and artists. Its members are people who have earned their authority by their fight against capitalism and Nazi occupation, people who were the initiators and organizers of the present process of regeneration of socialism and of the development of socialist democracy. Its cadres form the predominant part of the administrative and managerial structure of our society. All this creates an <u>historical reality,</u> a situation under which there is no other way ahead for really democratic and socialist development without undesirable upheavals and without unleashing a struggle for power, than the road along which the Communist Party of Czechoslovakia as the strongest organized political force in this country will lead the further process of development. It will naturally lead this process along the new roads and methods outlined in the Action Programme of the Party and which will be discussed as a new Party line by the extraordinary 14th Congress.

We should like to emphasize that we highly esteem the self-sacrificing and meritorious work of the old Communist guard

26

a

We want to continue along its revolutionary tradition of self-sacrificing, devoted and selfless service to the Party and the people which we regard as the revolutionary heritage of the Communist Party of Czechoslovakia. It is just these Communists, used to varied and manysided political work, who legitimately and sharply condemned the incorrect pre-January methods of Party work.

Just at this time, when unity of the Party is required as the basic guarantee of our new policy, we regard sporadic views wanting to "revise" the historical step of the unification of the two Marxist workers' parties as very harmful. The Party will resolutely counter them.

Another important factor in implementing the Action Programme is the policy in the sphere of the reconstruction of the socialist state and within it the first place is taken by the problem of <u>constitutional arrangement.</u> We have decided to draw all consequences from the slogan of self-assertion of nations and to go over to ensuring a full equality of Czechs and Slovaks, while guaranteeing adequate rights to nationality groups. The symmetric constitutional arrangement will enable the national missions and peculiarities of the Czech and Slovak nations to assert themselves more fully and at the same time will create a firmer basis for their mutual cooperation. Not only the Slovak, but also the Czech nation will be able in the future to better appreciate its peculiarities and conditions, formulate more precisely its national tasks and its place among the nations of Europe and the world. In the federative model of the Czechoslovak state the autonomous Czech and Slovak bodies are asserting themselves not only in the organism of the State, but also in mass organizations.

This gives rise to very important tasks. Some of which are being solved already, while the solving of others is just beginning. In the spirit of the Action Programme and the Go-

a

vernment Statement and at the initiative of the Presidium of
the Central Committee of the Communist Party of Czechoslovakia,
a committee for preparing the federalization of the Czechoslovak Socialist Republic and a government commission of spe-
cialists for preparing the bill on federation have been set
up. The work on drafting the principles of the federalization
law is being organised so as to get it ready for submission to
the National Assembly on the 50th anniversary of the foundation of the Republic. This constitutional law must outline the
structure of the new Czech, Slovak and all-State representative bodies. It would then be followed by the reconstruction of
State bodies and the preparation of elections.

Federalization creates a wide scope for the self-assertion of each of our nations. At the same time, however, it will
be the task of the centre and the national bodies to see that
the importance of the economy as an integrating factor and binding agent of Czechoslovak mutuality and united statehood be
respected in the federation. The Federal Government must have
instruments in its hands with which it will assert its role
in the development of the Czechoslovak national economy.

We have submitted a proposal recommending that the Government, in cooperation with the National Assembly, sets up
a representative commission for the preparation of Czech national bodies. The task of this commission will be to express
the Czech national interests in the process of solving these
problems in relation with all-State bodies, to act as a partner
of the Slovak national bodies and to help make it understood
among the public in the Czech lands that the federative regulation is in keeping with both the Czech and Slovak national
interests.

The federative regulation of the State demands corresponding changes in the structure of the bodies of the CPCz. This
is why we consider it necessary to set up a commission composed

28

a

of representatives of regional Party organizations from the Czech lands. The task of the commission will be to cooperate in drafting the principles on the organizational construction of the CPCz under conditions of the federation, so as to create pre-conditions for the fulfillment of the tasks which face the Party in the Czech lands, while ensuring the international unity of the Party.

For the time being there is not enough material to enable us to take a stand on the solution envisaged. However, we must realize that the CPCz will have to play the important role of an integrating force in the new federal regulation. We shall have to take care that in solving questions previously neglected the principles of socialist internationalism and objective integration tendencies be fully respected. The draft proposals will be submitted to the Party Congress for decision.

Now only briefly about the other questions. After January we finished in the Party with substituting the activity of the State and of economic bodies. This is why the political responsibility of communists working in these bodies is sharply rising; it is necessary that they contribute with their initiative to the fast, practical implementation of the objectives advanced by the Action Programme, that they help us perceptibly to move ahead with solving mainly those problems on which the attention of the public is being centred. In this sense it is really so that today the Party, the Communists, must literally daily achieve in the centre and in individual posts successes even though only in minor things, which will prove the consistency in implementing the Action Programme.

The new stage of development requires a speeding up on a new base of the consolidation of the State apparatus, certain elements of which have slackened their activity in the past few weeks. Special attention must be devoted to national commit-

a

29

tees to prevent the postponement of the elections from leading to a passive wait-and-see attitude. The result of the elections is now already being decided.

The plan of legislative work for ensuring a speedy approval of laws which embody the results of the democratization process and give it a firm order, strengthening the authority of law, is ready.

We consider of exceptional importance the consolidation of the bodies of defence and the defence of our socialist state.

The deformations of the past period affected also the Army. This is why not only the analysis of the mistakes and shortcomings has been started, but fundamental measures have been made in the Command of the Army, so as to attain a qualitatively higher combat efficiency of the armed forces.

There has been much talk recently about the People's Militia. We have said many times before and repeat it again that the People's Militia has an undeniable place in our society, in the system of the armed forces. With the whole authority of the Party we shall oppose attacks against its existence, in which we see one of the guarantees of the socialist character of our society.

In the spirit of the Action Programme we shall support the strengthening of the bodies of the security apparatus. The Central Committee is proceeding from the fact that it is necessary to emphatically dissociate from all that in the past led to profound aberrations, and to ensure full political and legal guarantees of legality.

The point is to ensure that the process now started might continue successfully, that the principles of the Action Programme should be realized also in this sphere. A consistent reconstruction of these bodies and their purging of all per- -sons responsible for the aberrations is a condition for their effective activity.

30

a

Every state, just as ours, needs an effective organism for the defence of its interests against forces violating it. This is why we cannot agree with a general abuse of the Security Force, the Army, the Justice, and their workers, who loyal to their country are truly guarding its interests.

The criticism of the shortcomings in the sphere of prosecution and justice was also justified. On the other hand, however, there have been all sorts of incorrect generalizations which could provoke mistrust in the valid law order. This is why it is necessary to lend support to political, cadre and legislative measures which will give guarantees that the mistakes of the past years be not repeated in this sphere. This also enables tendencies undermining the confidence of these bodies to be opposed.

Another fundamental demand conditioning the successful development of the socialist regeneration process is that it must help an all- round development of the life of our society. It cannot lead to anarchy, exposing the national property to risks, but must help such organization and specialized management of the national economy which would enable the solving of problems preventing an economic growth and the rise of the living standard. The close links between the democratization process in the political sphere with economic life in our country is evident. From the problem, when the political sphere was tying the economic dynamics we are going over to the necessity of thinking out how to correctly direct the emerging initiative in the political sphere into positive results in the sphere of economy.

I think it is necessary to underline the principle that no lasting progress of society can be achieved without a decisive progress in economy. Otherwise it is not possible to make use of the advantages of socialist democracy for a real development of the personality,for a self-assertion of people and

a

31

for such human development that would be a humane challenge
for real competition in social progress ensuring the people
a full and happy life.

I am pointing this out lest we should lose sight of certain strategic aspects and economic perspectives now that we
are exposed to a great pressure of economic problems. At the
same time, however, we must be sober realists and must not
fail to see the present economic situation as it really is,
and in keeping with the problems and needs this implies to
develop our efforts.

This year, too, the economic situation is characterized
by the continuance of controversial tendencies. On the one hand,
there is a fast growth in industrial, agricultural and building
production. It may be presumed that even this year we shall
achieve a relatively high increment of the national income.
On the other hand certain negative tendencies continue to arise
and make themselves felt in our economy, which deprecate the
positive production results, due to shortcomings in the composition of the supply of products, quality, technical and economic standard of production, piling stocks of unsalable goods
or ineffective exports reflected negatively in the balance of
payments.

The result is the growth of inflationary pressure and
worsening of the economic imbalance.

We are aware of the conflicting character of this economic trend started in the past years, and we do not want to
consider separate tendencies and draw exaggerated conclusions,
whether pessimistic or optimistic. In any case it is necessary
to develop the economic reform in a thorough, well premeditat-
ed way so that it might increase the economic pressure on the
rational activity of enterprises and all economic subjects. I
have in mind the urgent task of systematically strengthening

32   a

the forming economic policy which would lead to a reliable
economic consolidation.

Since we do not retreat from the basic sense of the
socialist revolution, we are obliged to oppose that the negative consequences of these necessary measures should fall
on the shoulders of the workers and the working people as a
whole, and we must ensure that the working people too should
have an opportunity of participating in solving these questions, so as to find a way which would not damage the worker
and the working people and at the same time would ensure the
necessary effectiveness of the whole national economy.

I should like to stress that great reserves still
exist in our national economy which provide conditions for
achieving a fast economic consolidation. When this will be
done depends upon the people, upon those who control the
economy, and upon all the working people. In this respect
we must create all conditions necessary in the sphere of political leadership.

Permit me now to say a few words on the work of the
press, radio and television. On different occasions we have
appraised their exceptional merit in clarifying the present
happenings and the development of socialist democracy.

We have also said that we continue to count with their
work in shaping and implementing the policy, and that we expect from them assistance in pushing through the basic ten-
cencies of our development while respecting the present state
of public opinion. We also expect that they will not speed
up the rate in an uncontrolled way, and table now problems
without considering the order of urgency, which might lead
to disorganization in solving the tasks of the democratization
process.

However, it is also necessary to give thought as to
why the work of the press, radio and television provoked such
sharp criticism at the Party working session and in our society

[251]

over the past one-and-a-half months, Party members and other workers could, in many cases, not find a reply to the question why there is not sufficient harmony between the standpoint of the Central Committee and the work of mass communication media, which of late have presented exceedingly one-sided views.

I think that some of the journalists did not see the objective consequences of their influence upon the society. The one-sided underlining of mistakes and shortcomings influenced public opinion to the effect that there arose a feeling of uncertainty and mistrust among part of the people towards our policy. Public opinion was often being more influenced by drawing attention to the problems of the fifties than to helping solve the tasks of the Action Programme, to positively overcoming mistakes of the past. A feeling of dissatisfaction was also provoked by the fact that the Party press and also Communists in television, the radio and in journalism are unable to react quickly to covert and overt anti-socialist attacks, which are aimed at the Party from the outside.

If communist and socialist-minded journalists want to support the regeneration of socialist democracy, they must take into consideration the real political situation which changes quickly, and the objective influence of their activity. They cannot proceed only from their subjective wishes. Unconsidered, even though well-meant appearances harm it objectively and play into the hands of both rightist opposition elements and dogmatic forces.

At present, mainly proceeding from the Action Programme, we believe that the main task of communication media is their positive work, their creative and organizational role, which not only will not disrupt the consolidation process, but will help to strengthen it, will create an atmosphere of political confidence and provide concrete critical analyses of the obstacles impeding the realization of a positive policy.

In this sense it is necessary to give the means of communication all round assistance and draw conclusions also for ourselves in learning to count more with the possibilities of these means, with their importance for increasing the·effectiveness of the Party policy.

We shall continue to call working meetings of communist journalists so that also communists in this sphere might participate in the creation and realization of Party policy.

I think that the demand for an active share in the implementation of the new and creative policy of the Party is a worthy demand and is fully in keeping with the mission of our journalists and publicists.

The Party has the right to ask of communist journalists to develop and defend the basic values of socialism.

In the foreign political sphere we expect that the mass information media will not affect negatively Czechoslovak State interests, that the editorial staff will see that there is no interference in the affairs of other socialist countries, and that they will react with consideration and in a matter-of-fact way to eventual expressions of anxiety or critisism of our development on the part of other countries.

The legislation prepared embodies freedom of speech, abolition of preliminary censorship. This, however, cannot be confused with the right to express subjective views before millions of spectators, listeners or readers, without sufficiently considering their social influence.

The government is responsible for State information media -- ČTK , the radio and television.

The Presidium of the Central Committee has devoted considerable attention to this sphere, because the influence of the press, radio and television assumes really great importance in the political development. In the Presidium we dealt in detail the work of the Rudé Pravo in the presence of the paper's editorial functionaries. We stressed that the Rudé Právo is the organ of the Central Committee and discussed the programme of measures to increase the effectiveness of its work. We approved that as soon as possible a Party political weekly should be issued to be devoted to analyses and commentaries of political development. We want to make of Nová Mysl a theoretical Marxist journal which would provide a platform for dialogue and polemics of Marxism with other indeological streams.

In other press too we must strive for increased responsibility and authority of the publisher and editors. We shall rely on communists in editorial offices and on the work of the National Front, whose components should exert influence on its press bodies in the spirit of its policy.

It seems that of late, during the past few days, sensations and one-sided negativism is dying down. A more serious tone begins to prevail. These are the first signs that communists in these places of work are aware of the critical notes which are being addressed to them by Party members and other working people.

We have rejected the conception which degraded journalists to passive interpreters of the policy of the Party. We believe that the Party press should mediate an exchange of suggestions between the leadership and Party members, between the Party and society. However another extreme would be if individual communists in newspapers considered themselves as autonomous makers of Party policy. Even in this respect it is necessary to advance the Leninist principles of broad joint creation of the Party policy, but also of action unity in implementing the adopted resolutions. On our part this presumes a more regular, more frequent and consistent cooperation with this group of communists.

The process of the development of socialist democracy in our country continues to be the subject of increased interest in the world. It is the centre of attention especially of communist and workers' parties.

We, of course, are in the first place interested in the attitude taken by the fraternal parties of socialist countries. It is a fact that their representatives, whom we met, express support and understanding for our party, support for the Party Central Committee, in its effort to build an advanced socialist society, but in these talks and sometimes in public they do not conceal their anxiety over certain anti-socialist, anti-communist and anti-Soviet tendencies which have emerged in the course of the regeneration process.

The countering of anti-communist expressions, of undermining our alliance and good relations with the Soviet Union and the socialist countries, of attacks on the international aspects of the policy of our Party, form an inseparable part of our policy, together with the combatting of past aberrations.

If we want to strengthen our friendly relations and prevent various misunderstandings, it is necessary to make it quite clear that we are not pressenting our policy as a model and an example to others, that we shall not judge the policy of other socialist countries according to our needs and that we cannot award good or bad marks. We have reserved the right to arrange our internal affairs according to our conditions and traditions. We do not deny this right to others and neither do we interfer by publishing various aspects concerning the internal affairs of other socialist countries.

We must on no account play into the hands of bourgeois propaganda, directed to splitting the unity of socialist countries and creating an atmosphere of mistrust by spreading not only distorted interpretations of certain different views, but even explicitly provocative reports, for example,

a

about prepared military intervention by the socialist states against Czechoslovakia, or by grossly distorted statements of our leading comrades, by quoting these statements out of context and so on. I do not know what good purpose is served by our news service taking over slanderous reports and information of bourgeois propaganda and giving them publicity without comment.

It is necessary to reassure our public that all meetings with representatives of the Communist Party of the Soviet Union and the government of the Soviet Union have been proceeding and continue to proceed on principles of equality and non-interference in internal affairs. As internationalists we are in the first place fully aware of our own responsibility for the development of the situation in this country, for the work of the Communist Party of Czechoslovakia in guiding the socialist development. I should like to repeat that the Soviet comrades are showing great readiness to help us solve our economic difficulties.

I can assure you of relations of full mutual confidence between the Presidium of the Central Committee of the Communist Party of the Soviet Union and the Presidium of the CPCz Central Committee, the National Assembly and the Government of the Republic.

We must still more often and in more detail inform the fraternal parties of our development, meet them and seek ways for further concrete cooperation. We do not think that we are and will be able to reach an ideal and complete unity in all questions of the development in the individual socialist countries, because while respecting international experiences and interests it is necessary to see also the peculiarities and specific conditions under which the different communist parties work. Certain differences objectively exist and will continue to exist between us and other socialist countries, in the political practice of building a socialist society, especially as we shall proceed from certain peculiarities which are characteristic for this or that country and the work of the communist parties in them.

We are convinced, however, that our cooperation with the fraternal Communist Party of the Soviet Union and the socialist countries will proceed on principles of mutual understanding and mutual asistance.

We are doing everything to promote cooperation with countries with which we are linked by bonds of alliance and common interests of the defence and socialist progress. In June joint staff exercises of the Warsaw Treaty armies will be held in Czechoslovakia as previously agreed.

The policy of our Party is and will remain international, as it corresponds to the basic principles of a Marxist-Leninist party, the most vital even fateful interests of both our nations. Defending the friendship and alliance with the Soviet Union and other socialist countries is not only a matter of communists, but of all citizens of this country who have not forgotten Munich, who do not lightheartedly want to endanger the basic condition of the existence of our country, its inviolability and independence. As we know the value of our friendly relations and bonds of alliance with the Soviet Union and other socialist countries, we would like our allies also to see that we repay like with like, that also our relations to them are of a lasting character.

The alliance with the socialist countries, our allegiance to the Warsaw Treaty does not prevent an active and flexible development of cooperation and relations with all other countries in keeping with our political, economic and cultural interests. In this lies the basic element of our active foreign policy, which we want to pursue seriously and responsibly.

In the first place this means to add to a gradual creation of a system of European collective security. The cardinal question is the German issue. For us and for the whole ef Europe it is a matter of historical importance that in one part of Germany, the German Democratic Republic, there exists today a socialist state, built on the principles of friendship and peaceful coexistence with the other European countries, a state which recognizes the realities of the outcome of the Second World War and which has our full support.

We also favour good neighbourly and friendly relations with the German Federal Republic. If, however, there exist causes for concern, provoked not only by the growth of neo-Nazi forces, but also by the fact that the German Federal Republic has still not decided to recognize the existing frontiers in Europe, to recognize the German Democratic Republic and the invalidity of the Munich agreement from the very beginning, then it is these very facts that stand in the way of normalizing mutual relations.

The international attitude of our Party expresses also the share in the preparations of the international meeting of communist and workers'parties to be convened in Moscow on November 25, 1968.

In this connection I should like to stress appreciation of the fact that the participating countries have reached unity on basic issues. This naturally does not solve everything. Much effort many consultations and discussions will be necessary if the meeting is to bring the expected result.

Our party considers two things as decisive. First: a political document should be worked out, and concrete measures adopted which would lead to a real activation of the international communist movement in the combatting of imperialism, and the striving for peace, socialism and democracy.

Second: the meeting should contribute to the utmost towards invigorating the action unity of the international communist movement and towards inspiring the development of extensive cooperation with all other anti-imperialist forces in the world.

We fully understand the difficulties involved in this task. However, in the spirit of our international traditions and according to our capacity, we want to contribute to the unity, action capacity and authority of the entire movement.

Comrades, permit me to sum up the main tasks confronting the Party in the nearest future.

1. The development since the plenum in January is in keeping with the needs of the regeneration of socialism. The content of our policy must therefore be a consistent implementation of the Action Programme of the Party. By their initiative and honest work in solving the problems of the society, the communists want to persuade all citizens of the correctness of their course, that they are capable and entitled to lead the society. Therein lies the main content of the struggle against a possible danger of creating an anti-Party and anti-socialist opposition.

2. A condition of the success of our policy is to enhance the authority of the Party and strengthen its leading role. This is not possible without dissociating the Party in all respects from past aberrations of socialism. To strengthen the Party, its unity and action capacity we shall centre on the preparations of an extraordinary, the 14th Congress of the Party, to be held in September 1968, so that the Congress might be an impetus for political activity in the whole country; we shall develop political and organizational activity, work in social organizations, mainly in the trade union movement. We shall resolutely oppose sectariamism and dogmatism. We shall strive to win over for the Party socialistically minded citizens, especially progressive youth.

We consider the strengthening of Party unity as a necessary precondition of its leading role, while observing the principles of intra-Party democracy. We shall insist on the consistent rehabilitation of those un-

[259]

justly affected. We shall not however retreat from the
results of socialist revolution, we shall back up all
honest members and functionaries of the Party, workers
of national committees and state bodies against scandaliz-
ing.

3. We see the prime task in creating conditions for
an active participation of the working class, which is
the leading force of our society, in implementing the
present social changes. The Party policy must express
the interests and needs of the workers and strive to
strengthen their influence on the management of society.
Proceeding from the Action Programme, we shall make
proposals for setting up workers' bodies in enterprises.
With our policy we shall express the interests of farmers, the intelligentsia and primarily of the youth.

4. We shall implement consistently the policy of the National Front. We shall lay stress on its socialist content
and help in uniting all honest forces for concerted
work – members of all social groups and their social
organizations, political parties, all citizens. We exclude the possibility that forces standing in opposition
to its socialist programme might organize legally outside the National Front. In the interest of the development of socialist democracy and in the interest of preserving the socialist attainments of our people we shall
put up a resolute political challenge to efforts
formulating opposition, anticommunist forces in any
form.

5. We shall strengthen the socialist legal order as the
basis of democratic life. We shall insist that legal
amendments ensuring the development of socialist democracy be approved as soon as possible. We shall support the authority of bodies of the socialist state:
national committees, the Czechoslovak People's Army,

42

the Security Force and Justice. We consider the People's Militia, which arose as a result of the victory over reaction after February 1948, as an important achievement of the working chass and the workers, and we categorically reject attempts to weaken them.

6. The Central Committee asks communists in the press, the radio and television to help concentrate all forces of the society on the positive tasks of the Action Programme and to actively defend and develop the policy of the Party and the National Front and reply to anti-communist and anti-socialist voices.

7. We shall strive to speed up the preparations for the federative regulation of the Republic. Along with changes in the structure of representative and State bodies we shall draft a proposal on the reorganization of the bodies of the Communist Party of Czechoslovakia in the future federative state.

8. We shall defend the interests and needs of our nations, cultivate national traditions, fulfil all international duties and commitments. In the spirit of proletarian internationalism and mutual equality we want to strengthen in every way possible the fraternal links and bonds of alliance with the socialist countries, primarily with the Soviet Union.

When deliberating on the further advance of the Party we realize that it must be essentially based on the working class becoming in practice the main creative economic, so-cial and political force in our country, on its occupying the key position in socialist society. The Party must draw a lesson from the fact that many critical voices and com-ments of workers were hardly ever heeded in the preceding period.

a

43

It is, therefore, our prime duty to study the real needs and interests of the working class. This is the leading force and the vanguard of society, the most numerous social category. We must approach the needs of the workers with full responsibility and, at the same time reveal the political meaning of the demagogy which is being developed around the concept of working class by various false "friends of the workers and friends of the people", whether they come from left or right.

One of the key problems of the working class policy is the creation of organizational norms for a direct participation of workers in the management of society. I shall speak on the extension of forms of the political influence of the working class on the management of society in connection with the policy of the National Front.

It is very urgent, however, to prepare concrete proposals for the implementation of that part of the Action Programme which suggests formation of collective bodies of democratic administration of enterprises. However, this still calls for discussion, not only among experts, but also in Party and trade union organizations, in works, discussion of workers and other working people.

We assume, being aware of the high standard of our working class in whose memory the activity and the tradition of revolutionary works councils of 1945 to 1948 is still vivid, that this step towards democratization will result in a strengthening of cooperation between the working people and the bodies responsible for management of the enterprise, that the relationship between the workers, economists and technicians will continue to improve, that their initiative will be spurred and the management of enterprises will become more efficient thanks to the support they will find in enterprise councils as elected organs of the working people.

We are of the opinion that this is the real way towards setting many economic, social and political problems inside the works which are very pressing and which the old system was basically unable to tackle. The enterprise itself will remain the property of the society, it will not be owned by the collective of the works. A suitable way must be found to safeguard institutionally the interests of the society and the State in establishing the working people's councils in enterprises.

The establishment of enterprise councils does not exclude, in fact it presupposes, an increased importance of the role played by trade unions as a distinctive form of social activization of workers and of all working people of our socialist society. It may now clearly be observed that already the trade unions are changing into an organization which intends to express, represent, and enforce in an unambiguous way, the real social needs of the working people.

This calls for a political character to be imprinted on the trade unions. If the trade unions are to represent and defend social interests, if they are to be an important political force of socialist democracy, they should once again become an organization which, even if based on direct partial interests of individual groups, must reach the stage of grasping and expressing these needs from the point of view of society as a whole. They should once more become that important political force in the National Front which they were before February, 1948. We, communists, will give all-out support to this political and economic standing of the trade unions in our system.

Thus a new political activity of the workers will spring from, take shape and expand in the trade unions and will spread from here to the political life of our country. This was the tradition of the revolutionary trade unions from 1945 when they represented the main political support of the Party.

[263]

a

45

The communists in the trade unions will make a point of defending concrete economic and social claims of the working people in works and of ensuring that the trade unions as representatives of an all-society organization of workers and working people express their all-society interests, oppose one-sidedness and narrow-mindedness, send highly qualified people to enterprise councils, and raise the level of political-mindedness of the working people, bring partial interests of individual collectives into harmony with the general interests of the working class and of our socialist society.

This dual role of the trade unions, in representing the interests of the working people against State power and in correctly enforcing partial and society-wide interests of the working people against enterprise management, this, in our opinion, is the new role of the trade unions in the system of socialist democracy. This role will necessarily result in making the trade unions a platform for the form-ing of a new political-awareness and of a new political activity of the working class without which the progress of our socialist democracy is hard to imagine.

The importance of this new role of the trade unions is emphasized especially in connection with some spontaneous social pressures and one-sided claims. We should stress all the more now the principle of "each person a manager at his place of work." The trade unions are an irreplaceable part of the social mechanism which must help us solve the con-troversies mainly in the economic field, as well as in the political sphere, too, without any upheavals.

The post-January developments opened new prospects also for cooperative farmers to become a real part of po-litical life, to have a more productive say in the develop-ment of socialist society. At the congress of agricultural cooperatives and especially in the Action Programme we ex-pressed our basic conception of agricultural policy. Then we were witnesses to discussions, debates and all sorts of views on the way of organizing farmers and agricultural workers generally. The time is now ripe, in our opinion, to close the discussions and to act: to give definite shape to the proposals and submit them to the agricultural public.

I think that we, communists, who initiated the idea of building up an agricultural organization in the spirit of post-war traditions, should now use the same initiative in helping to set it up as special-interest organization of cooperative farmers. It is going to be an organization with individual membership of cooperative farmers, a union of cooperative farmers opening its ranks also to individual private farmers, an organization that would give expression to the main social interests of people working in socialist agriculture who are not organized in trade unions.The organization would take up all the positive aspects of the farming folk's contribution towards the development of socialist society in the past years. That is to say, and this was also expressed in the standpoint of the Presidium of the Central Committee, not only to defend individual interests of cooperative farmers regarding their wages and so on, but also to represent the cooperative farmers politically in the National Front with all the rights pertaining to their political representation in society, and to take an active part in tackling the problems of the life of our countryside.

Another key point of our march forward is a consistent implementation of the policy of the National Front.

We want to set up such a system of political relations in society, such a political system, in which our Party will share decision-making and power with non-communists, in which the Party will not become directly identical with the monopoly of the State power centre.

At the same time it would be a distortion of facts to state that the Party does not express the interests of society. Its leading position in society is based primarily on the

a

47

fact that it represents the most progressive and perspective social interests. The problem is that the range of interests expressed by the political direction of our State and society should be as broad and concrete as possible. This is the most profound sense of our present efforts at developing the National Front policy which is and should be pivoted on a policy aiming at an intensification of socialist democracy, a democracy providing ample room for active participation of all people in socialist construction. However, it would be a misunderstanding to think that the essence of democracy consists in mechanically transferring the formal democracy of bourgeois parliamentarism into socialist society.

The present process of development is essentially a process of the revival of socialism. To speak only of a process of democratization without this clear-cut socialist content would equal a distortion of the underlying efforts of our Party to develop socialist democracy.

The new face of the socialist democracy we want to form will differ from a formal democracy in at least two respects:

First of all it will have to settle the problem which no bourgeois democracy has so far tackled or even formulated: how the working people themselves, workers and technicians in production and working collectives in other fields, can and should have a say in the management and administration of society. How to make sure that no system of various procedural forms and by-passing can carry out State policy without reference to or even against the interests of workers and working people. It is well known that this is not only possible under formal democracy, but actually made use of by the bourgeoisie as part of their programme.

Socialist democracy cannot develop as a system in which policies are decided by political parties alone. Our

[266]

experience from 1945 to 1948 brings sufficient proof that such a "party" in political life is detrimental to the interests of the working people. Our democracy must therefore provide also for the right of the working people to take a direct share in the power of the State, to have their representatives in elected bodies: through the trade unions, through an organization of farming people, organizations of youth, women's organizations, and the like. The Communist Party is of the opinion that these organizations are equal political pertners in the National Front. We shall defend the idea that even people who are not members of any political party should have a factual opportunity of participating directly in policy-making in a socialist state. The National Front cannot ever be changed into a mere coalition of political parties. The chief political organizations mentioned ~~shou~~ should get an appropriate position in the National Front.

The National Front will certainly clearly define as soon as possible, the programme of its socialist basis, the violation or rejection of which will be incompatible with membership in the National Front.

The Communist Party of Czechoslovakia will submit its proposals suggesting that such a basis be constituted by the acceptance of a socialist, class ownership system of social relations and activity supporting their development. Further conditions are, activity complying with the Constitution of the Czechoslovak Socialist Republic, rejection of activities against the people's interest, of anti-communist, fascist- and similar nature, inciting nationalist or racial controversies; any activity aimed against the foundations of the State and national independence, as expressed by the alliance with the Soviet Union and the socialist countries is impermissible; it is further essential to respect the principle that the Marxist conception of the construction of socialism forms the programme basis of the development of our society and that the leading political position of the Communist Party of Czechoslovakia is a historical fact.

[267]

a

The common platform should include a declaration that
the National Front has endorsed the contents of the Action
Programme and of the government statement.

As regards parliamentary elections, they will probably
take place in the first half of next year and will refer to
bodies extablished under the new constitutional pattern of
the State.

All of these problems will be subjects of debate in
the National Front so as to reach binding agreements.

The basic difference between bourgeois parliamentarism
and socialist democracy is that the relation between political
parties, which preserve the basis of the National Front, must
be a relation of partnership and cooperation, not one of
struggle for redividing power in the State, which is characteristic for a bourgeois political system. This does not
mean to eliminate political autonomy, to eliminate controversies and mutual opponency inside the National Front. The
clashing of views must be based on a common socialist programme. This programme is guaranteed by the leading role of
the Communist Party of Czechoslovakia, as there is no other
real programme of the building up of socialism but the
Marxist one based upon scientific cognition and the most
progressive social interests.

We exclude the possibility that socialist democracy
would develop in our country at the present time by forming
an opposition political party which would be outside the
National Front, as this would result in a revival of a
struggle for power. Our Party will oppose such tendencies
with all its means as they would, under existing conditions
and independently of the wishes of those who advocate such
ideas, lead finally to an attempt at undermining the position
of the Communist Party of Czechoslovakia in society and
ultimately even of the socialist development.

Therefore we are radically opposed to the setting up of any opposition party that would be outside the policy of the National Front. This is the principle we adopted as early as 1945.

In the new conception of the National Front there will be room enough for controversies, clashes of views and for mutual opponency of various forces inside the National Front.

These principles will also be the basis of our stand-point in formulating new laws, especially the electoral law and the law of association and assembly. We shall maintain the principle that the organizations that want to carry on political activities, want a share in the elections and a share in State power, must be organizations of the National Front, and cannot stand in opposition to its programme.

ɔ o o

It is not only communists who want to gain favour with the young people of our Republic. We must do all we can to win them over for our policy. That means to work with the youth and open the gates of the Party to them. With the Action Programme as our foundation we should work out a comprehensive programme for the young generation which would open prospects of their fuller assertion. The care of the Government of the future builders of our socialist Republic is one of the key duties of communist policy in the Government. We should, therefore, consider the ways and means to be used by the State, Government and its policy in order to exercise a greater influence on the youth.

As regards a youth organization, the Central Committee Presidium lends support to all the efforts tending to achieve an agreement and unification of all the various organizations of young people, in accordance with their individual interests, in an organization of the federative type. We favour a unified organization of young people, the unity of youth. This is the agency through which the youth may achieve a greater influence

[269]

in the National Front, on the policy of our country, in elected bodies. They can win the support of the Government and State authorities in realizing common interests of all the young generation and its individual groupings. An atomization of the movement can only harm the common interests of the youth.

- - - - -

RESOLUTION ON THE PRESENT SITUATION
AND THE FURTHER COURSE OF THE PARTY

After the plenary session in April of the Central
Committee of the Communist Party of Czechoslovakia, at which
the action programme of the Party was approved, the government programme drawn up, the new government formed, and a
new (Party) presidium and secretariat elected, a new stage
of the development, initiated by the plenary session of the
Party Central Committee in January, has begun. Newly elected
Party bodies have started working in regions and districts.
The Party Central Committee considers the most important task
of this stage to be full exertion of positive effort aimed
at fulfilling the Action Programme, to ensure the offensive
of the whole Party towards carrying out its unified political
line so that the confidence of the people, won over for the
Party policy by the plenum in January, is strengthened and
further augmented.

We cannot be fully satisfied with the development of
our internal political situation since the April plenum,
because not all its objectives have been always achieved to
the full. Along with certain attempts to support the consolidation process, fears have also been arising within the
Party and among the general public as regards the further
development of socialist democracy in our country. On the
one hand, fears are being voiced that the process of developing socialist democracy might give rise to anarchist tendencies and create scope for endangering the very foundations

a

of socialism, for <u>attempted attacks of anti-socialist and</u> <u>downright anti-communist forces.</u> On the other hand, fears are also being expressed lest the development does not get stuck half way, and <u>lest attempts be made to revert to the</u> <u>state existing before January 1968.</u>

The Party Central Committee notes that negative tendencies in our internal political development, justifying the fears of both kinds, actually exist. The Central Committee considers it the main condition of further successful development of socialist democracy in Czechoslovakia for the Party to strengthen its political authority in a determined way, and to win over for the support of its new policy <u>working</u> <u>class, cooperative farmers, youth, intelligentsia</u> and wide strata of the working people, to remain within the actual conditions of the present stage, and not to <u>ourstrip the</u> <u>development which is realistically possible.</u>

The Party considers it of decisive importance in the present stage <u>to shape, strengthen and develop unity of the</u> <u>communists</u> on the basis of the new policy line, as laid down by the Action Programme, and <u>to create all necessary safeguards</u> <u>in the Party leadership for clear-cut and consistent carrying</u> <u>out of this policy.</u> The Party will execute its policy so as <u>to make the broad masses of the working people, especially</u> <u>workers, sure that in Czechoslovakia there will be no return</u> <u>to class, ownership, social and political conditions as they</u> <u>existed before the victory of the working people in February</u> <u>1948,</u> that the political leadership of the society by the Communist Party will be strengthened by the new methods and will be more effective, based upon mass support of the people. This will above all require the Party to dissociate itself, clearly and in a way comprehensible for the broadest masses of the working people, from the deformations of the past, and to formulate a fundamental stand of the Party on contemporary problems and questions which have recently been the subject of various speculations, that have often been one-sidedly dis-

54

a

torted, give rise to apprehension, and spread distrust among
the working people in the leadership of the Party and its policy. The Party Central Committee considers it a serious
shortcoming that so far, the Party, social and State bodies
and organizations, as well as the mass communications media
which shape public opinion (press, radio, television) have
been making only few and insufficient efforts to make the
new policy of the Party known, in an intelligible, positive
way, to wide masses of the working people, especially to
workers, and that they have been taking little care to make
their voice and their views more pronouncedly heard in our
whole public and political life. This creates a favourable
atmosphere for the spreading of distrust and uncertainty,
for the possibility of exacerbating disputes and conflicts
which by their consequences would tend to disorganize our
life, and might also encourage the hopes of anti-communist
forces that they might gain something from the development
of the process of socialist democratization.

In the present situation, the Party considers it to be
the main issue to ensure that the socialist character of power
and social order could not be endangered from either side -
neither by rightist, anti-communist tendencies, nor by conservative forces which would welcome a return to pre-January
1968 conditions, which were incapable of ensuring the development of socialism.

The foundation, on which we stand firmly, is the
Action Programme of the Party. The political line of the
Action Programme must be discussed by the Party Congress,
which alone can set up in a democratic way such central bodies which will fully guarantee consistent implementation of
the new policy. This alone can repel the attacks against the
Party, fostered by doubts as to whether the Party will be
able to dissociate itself absolutely from the past mistakes
and deformations, by mistrust in the unity of the Party and
its leadership. The new form of socialism, to which the Action

a

[273]

55

...rogramme shows the way, has not yet been shaped, and necessitates solving not only a number of practical problems,
but also a number of theoretical questions concerning the
programme. This final objective of the course which has been
adopted must be viewed apart from the conditions and possibilities of individual stages of the transition from the
past to the ultimate goal. The concrete policy of the Party
must at all times proceed from the conditions existing in
every stage of this transition, which is a realistic possibility. It is, therefore, harmful for the policy of the Party
when some comrades do not realize this necessity, and confuse
the final objectives with concrete, practical tasks of the
present stage.

To ensure a uniform, politically effective course of
the Party in the present political situation, at the time
when the Party Congress is being prepared, the Party Central
Committee considers it necessary that all communists, at any
sector of their social work - in factories and in agriculture,
in political work and in journalistic work, in their influencing of public opinion - should uniformly observe the following main principles of the political course of the Party:

1. To ensure political leadership of the society by
the Communist Party, and to effectively repel all attempts
aimed at discrediting the Party as a whole, attempts to
create distrust in the Party and to deny it the moral and
political right to lead our society, to be the decisive political force of socialist power.

The Party has led our society since February 1948, and
thus claims as its own the achievements of socialist construction, and admits responsibility for the deformations
which distorted the socialist ideal. Some communists have themselves been victims of the deformations and crimes of the
1950s, for which quite specific individuals and groups in
the Party leadership are responsible. The communists were at
the same time initiators of the fight against these deformat-

ions, and the culmination of the fight into the results of
the January plenum of the Party Central Committee and into
the Action Programme of the Party gives them full moral and
political right to strive for the leadership role in Czechoslovakia during the further development of socialism.

To deny these facts, to try to discredit the Party as
a whole and to fight against its being the decisive political
force of socialist power - those in the opinion of the Party
are the concrete anti-communist and anti-socialist tendencies
which exist at present. The Party has already carried out
rehabilitaiton in a number of cases, and is at present engaged in consistently rehabilitating all those communists and
non-communists who had been unjustly victimized in the past.
To raise doubts about this means causing distrust in the
Party. The Party is determined to purge itself of those who
are responsible for the past deformations, and will see to
it that all those found guilty will be punished, without
regard to their position. The Party will, however, proceed
according to legal and Party norms so that the guilt and
responsibility of everyone could be justly determined. The
Party is quite resolutely opposed to all attempts to create
an atmosphere of hysteria and all-inclusive distrust in Party
and state functionaries by means inconsistent with just and
legal procedures, and which could be politically beneficial
only to anti-communist forces and their designs. The revolutionary measures which affected the bourgeois class after
February 1948 - regardless of whether they were political,
economic or state power measures - will not be the subject of
any "revision".

The Party Central Committe proceeds from the fact that
consistent regeneration of the Party needs <u>convening an extraordinary 14th Party Congress</u> at the beginning of September
<u>1968</u>, because without this,all guarantees of consistent im-
plementation of the new policy could not be provided. The
Party Congress will:

a

a) discuss the development after the 13th Party Congress, and especially after the January plenum of the Communist Party Central Committee, assess the main tendencies in the development of society and the Party; on this basis, it will lay down the political line of the Party for the next period, including the political line of the Party for the solution of the constitutional (federative) structure of Czechoslovakia, and will lay down the political line of the Party for the development of the whole political system (especially the structure of representative bodies as organs of state power, and elections to these bodies),

b) discuss the results which will have been achieved as regards the rehabilitation of unjustly victimized comrades, and the responsibility of the old political leadership for the unlawful acts;

c) adopt new statutes of the Communist Party of Czechoslovakia, which will express in detail the principles of intra-Party democracy and methods of Party work;

d) elect a new Central Committee of the Communist Party, and new central inspection and auditing commission.

The Party Central Committee considers it necessary to ensure the preparation of the agenda of the extraordinary 14th Party Congress very speedily and at the same time in a responsible way. All this work, and the process of electing delegates to the Congress, should be organized so that the extraordinary 14th Party Congress could be held at the beginning of September, and that the outset of the development of political activity in the autumn (congresses and conferences of all National Front organizations, legislation on federalization, celebrations of the 50th anniversary of the birth of the Republic) could begin by an offensive of the Communist Party as the leading political force in the country.

At the beginning of 1969, the new constitutional relations in federalized Czechoslovakia would be expressed by a

58

a

constitutional law, the structure of representative bodies
would be adopted, and a new election law passed, according
to which elections to the representative bodies of the State,
on all levels, would be held.

The Party Central Committee considers the views, spora-
dically cropping up, that the Party should dissociate itself
from the past shortcomings and create final, firm guarantees
for the new policy in another way than by convening speedily
the extraordinary 14th Party Congress, to be wrong. This applies especially to those infrequent views which in essence
call for a split of the Party, and for the establishment of some
other Marxist workers party - regardless as to whether they
are based on instigations of certain individuals describing
themselves as "progressive communists", or, to the contrary,
whether they are being instigated by those social democrats
who want to "revise" the historic step of 1948, when the two
Marxist workers´ parties merged. These views are considered
by the Party Central Committee, at a time when the unity of
the Party is of prime importance as a fundamental safeguard
of the new policy, as attempts whose political character is,
in the last analysis, downright anti-communist.

The Communist Party of Czechoslovakia is the only political force in this country which has a scientific, socialist programme. It is the main guarantee of good relations
between Czechoslovakia and the other socialist states, and
thus also the guarantee of a stable international position
of our Republic. It is a unifying force of both our nations -
Czechs and Slovaks. It associates hundreds of thousands of
workers, farmers and members of professions who enjoy the
personal respect and esteem of people in their proximity;
within the ranks of the Party the overwhelming majority is comprised of the best creative forces of our society - scientists,
technicians, artists. There are also such Party members who
have gained their authority by their participation in the
fight against capitalism and Nazi occupation, there are people

a

59

in the Party who were initiators and organizers of the present process of regeneration of socialism and the development of socialist democracy. The Party cadres form the decisive part of the administrative and managing structure of our society. All that creates, as a historic reality, a situation in which there is no other way for a really democratic, socialist development without conflicts, without undesirable upheavals, without unleashing a struggle for power (and thus for the very socialist character of power) than the way, along which the Communist Party of Czechoslovakia, as the strongest organized political force in this country, will lead the whole development process - by those new means and methods, however, which are clearly outlined by the Action Programme of the Party, and which will be laid down by the Party Congress.

The Party Central Committee declares that if anti-communist elements should try to attack this historic reality, and if they should try to lead astray the development of our nations, the Party will mobilize all forces of our people and of the socialist state, and will repel and suppress such an adventurous attempt. That would, however, considerably endanger the whole development to date, and would also endanger the implementation of the line of the Party Action Programme: the Communist Party will therefore strive by all available means to prevent such a situation from arising in our development.

The Party Central Committee is of the opinion that anti-communist forces, as such, are numerically weak in Czechoslovakia: they are the small remnants of the former members of exploiting classes still living, a handful of still living political representatives of the reactionary, right-wing pre-February politics, unless they have already renounced their political ambitions; this is but a handful of enemies, who sold themselves to foreign imperialist forces, who were justly punished by the state in the past, and who in certain cases, having served their just sentences, did not change their real

60 a

designs, and the like. These anti-communist forces have indeed their supporters abroad, but they could gain major political influence only if they succeeded in taking advantage of dissatisfaction and in creating chaos, disorganization and situations of conflict. In order to prevent this from happening, it is necessary to ensure that:

   – our policy expresses the interest of workers and farmers, and that it solves the problems which affect them. The support of the working class is of prime importance for the policy of the Party: it is on the attitude of the workers that the character and possibilities of developing socialist democracy above all depend;

   – sectarian mistakes are not repeated in the Party policy towards the intelligentsia and youth, and that consequently conflict situations do not arise; the intelligentsia and youth must be won over to actively support the Party;

   – non-communists are given the opportunity to participate, with full rights, in the government and management of the society, and that the National Front policy is consistently implemented;

   – all vestiges of sectarian, bureaucratic and directive methods in the Party and society are overcome: it is not possible to enforce political leadership by old, administratively authoritarian ways, and to restrict by these means the freedom of expression of different views and interests, socialist in character (freedom of the press and so forth).

   The Party Central Committee instructs all Party bodies and organizations, as well as all communists, to direct their efforts – in accord with all of the above principles, and in a united organized way – towards strengthening the political guiding influence of the Party, especially at present, when our society is engaged in preparations of the Party Congress;

a

61

the Central Committee calls on all honest and socialist-minded organizations and citizens to extend the communists help and assistance in their efforts.

2. <u>Our democracy is socialist in character. It strives for the development of socialism, for freedom of workers and all working people.</u> To speak today only about the "regeneration" process and about democratization without this clear content means to distort the essence of the present stage of development.

The development of political democracy, and civil rights and freedoms, belongs inseparably to the development of socialism. Actual possibilities of a free life of workers and all working people stem, however, from conditions provided by the stage of development of the economy. Our whole socialist democracy must ensure <u>the development of social wealth,</u> the development of production, progressive development of our economic and civilization base in the direction which will make it possible for people to enjoy in future all fruits of the scientific and technical revolution.

Socialist democracy does not deny the workers their traditional rights of defending their own interests, including the right to strike. The Communists declare openly, however, that those slogans urging the workers to seek <u>the main problem of their freedom</u> in, for example, the right to strike, and to seek their freedom in adopting a stand against the technical intelligentsia, against the necessary expert management of large-scale production (slogan inciting the workers against the "technocrats") – all that is <u>demagogism, which does not further the real interests of the working class.</u>

The technical intelligentsia represents an inseparable part of socialist producers, and together with the workers, it is a decisive force for the development of socialism and the perspective of the scientific and technical revolution.

62

a

The Party Central Committee also notes critically that the explicit appeal of the Action Programme - to set up democratic bodies for the management of socialist enterprise and other places of work - is being carried out slowly, insufficiently and hesitatingly. State and economic bodies, as well as the trade unions, have not yet fully taken this to be their task. The Party Central Committee considers it a political necessity to solve these questions, concurrently with the questions concerning the status of enterprises and their associations, to make the problems the subject of discussions not only in management bodies, but also directly among the workers and all working people. The Party is for a consistent, speedy solution of problems of democratic forms of management in the socialist sector (workers' councils or similar bodies), carried out so that the planned assignments are nor affected, that no disorganization of interconnections in the economy takes place, and that working discipline and authority of the executive management does not deteriorate. That would endanger the functioning of the economy, and thus also the establishment of realistic prerequisites for a higher standard of living of the people.

The problems of democratic, self-administrative forms of management should be solved, as outlined above, so that the new system of management might become operational already this year. This will have established one of the fundamental features of our democratization development, guaranteeing that the development of socialist democracy is not a return to a formal political democracy of bourgeois type.

The socialist character of democracy as a democracy for the workers and other working people must be expressed in the content and methods of the whole economic policy in our society. We already know today that not even in socialism shall we be able to avoid the effects of several inevitable consequences of commodity production and of the market, especially the pressure of economic profitability and profits as a

[281]

63

the "engine" of the economic and technical progress. If we did not permit these pressures to be felt, we would not be able to ensure meeting the requirements of the working people on a permanent basis and to an increasing degree.

At the same time, however, certain short-term interests of workers and working people (their groups, various professions or various territorial divisions) may in this situation get into conflict with long-term perspective requirements of the economic development. In this connection, the Party Central Committee declares plainly: the necessary changes in our economy – e.g. the changes in the structure of the national economy, the closing down of ineffective enterprises and withdrawal of state subsidies to unprofitable production) which is a form that makes workers and employees of enterprises with better economic results partly pay for the losses of less profitable ones), movement of prices according to market laws and so on – all that must be solved by the policy of a socialist state so that the working people, whose immediate interests and social security are tied to these, in principle unsound economic features, would be given democratic possibility of participation in decision-making concerning these questions. Without an agreement, without finding ways of meeting social interests and at the same time not harming the immediate interests of workers as they are harmed by the capitalist ways of solving similar problems, we would be departing from the principles of socialism. The Communist Party will promote perspective economic requirements of the society as a whole, but the methods of solution must be in keeping with these principles of socialist democracy for workers and the working people.

This applies to a number of specific questions, e.g. to the problems connected with the prospects of development of our mountainous areas, development problems of backward areas, the border regions, and so forth.

3) The new political system must be consistent with the development of socialism; it cannot be a return to a merely formal political democracy.

The Party proceeds from the principle that contrary
to the formal political democracy, as known also to bourgeois
parliamentarism, in which a system of various procedural forms
and tricks makes it ultimately possible to pursue a state
policy even against the vital interests of the workers and
the majority of the working people, <u>socialist democracy must
ensure that nothing like this can be done</u>: state policy must
<u>correctly bring into accord, express and ensure</u> the meeting
of the interests of workers, farmers and intellectuals of
all strata and groups of socialist society. Since our political system in the preceding period did not meet these requirements properly, the Communist Party is starting to reform the whole system of political democracy. To ensure that
a real <u>development of socialism</u> is the outcome, the Communist
Party will pursue the line of the Action Programme with the
following aims in sight:

a) <u>All forces standing on the base of the socialist
system</u> should participate in the building of an advanced
socialist society, and thus also in state power and administration. It is necessary to establish real guarantees
against consequences resulting from monopoly of directive,
undemocratic decision-making in politics, which prevents
the various socialist interests, needs and views of various
groups and strata of society from being expressed in a democratic way, and to achieve unity through democratic agreements, which prevents them from <u>formulating their common interests as a political line.</u>

b) It is, therefore, necessary to build a unifying
political platform, within the framework of which the individual elements of our society will democratically seek solutions even to conflicting interests, approaches and views
so that the result might benefit the building of socialism.
We see such platform in the <u>National Front</u>. So that it can
fulfil this role, it will be necessary to ensure the following in its development:

a

65

- the establishment of an association of the <u>main political organizations</u>, whose purpose is direct political activity, and the <u>separation</u> from this association (the membership in the National Front in the broad sense of the term being retained), as the second component part of the National Front, of organizations expressing specific, but not the fundamental social and political interests (organizations such as the Czechoslovak Red Cross, Cezchoslovak Fire Service Organization, more specialized group-interest organizations, group-interest unions, clubs and the like;

- the association of <u>the main political organizations</u> should in no case be restricted to an association (coalition) of political parties; the trade unions, organizations of cooperative farmers, intelligentsia, youth, women, the Union of Anti-Fascist Fighters, the Czechoslovak-Soviet Friendship Society, nationality interest groups etc. should be accorded representation with full rights, while striving at the same time for the interests of e.g. the intelligentsia or youth to be represented by an organization of a "roof" character (federation etc.), not by separate organizations.

- for the membership in the association of the main political organizations, a certain statute should be worked out in the National Front by mutual agreement of its representative elements of their mutual relations and activities, their position in political life, their relations to the State and so on, as well as certain - <u>binding for all member organizations</u> - principles of political programme, whose infringement would rule out the possibility of participation in political power and State administration. It will be necessary to express in these principles certain fundamental (and at the same time constitutional) features of our socialist society, against which no political force can at the present stage of development legally pursue any political activities, as it would endanger the socialist character of the social development: consent with socialist class and

66

a

ownership structure of social relations, not to permit political activity which is anti-communist, fascist-minded,
inciting nationality or racial disputes and discrimination,
as well as political activity which would impair the alliance
with the Soviet Union and the socialist states as the basis
of our State and national independence.

c) the Party is for co-government of all elements
standing on the basis of this clearly formulated political
programme framework of the National Front, but at the present
stage of development, it rejects on principle the establishment of an opposition political organization (party) outside
the National Front, because this would, under the existing
conditions, necessarily mean legalizing the formation of
political forces directed against the socialist political
programme within the broadest meaning of the National Front
platform.

The Party Central Committee considers it necessary to
create already in June 1968, in agreement with the main political organizations of the National Front, a clear organizational and political programme base for the activities
of the National Front, with which the whole National Front
would come before our public. By its initiative proposals the
Party Central Committee will ensure that these questions
will be discussed in the National Front within an appropriate time. In the National Front, the Party will fight
relentlessly against attempts to "party-ize" our public life,
and will promote full possibilities for the main social, generation, nationality and other interests of people, who
need not be members of any political party, to manifest themselves directly as a politically influential force in the
National Front and in the State. Especially the trade unions
must become a political force in our democracy, as an organization of the strongest social element in our society - the
workers; political questions concerning the whole development of our political system must not remain outside the

a

67

scope of attention of the trade unions; they must, on the
contrary, strive by their policy for guarantees enabling
free expression of the interests of the workers and the
other working people. Of similar importance is also the
speedy establishment of another social political organization
the Union of Cooperative Farmers, whose representation with
full rights in the National Front will be supported by the
Party.

These principles will also be the base for the Party's
stand on the drafting of new laws,especially the law on the
freedom of assembly and organization (which should be passed
early in summer) and the electoral law.

As regards the guarantees of socialist character, the
Party Central Committee will submit to the Party Congress
certain proposals concerning the development of our democratic representative state bodies so as to ensure the greatest
possible direct influence of the interests of the working
people on the decision-making on State affairs. This might be
served, for example, by the concept, which in addition to
elected bodies of generally political character (to which
candidates nominated by National Front organizations would
be elected on a territorial division system) – provides for
certain auxiliary, corrective bodies (with fixed authority),
to which representatives of the working people could be
elected according to places of employment,-without any party
key. In these bodies (chambers), working people from the industries, agriculture and the sphere of social services
(health, education, culture) would be directly represented
by elected deputies.

An inseparable part of the development of our political system is the federalization of Czechoslovakia, based
on consistent application of the principle of equal rights
of the Czechs and Slovaks, and ensuring national development to all other nationalities in our Republic. The Party

68

a

Central Committee considers it politically necessary that
preparations for the federalization of the country do not
proceed only along the line of specialized government bodies,
and that political initiative does not rest mainly on Slovak
national bodies. The interests of both nations are involved,
and the political aspect of these questions must also be
dealt with in the Czech lands. The Party Central Committee
will, therefore, set up a collective Party organ, consisting
of delegations of Czech and Moravian regional Party bodies,
which will be instructed to analyze – in conjunction with
the preparations of the Party Congress – and to initiatively
deal with political questions, both as regards the attitude
of the communists in Bohemia and Moravia to constitutional
questions, as well as from the point of view of the future
organizational set-up of the Party in the federative Republic.
The Party Central Committee also recommends setting up by
the government and the National Assembly, i.e. also on state
level, a preparatory political body representative of Czech
and Moravian regions.

The means of mass influence upon the shaping of
public opinion and political attitudes of people – the press,
radio and television – are also a part of the political system. In the resolution adopted by its plenary session in
April the Party Central Committee appreciated fully the positive role played by these media at the time of the Party's
inception of its new policy after the Central Committee plenum in January. Those communist journalists, who are discharg-
ing the duties of their difficult mission in a responsible
way, will continue to be supported by the Party, which will
oppose all attacks directed against them, frequently by both
rightist and anti-communist forces, as are also communists
in other fields of work.

In the present political situation, the Party Central
Committee sees the main role of the mass communication media
in the necessity of their positive political influence: the

a

communists in this sector must strive to adopt such a
course which would not impair the positive political line
of the Communist Party programme and the present political
line of the Party on individual problems as expressed by
this resolution, but which <u>will help implement it.</u> The political influence of these media must ultimately result in
shaping a political atmosphere conducive to <u>confidence</u> in
the present process of developing socialist democracy, and
specifically help to recognize the objectives and plans of
the Action Programme, to show how they can be realized and
to critically and factually draw attention to obstacles impeding the positive policy of the Party in the new period.

The press, radio and television workers have <u>social
means</u> in their hands, and social bodies have the right to
ask and to ensure in practice that the influence of these
means upon the political actitude of the people be not directed against positive efforts of the socialist society and
their organization. <u>The communists working in the mass media
are responsible to the whole Party</u> that no moods of distrust
in the Party and its new positive programme will be spread
through the media, and that the main interest of public opinion will not be drawn to questions which impede, make difficult and sometimes even impossible an initiative start of
the Party towards the fulfilment of the Action Programme.
Especially during the period of preparations for the Party
Congress, is it necessary to ensure such political influence
of the mass communication media as outlined above, to draw
the attention of all citizens to new, positive proposals
and to prevent the solution of <u>intra-Party questions</u> from
becoming a means of pressure of forces often even anti-communist in character.

The Party Central Committee considers as quite justified the demand to pass legislative measures <u>already in June</u>
which would give expression to the conclusion of the Action

70

a

Programme on the abolition of preliminary censorship, and would thus preclude the appearance of moods conducive to distrust on the part of the press, radio and television workers in the validity of the principles of the Party Action Programme. The Party Central Committee also considers it necessary for the communist journalists and publicists to be not only systematically informed of the political and tactical line of the Party, but also to have – just as communist activists in other sectors – real possibility of participating in shaping the Party policy within the Party and in accordance with its inner principles. It is, however, not consistent with the principles of the life and work of the Party – especially in the present situation of necessary consolidation of internal political conditions – for individual communists in editorial offices to regard themselves as autonomous architects of a "progressive policy of the Party", and not to respect in their public political influencing millions of people, the political and tactical line of Party bodies, including the Central Committee, and the need of the whole Party to prepare the extraordinary Party Congress according to the principles of intra-Party democracy.

The influence of mass communications media is, in conditions of a modern society, one of the most important forms of political influence upon the society in general. As a part of the political system, this sector must in its development proceed according to the same principles as the development of the system as a whole: it must ensure the strengthening of socialist relations, prevent the formation of scope for excessive disintegration and anarchist tendencies, support constitutionality and legal forms of the development of our political reform, actively counteract the influence of anti-communist tendencies and attempts at discrediting the Communist Party and the positive results of the socialist development in our country to date.

a

71

4) <u>To counter attempts at infringements of legal order
and disrupting the State apparatus</u> is held by the Party
Central Committee to be one of the prime political tasks in
the present situation. The development of socialist democracy
in this country can proceed successfully only as a process
that is <u>fully constitutional and respecting legal order.</u> It
is obvious that the existing legal order must be subjected
to qualitative changes, specifically indicated by the Party
Action Programme. But the principle must be observed that
those laws which have not been abolished and replaced, are
in force and must be respected. The Party Central Committee
considers criticism to be justified which points to hesitancy
and indecision as regards such fundamental legislative amendments as those concerning the assembly and press laws, where
the vague legal situation leads to nervousness, facilitates
the sowing of distrust in the positive programme of the Party
and State bodies, and at the same time creates conditions for
not always a sound development of social organizations (e.g.
the rise of organizations such as the "Club 231"; extensive
press publicity of each "initiative from below" even in cases
where such organizations actually lack any legal basis, and
so on.)

These principles are also served by the efforts aimed
at adjusting and improving conditions for the activities of
<u>all state bodies, national committees and bodies of State
administration.</u> To weaken their function in the present situation would mean to seriously endanger the necessary organized, democratic and legal character of the development of
our democracy.

The Party Central Committee is resolutely opposed to
attempts seeking to misuse the development of socialist democracy for all-inclusive accusations and the sowing of distrust in such <u>elements of the state power structure</u> as the
armed forces, security, the institutions of prosecutors and
the courts. The position of the Party, with regard to these

72 a

bodies, as expressed in the Action Programme, remains fully valid, and will be consistently realized. The process of reconstructing the security forces and the system of prosecutors and courts, as well as the process of purging them of people responsible for the past deformations continues, and will be completed. It must not be permitted, however, to raise doubts about the sincerity of these efforts just because a number of the complicated problems cannot be solved overnight, and will take some time.

The Party Central Committee also considers if necessary for all communists to be united in their stand against all attempts to discredit the People's Militia, which came into existence as an instrument of the workers and working people for the defence of the achievements of the socialist revolution; at present, the Party will not change anything in the status of the People's Militia.

5) Our relations to the Soviet Union, the socialist countries and the international communist movement are based upon the principles of internationalism and full respect for special conditions, under which in every country and in every period, a fight is waged for universal, common aims of the communist movement. Our development today is a development corresponding to our present Czechoslovak conditions; it was with the awareness of responsibility before our nations that the Party has taken this road. That is why, however, the Party Central Committee considers it necessary to stress in the present situation that attempts to present our course as a certain obligatory "model" for all socialist countries are wrong in principle as to content, and politically harmful both for us and for the development of our relations to the allied socialist countries.

It is impermissible for communists to forget that distortions and exaggerations of certain decisions up to the spreading of false information about a "danger of military

a

73

intervention" (e.g. in conjunction with the manoeuvres of units of the Warsaw Treaty armed forces,etc.) are highly detrimental to the whole course of our present policy, and play into the hands of certain circles in the capitalist countries, intent on disrupting the unity of the socialist countries.

The Party Central Committee declares that all negotiations which were and are being held, on Party and government levels, with representatives of the Soviet Union, lead to positive conclusions, and provide possibilities of extending mutual cooperation and assistance which is very important for the solving of some of our topical economic difficulties; the Soviet comrades have shown good will to extend such help to us.

In the past hew years , grave ideological differences have been appearing in the international communist movement in an especially marked way, as regards significant questions concerning further progress. The Communist Party of Czechoslovakia will actively assist in overcoming these differences, and will promote the development of action unity of the international communist movement. The existence of differences among communist parties should not, however, negatively affect their mutual relations. In accord with the Action Programme, we shall explain and defend our standpoint that our internal development is the sovereign affair of Czechoslovakia. We do not interfere with internal political questions of other countries, and we demand the same as regards their relations to our country.

<u>The action unity of the whole Party during the preparations of the Party Congress is an essential condition for the further successful development of socialism and democracy in our country.</u> The Action Programme of the Party is at the

74

a

moment the conceptual basis of this unity. To know, develop and concretize the Action Programme, as an open political document on the basis of which communists in all sectors, in places of residence and work, should set themselves concrete tasks and solve them — that is one of the prime requirements of Party work today. The Party bodies — regional, district and local organizations — must, on the basis of analyses of their specific situation, seek such problems whose solution is of prime importance with them for a further raising of Party authority, for winning and strengthening the confidence of the people in the Party and its concrete policy.

The initiative and the proposals submitted by communists must not only come in time — they must not only be the first, but they must also counteract the cheap, often bargain-type and therefore questionably "popular" demands which irresponsible individuals are putting forward in various sectors. The principle of the new Party policy is to tell people the truth, even the bitter truth about the limited possibilities of our present economic situation. The communists must sound truthful warnings against demagogism, must win the people over by a well-reasoned responsible approach. Let us point our that: chaos and want of method, subjectivism in management account substantially for our present difficulties. If democracy were understood to be a chaotic pressure of various unrealistic demands, it would be impossible to improve the living standard of the people, and to meet their other requirements.

The Party Central Committee considers it necessary at present to create an action unity of the Party around such a concept of 5 fundamental problems of today, as formulated in this resolution. In the spirit of the principles of this resolution the communists in all spheres of their political work must:

1/ strive in accord with the Action Programme for the strengthening of the influence of the political leadership of the Party, fight against the possibility of anti-com-

a

[293]

munist tendencies asserting themselves, and determine the character of the future development; they must prepare the extraordinary 14th Party Congress as the prime guarantee for the strengthening of Party authority and for inspiring confidence in the consistence of its new policy;

2/ strive to achieve that the working class has its influence in the management and administration of socialist enterprises, and that the economic policy brings short-range interests of the workers and other working people into harmony with perspective requirements of an effective development of the whole national economy;

3/ strive to achieve that the development of our political system is not understood as a return to formal political democracy as it existed before 1948, or even before 1938, but that it becomes - by the concept of the National Front, the concept of the role of the main political organizations of the people, the concept of the role of mass communications media and by the concept of nationality relations - a truly new, higher and socialist stage in the development of the political system;

4/ strive to achieve that legal order is respected, and that our democratic development is a constitutional reform, and not a process in which anarchist tendencies would prevail and the State apparatus of socialist power of the working people would be distrupted;

5/ strive to achieve that our ties of alliance are not impaired with the socialist countries, with the Soviet Union and with the whole international communist movement, and that we have full sovereignty in solving our internal affairs.

The unified course of the whole Party as regards these matters must also be ensured by practical organizational work in the Party. This was, however, one of the weakest spots, from the highest to the lowest Party level, in the period

76   a

following January plenum. Therefore the Party Central Committee considers it necessary to:

a/ <u>rebuild</u> qualitatively <u>the Party apparatus</u> so that it will, under the new condition, above all organizationally ensure the policy of the Party. All-inclusive attacks against the Party apparatus in the present situation would ultimately lead to the weakening of the Party's capacity to act. We shall not "liquidate" the Party apparatus, but we shall rebuild it in an expedient way. The main condition is that the <u>communists working outside the Party apparatus</u> - in State and social bodies and organizations, in various fields of social activity - should be able, given active help of the apparatus, to regularly and collectively assess and solve, from the point of view of Party policy, problems of their political work in any sector. <u>The apparatus in to serve the communists who implement the policy of the Party in society, and not the other way round - to think up assignments for them.</u> Otherwise, the overwhelming part of the communists would be kept away from the process of shaping the policy of the Party. It is, of course, obvious that both the Party apparatus and the communists in individual organizations and in various sectors must be guided by the line and directives laid down by elected Party bodies, in accord with the principles of intra-Party democracy and democratic centralism of Party work.

b/ ensure an improved and fast method of <u>intra-Party information</u> of all Party bodies and communists from top to bottom, so that the communists receive information about specific questions of the Party's political course and line in advance, before they are to adopt the course and tactic in practical work. The practice as it has been developing in the past few months, as if the Party bodies including the Central Committee had no right to inform and direct the Party, and were obliged to make known all their standpoints immediately to the whole public through mass communications

a

media, is considered wrong by the Party Central Committee.
The Party bodies do not want and will not conduct any
closed chamber policy, and conceal anything from the rest
of the people. Nevertheless, to formulate political standpoints of the Party on definite matters within the Party, to
first of all inform Party members and only then begin to
publicly defend the viewpoints and win over others for them —
that is a normal political procedure in every organization
and in every political party.

The Party Central Committee considers it necessary at
present to employ very intensively and on a broad scale such
methods of Party work as are prompt calling of meetings of
Party activists — from central to district levels — so as to
pass on information and instructions (including discussions).
This should be done according to need, withour any bureaucratic prescriptions; differentiation should be made as regards the requirements (and questions necessary to answer)
in view of the type of organization concerned (industrial,
rural, other sectors of public work) and so on. The Party
Central Committee will use this course, while organizationally
ensuring the political work of the Party after the present
plenary session and during the whole period of preparations
of the Congress;

c/ actively develop ideological work and political
education in the whole Party. It is necessary to ensure,
fast and effectively, forms of ideological education and
frequently of re-education of the whole Party membership so
that the dogmatic ideas, systematically brought into the
thinking of communists in the past, do not impede the new
directions and methods of the Party's political work. The
Party Central Committee will create the prerequisites for
this by providing necessary propaganda material (brochures
etc.) so as to enable all Party sections, down to branch
organizations, to execute this work effectively, especially
in conjunction with the campaign marking the 50th anniversary
of our Republic.

78

a

It is of decisive importance in the present situation to bring about a fast and effective reversal of the Party policy from the previously predominant orientation inward to Party organizations <u>to an open policy towards the masses of the working people.</u> The aim is <u>to openly and unitedly defend the principles of our present line, and to apply them in the influence of the Party upon the society,</u> upon all working people. This does not rule out, but directly presupposes the possibility of intra-Party discussions; their purpose and outcome must be, however, to reach united views in all Party bodies and individual organizations as to how to implement the common Party policy in the most effective, united way, all within the sphere of their competence. The communists must not avoid newly arising organizations (group-interest organizations, associations and the like); on the contrary, they must join these organizations and win them over for the policy of the Party, see that the ideas of the Action Programme are adopted, and strengthen confidence in the Party and its policy.

The Party Central Committee will do everything to increase confidence in the policy of the Party by consistent realization of the principles of the Action Programme; it will do everything with the help of communists in the National Front and State bodies to repel the attacks of these who want to discredit the Party. The Party Central Committee will cooperate systematically with communists in central communication media, with communists in the National Front and central State bodies in order to ensure that positive plans are actually realized and not blocked, that delays do not occur, and even less attempts to sow distrust, uneasiness, to create an atmosphere of uncertainty, tension and so forth.

<u>Yet if these efforts were not supported by the independent activity and political work of all bodies and organizations of the Party, and of every individual member of the Party, we would not achieve full success.</u> There is no

[297]

reason for nervousness and panic, but there are
reasons for far of further successful progress of our development. We do not fight for power, because we are its
decisive force. But we fight for confidence, for increasing confidence, for permanent and stronger support of the
masses of non-communists, workers in enterprises, in villages
and in all other sectors. We are concerned with having the
confidence of workers, farmers, intellectuals, youth , women, the confidence of both our nations and citizens of all
nationalities living on the territory of our Republic. Only
this confidence will strengthen the strongest political power and the political leadership role of our Party. The
result of this fight of the Party for the confidence of the
nation depends today, just as in the past when we were still
seeking to win the leadership role in the nation, on independence, the activity and initiative of every communist,
just as on fundamental political unity of the whole Party.

80

THE PROCLAMATION OF THE CENTRAL COMMITTEE

OF THE COMMUNIST PARTY OF CZECHOSLOVAKIA
TO MEMBERS OF THE PARTY AND ALL THE PEOPLE

We are turning to all citizens of the Czechoslovak Socialist Republic, to all the sincere patriots to whom the welfare of the Republic and its successful growth is dear. We are
doing this after having evaluated at our session the implementation of the Action Programme of the Communist Party of Czechoslovakia and the programme statement of the Government and
drawn conclusions from it for the future activity of communists.
If this work is to bring permanent success, we appeal to all
citizens for active cooperation. We are convinced that this is
the only way of developing socialism.

The communists do not want to close themselves up with
their initiative in their own ranks and they will accept all
suggestions and proposals which will realistically contribute
to the socialist progress of the country.

Five months have elapsed since the December and January
session of the Central Committee of the CPCz, which opened up
the way to a new policy of the Communist Party. In this short period we have done quite a lot of work with you. We want to give
you our opinion on how we should proceed, and ask you for further support and initiative.

The development begun on the stimulus and initiative of
the Communist Party is bringing positive results. At the same
time we must all realize that all the social problems cannot be
solved at once, that the current development has its stages.
Gradually conditions are being created for an atmosphere of political confidence. In evaluating their common problems, the

a
[299]

working class and intelligentsia are finding ways towards a rapprochement. The political weight of co-operative farmers in society is growing.

We are striving for a perfect system of legal guarantees, which must gradually safeguard the real legal security of citizens. We have created conditions for freedom of expression, for public criticism, for an open exchange of views. The public is now better informed about both internal and international affairs.

The Party is resolutely settling deformations of the past. Honour is being returned to all who suffered unjustly, and injustice is being rectified. Right and justice will take their course in the life of society. Of course, the justified criticism of the shortcomings in the application of legality must not lead to the general dissemination of want of confidence in state bodies, in the armed forces, the Security Force and justice.

Social organizations are starting to live an independent and active life according to the interests and needs of their members.

We are eliminating political obstacles so that the citizens have equal possibility of asserting themselves according to their abilities and their work regardless of differences of political conviction, nationality or religion.

We have begun to solve in a consistent manner the relationship of the Czech and Slovak nations on an equal, federal basis. We are bringing much more of our own initiative into Czechoslovakia's foreign policy.

The main representatives of the old course, those who lost the confidence of the people, are leaving political life. The country has a new President. The Party has new leadership composed of people who played a decisive role in the turn of its policy. The role of the National Assembly, as a representative of the will of the people and body of social control, has grown. The new government is starting to implement consistently,

82

a

and in a qualified way the government programme. Our people are filled with new hope, our young people with new stamina. The problems accumulated are starting to be solved. At least the most acute social problems are being eliminated in spite of economic difficulties.

We are now entering a new period. The Party will prove the vitality of the new policy by concrete results. The criticism of past shortcomings has hitherto been the centre of attention. The time has now come to concentrate attention and strength upon active work, when it is necessary to provide the socialist society with a firm order and rules which will safeguard the rights and also the fulfilment of duties.

If we do not want to repeat the mistakes of the past we must guard against impatience and nervousness, imprudent steps and hasty improvisations. The aim we are pursuing can be achieved only gradually, in stages. All the tasks cannot be solved at once. We intend to resolutely eliminate everything that has become outdated, but also to wisely make use of all the positive that has been created by the devoted work of the people over the past years.

We want to consistently pursue the road we set out on in January. The communists will ensure that new laws, such as the Press and Association Laws and other legal measures to incorporate in terms of law the principles of the Action Programme in the constitutional rights of citizens, be approved soon.

Work on the new constitutional structure of Czechoslovakia on a federal basis has begun at the initiative of the Party. Our country will become a real home, offering equal rights to the Czech and Slovak nations as well as to all other nationalities, and a guarantee of real unity of the State. The draft on the principles of the new structure will be submitted to the people for consideration on the occasion of the 50th anniversary of the foundation of the Czechoslovak Republic.

The Communists think it their duty to help in developing the activity of the National Front in which all political forces

a

that want to contribute to the patriotic work for a socialist Czechoslovakia can find a place. We are in favour of honest political cooperation based upon a socialist programme with the other political parties. We support the view that the principle to which the National Front has adhered since 1945 that there should be no place in our political life for opposition parties and political forces not included in the National Front, should be maintained.

In the economy, wa shall pursue the line of higher profitability, better ecohomy and such operation which will ensure economic balance, improvement of the standard of living and a stable currency. We intend to initiate the decrease of all unjustified expenditure of the State. We shall take the initiative in making use of all possibilities to more efficiently incorporate the economy into the international division of labour.

We are not promising that new economic growth is possible without hard work, without resolute measures against unprofitable production, bad and slipshod work, as well as against bureaucracy in economic management. Therefore we shall consistently implement the new system of management, and promote the socialist spirit of enterprise on the basis of expanded independence of enterprises.

Our aim will be to create pre-conditions that would ensure a really democratic participation of work teams in making decisions on basic matters concerning their enterprise, by means of enterprise councils.

The extraordinary 14th Congress of the Party, which will take place in September, is to be the start of the development of the political activity of the CPCz as the leading political force in the country. We shall submit the proposal for the future course of the Party and its attitude towards solving the main problems of the development of our society, for consideration to communists and all citizens.

In the past few months the communists have proved that they have been resolutely pursuing the new road. For this they have been given the support and understanding of the broadest strata of the people. We shall not dissapoint this confidence. We are determined to completely eliminate and put right all that was incorrect in the past years and we believe that wou will support us also in the view that the basic values   of socialism achieved by our people over the past 20 years are a necessary pre-condition for successful advancement.

The positive results of the past 20 years, in which our people have done so much self-sacrificing work, must not be rejected. These results cannot even be negated by the serious shortcomings which appeared especially in recent years. It cannot be permitted that the very outcome of the revolution and socialism be jeopardized.

With the same resoluteness with which we expose the distortions and unlawful acts of the past shall we defend the results of the self-sacrificial work of the millions of honest people who made the victory of socialism possible. Communists and members of other parties as well as non-party people worked just as well. Our Party thinks it its duty to defend them against any attempt of deliberate discreditation.

For us, democracy is as inseparable from socialism as is socialism from democracy. We are aware that the sovereign people is the decisive guarantee of present socialist democracy. In the Communist Party of Czechoslovakia our people have a leading political force which has enforced and put into motion present developments. It gives them a realistic programme and takes care of its implementation. In the contemporary divided world much depends upon the firmness of the alliance with our friendly socialist countries, in the first place with the Soviet Union. This is a pre-condition of the independence, sovereignty and security of our conutry. We want to express the conviction that the solidarity of the socialist countries and other democratic forces of the world will be a support for us in our work.

a

Just as we quite frankly say what we are striving for
so we want to say what we shall oppose and struggle against.
In our opinion it is not good for the common work if some
groups of working people present ultimatum-like demands for
the satisfaction of their interests which pay no need to the
interests of others and which jeopardize common interests and
aims. Wilfulness and demagogy must be confronted with socialist discipline and organization. Neither does it help the
process of democratization if the existing legislation and
laws are violated.

We cannot conceal either that some discredited political forces of the past, which,thinking their opportunity has
come again, are trying to take advantage of democratization
and to revert the political stage. Attempts to bring about an
atmosphere of distrust against the Party and its members are
evident in several places. Under the pretext of combatting
distortions, attacks are also made on the work done by the
working class and all people in the past years.

We do not want to attribute hostile views to anyone
without any reason. But independent of subjective intentions
the ultimate political aim of such trends is only one – to
evoke distrust of communists,distrust of socialism, weaken
the ties with our allies, bring the danger of a split and a
conflict into our society.

A menace is hidden in these trends, which might not
only impede the process initiated in January but which would
also be accompanied by the risk of most serious consequences
for a peaceful development of the country.

We express deep conviction that the working class and
the broad masses of the people will not permit such a development. In the name of socialist democracy, in the name of creative and harmonious work, for the protection of the socialist
system guaranteed by the constitution the communists will wage
a decisive political fight against everything that harms the
people and the Republic.If during the last few months and weeks,s

86   a

full of revolutionary events, our people maintained both a sincere sense for the requirements of new roads and a sober sense of reality so right now when the new policy is going into practice they will not allow its implementation to be menaced. Just as there is no return to the pre–January situation, so there is no return to the situation existing before February 1948 and the more so before September 1938! In the defence of socialism, in the defence of the results of May 1945 and February 1938 all working people will find resolute support in the Party! The Party is opening the door to all honest, capable and especially young people who want to work actively in its ranks for the development of socialism in this country.

By the rectification of the shortcomings of recent years the Communist Party is determined to fully restore the famous revolutionary tradition of its past, the tradition of self-sacrificial and unselfish struggle for the interests of the people so well tried in the years of capitalism, at the time of the Munich Pact, in the struggle for national liberation, in the building of a new life in the post-war years and in February 1948.

In the spirit of this tradition we shall erase everything that was distorting the true face of socialism, which is qualified to be the most humane social order in the contemporary world. We see its basic values in the means of production owned by society, in the co-operative life of the village, in the fact that power in the State does not belong to powerful individuals but to the organized people, in the fact that the security of our socialist state is safeguarded by the alliance with the Soviet Union and association with the socialist countries.

The issue is now that socialism in this country should develop by democratic means, that is should be a truly human socialism. We want to accomplish such a work together and to guard it against all internal and external intrigues.

We appeal to all the honest citizens of our State to
support the aims of the Communist Party of Czechoslovakia and
actively help to implement them.

CENTRAL COMITTEE OF
THE COMMUNIST PARTY OF CZECHOSLOVAKIA

THE RESOLUTION OF THE CENTRAL COMMITTEE ON THE CONVOCATION OF THE EXTRAORDINARY 14th CONGRESS OF THE COMMUNIST PARTY OF CZECHOSLOVAKIA

The plenary session of the Central Committee of the CPCz, held from May 29th to June 1st 1968 decided in accordance with article 24 of the Statutes of the Party to convene the extraordinary 14th Congress of the CPCz in Prague on September 9th 1968. The Central Committee of the CPCz reached this decision after the evaluation of the situation in the Party which requires that a new political course of the Party be set for the next period and that a new Central Committee be elected which will have full confidence and authority in ensuring a united advance of the Party.

The extraordinary 14th Congress of the CPCz will have the following agenda:

1. Report on the activity of the Party and development of society since the 13th Congress of the CPCz and main tasks of the Party in the approaching period.
   Delivered by: comrade Alexander Dubček

2. Report of the Central Control and Auditing Commission of the CPCz.
   Delivered by: comrade Miloš Jakeš

3. Proposal for the political guideline of the constitutional structure of Czechoslovakia.
   Delivered by: comrade Oldřich Černík

4. Draft of the new Statutes of the CPCz and reorganization of the Party and the principles of Party work in the conditions of the federal structure of the State.
   Delivered by: comrade Alois Indra

a

5. Election of the Central Committee of the CPCz and the Central Control and Auditing Commission of the CPCz

6. Resolution.

The election of delegates to the Congress will be done according to Party Statutes at extraordinary regional conferences and extraordinary city conferences of the CPCz in Prague and Bratislava. One delegate with full voting rights is elected for every 1,100 members of the Party. The plenary session of the Central Committee of the CPCz also decided that:

- Meetings of local Party branch organizations be held between June 10th and June 23rd 1968 at which delegates will be elected to extraordinary district conferences of the CPCz

- Extraordinary district conferences of the Party be held on June 29th and 30th 1968; these conferences will elect delegates to extraordinary regional conferences of the CPCz. (The decision on whether two or one-day extraordinary district conferences will be held following an agreement with the Regional Committees of the Communist Party of Czechoslovakia and the Communist Party of Slovakia, should be left to the District Committees of the CPCz and the CPS.)

- Extraordinary regional conferences and extraordinary city conferences in Prague and Bratislava be held on July 6th and 7th or July 13th and 14th 1968. At these conferences delegates to the extraordinary 14th Congress of the CPCz should be elected also by communists from Party branches in the army and the Security Force. (The date will be chosen by Regional Committees of the CPCz in agreement with the Central Committee of the CPCz and the Central Committee of the CPS.)

IV

THE PRESIDIUM'S WARNING

THE document that follows helps to set in perspective not only the recent crisis in Czechoslovakia, but those factors which, either individually or in concert, contributed to that crisis.

Written in response "to the letters of five Communist and workers' parties"—letters which, it should be noted, expressed concern over the course of recent developments in Czechoslovakia as well as over the implications of these developments for the future of the bloc—the document speaks as much to the internal as to the external audience. The message in both cases appears to be the same: that the process of change going on within Czechoslovakia will not be permitted to threaten either the primacy of the CCP or the integrity of the Soviet Bloc and, therefore, should be accommodated by all concerned.

The Internal Audience

To the internal audience the message is presented in the form of a warning. The warning is directed, in the first instance, to those within Czechoslovakia who seek an end to Communist rule in that country. They are told in no uncertain terms that the CCP is aware of the danger and is prepared to act decisively when and if it becomes necessary to do so. They are also told, albeit implicitly, that the Soviet Union and the other members of the bloc are aware of the danger, and might decide to intervene should the CCP lose control of the situation. The implication, apparently, is that in Czechoslovakia, if not in the United States, "extremism in the defence of liberty" is indeed a "vice."

Turning to those, particularly within the CCP itself, who might wish a return to the period before the January plenum, the letter carries a warning of indictment. They and those who shared their views are assigned responsibility for the ills which characterized Czech society. It was their policies that drove the people and the Party apart; that divided Czech from Slovaks; that contributed to economic chaos and stagnation;

that, in short, threatened the survival of the CCP and, by implication, the integrity of the bloc. These same individuals are also warned, although again in a less explicit fashion, that they can expect no help either from the "masses" or from external sources in their opposition to reforms initiated by the Party. The CCP and the "masses" are as one, or so the letter suggests, in their pursuit of a better future under socialism. Because their cause is "just" it will, moreover, meet with the approval of the "socialist camp." The "letters from the five Communist and workers' parties" are thus attributed to a misunderstanding of, rather than genuine opposition to, the policies of the CCP. Accordingly those who would oppose these policies are, in effect, notified that their cause is hopeless and therefore should be abandoned.

Finally, there is the warning to the "masses." It is a warning against excess which might be misconstrued by sources outside of Czechoslovakia as a danger to the continued primacy of the CCP. In this period of uneasiness, there is a need for patience and moderation. The Party, or so the letter suggests, has the situation under control and the Presidium of the Central Committee is now endeavouring to clear up whatever doubt might exist in the minds of other members of the bloc. Consequently, there must be restraint lest these efforts be jeopardized.

The External Audience
The presentation of the message to the external audience takes the form of an explanation, if not a lecture. To the Soviet Union, members of the bloc and other "fraternal parties" the Presidium offers a review of events which led up to the decision to initiate change. In its own way, this review is apparently intended to explain not only what had occurred in Czechoslovakia prior to the January plenum, but why the decisions taken since that meeting have been both necessary and correct. The implication is that the concern reflected in "the letters from the five Communist and workers' parties" is simply the result of a lack of information or a breakdown in communication.

It is unlikely, however, that the Presidium actually believed this to be the case. On the contrary, it is quite probable that the members of the Presidium and, for that matter, the entire membership of the CCP, understood only too well the reasons which prompted the "letters."

This impression would appear to be confirmed by those portions of the letter that deal specifically with the course of events since Novotny's removal as Party leader. Here, as throughout, an attempt is made to explain these events to an apparently confused audience. Yet it is significant that the explanation is, in each instance, related either to the ability of the CCP to maintain effective internal control, or to the relationship of Czechoslovakia to the bloc, or both. The letter emphasizes, for example, the Party's awareness of the dangers that might arise as a result of the liberalization effort; it goes to great lengths, however, to minimize those dangers and to point out that the CCP not only did not agree with the sentiments expressed in the "Statement of 2000 Words," but said so publicly.

The same pattern is followed in "explaining" the "doubts" concerning Czechoslovakia's position within the bloc. Those portions of the letter that deal with the relationship of the Czechoslovak Socialist Republic to the German Democratic Republic (G.D.R.) and, more importantly, to the German Federal Republic (G.F.R.) are preceded by a reminder that not only has Czechoslovakia suffered at the hands of German imperialism and militarism, but that it moved to normalize its relations with the GFR only after other members of the bloc had done so. As for Czech participation in the Warsaw Treaty Organization (WTO), the letter emphasizes the recently concluded treaties of alliance with the Bulgarian People's Republic and the Rumanian Socialist Republic, as well as the fact that Czechoslovakia, after permitting staff exercises of the WTO on its territory, became somewhat concerned about the purpose of these exercises only after delays had occurred in the departure of foreign forces from Czech soil. In explaining its absence from the meeting held in Warsaw on July 14th, the Presidium assumes a posture of injured innocence. The explanation offered stresses the fact that the meeting was held without the knowledge of the CCP which found out about it only through the official press agency CTK. It also stresses the fact that proposals made by the CCP for bilateral talks prior to such a meeting did not imply a desire on the part of the Czechs to isolate themselves from the bloc.

When these references are read together they leave little doubt as to the growing concern of the Soviet Union and other members of the bloc regarding the situation within Czechoslovakia and its possible consequences for the survival of the bloc. The message as stated in the letter appears to be that the CCP is in control of the internal situation, that it intends to retain control, and that, consequently, the concern expressed in the "letters" is unfounded. To underscore this message, the letter concludes with an appeal for support of the CCP by "fraternal parties" and an all-too-obvious reference to the principles that have supposedly governed intra-bloc relations since the Moscow Conference of November, 1957.

To the non-Communist world the message is expressed as a reproval to those who would seek to exploit either the situation within Czechoslovakia or the concern with this situation which has been expressed by other members of the bloc. Thus, we are told that internally the position of the CCP is strong, and that externally its ties with the "socialist camp" are secure. Admittedly, the letter does hold out the prospect of greater co-operation between "socialist" and "non-socialist" countries. Yet, stated as it is in the context of this letter, the offer would seem to be a notification that such co-operation will come slowly, if at all, and that it will have to be on Czech terms.

Conclusion

Although the intended message of this letter suggests strength, the reverse appears to be the case. The fact that the letter had to be written at all is sufficient to indicate deep concern on the part of the Soviet Union and other members of the bloc as to the ability of the CCP to manage the process of change. Despite numerous references to "doubts" and "confusion," the Presidium seems to be fully aware of the fact that this concern is based not, as it suggests, on misunderstanding, but rather on a full understanding of the possible implications of the Czech experience for the bloc as a whole as well as for the individual members. Thus, while endeavouring to "explain," the letter also offers assurances of internal stability and continued participation in the bloc. The intervention that began on August 20th would appear to suggest that these assurances were not enough—that the message as read in Moscow conveyed weakness, not strength, and that as a consequence the Soviet Union thought it necessary to move decisively against the Czechs.

STANDPOINT OF THE PRESIDIUM OF THE CENTRAL COMMITTEE OF THE COMMUNIST PARTY OF CZECHO SLOVAKIA TO THE LETTERS OF FIVE COMMUNIST AND WORKERS' PARTIES

STANDPOINT OF THE PRESIDIUM OF THE CENTRAL COMMITTEE OF THE COMMUNIST PARTY OF CZECHO-SLOVAKIA TO THE LETTERS OF FIVE COMMUNIST AND WORKERS' PARTIES

The Presidium of the Central Committee of the Communist Party of Czechoslovakia has thoroughly studied the letter received by the Central Committee of our party from the meeting of the representatives of the parties of five socialist countries in Warsaw.

In the letter it is stressed that it is motivated by anxiety about our common cause and about the strengthening of the positions of socialism. Proceeding from this fact and led by the same striving, we wish to express equally frankly also our own attitude on the questions mentioned in the letter.

We are at the same time fully aware that an exchange of letters cannot fully explain such a complex problem as is the subject of attention and our standpoint therefore does not even aim at such ends but, on the contrary, presupposes direct mutual talks between parties.

A number of fears explained in the letter were expressed by ourselves in the resolution of the May plenary session of the Central Committee of the Communist Party of Czechoslovakia. However, we see the causes of the political situation, which is full of contradictions mainly in the accumulation of these contradictions over the years preceding the January plenum of the Central Committee of the Communist Party of Czechoslovakia. These contradictions cannot be satisfactorily solved

a 3a

at once in a short time. In the process of the realization of
the political line of the Action Programme of our party it
therefore necessarily happens that the wide stream of healthy
socialist activity is accompanied by extreme tendencies,that
the remnants of anti-socialist forces in our society are also
trying to tag along and that at the same time activity is
being also developed by the dogmatic-sectarian forces connected with the faulty policy of the time before the January plenum of the Central Committee of the Communist Party of Czechoslovakia. Not even the party itself can in this complex situation remain untouched by internal contradictions accompanying
the process of unification along the line of the Action Programme. The negative phenomena of this process also include
violation of the principles of democratic centralism in the
dealings of some Communists which is mainly the consequence
of the fact that, for many long years, the old party leadership applied bureaucratic centralism and suppressed internal
party democracy. All this prevents us from always achieving
in political work only those results we ourselves would wish.

We do not wish to hide these facts and we do not hide
them from our own party and people either.

For this reason the May plenum of the Central Committee
also clearly stated that it is necessary to mobilize all forces to prevent a conflicting situation in the country and the
endangering of socialist power in the Czechoslovak Socialist
Republic. Our party has also unequivocally stated that if any
such danger occurred,it would use all means to protect the socialist system. We thus ourselves saw the possibility of such
a danger. We understand that the fraternal parties of the socialist countries cannot be indifferent to this either. We do not,
however, see any realistic reasons which would justify assertions calling our present situation counter-revolutionary,
assertions of an immediate endangering of the basis of the socialist system, or assertions that a change is being prepared
in Czechoslovakia in the orientation of our socialist foreign
policy and that there is a concrete threat of a separation of
our country from the socialist community.

4 a

a

Our alliance and friendship with the USSR and other socialist countries is deeply rooted in the social system, in the historical traditions and experience of our nations, in their interests, their thoughts and feelings. The liberation from Nazi occupation and the entry onto the path of a new life is for ever connected in the consciousness of our people with the historical victory of the USSR in the Second World War, with respect for the heroes who laid down their lives in this fight.

This is also the basis of the Action Programme of our party, where we proclaim this tradition to be the starting point:

The basic orientation of Czechoslovak foreign policy was born and confirmed at the time of the national liberation struggle and in the process of the socialist reconstruction of our country - it is alliance and cooperation with the Soviet Union and the other socialist states. We shall strive for the friendly relations with our allies - the countries of the world socialist community - to deepen also in future on the basis of mutual esteem, sovereignty and equality, mutual respect and international solidarity. In this sense we shall contribute more actively and with a well-conceived concept towards the common activities of the Council of Mutual Economic Assistance and the Warsaw Treaty.

The letter mentions attacks against the socialist foreign policy, assaults against the alliance and friendship with socialist countries, voices calling for a revision of our common and coordinated policy in relation to the GFR and it is even asserted that attempts at making advances on the part of the authorities of the GFR and revanchists are finding response in the leading circles of our country. We are surprised at such assertions because it is well known that the Czechoslovak Socialist Republic is implementing a consistent socialist foreign policy, whose principles were formulated in the Action Programme of the Communist Party of

Czechoslovakia and the Programme Statement of the Government. These documents, statements made by leading Czechoslovak representatives and also our further actions consistently proceed from the principles of socialist internationalism, alliance and the development of friendly relations with the Soviet Union and the other socialist states.

We are of the opinion that these facts are decisive and not the irresponsible voices of individuals which are sometimes heard in this country.

In view of the bitter historical experiences of our nations with German imperialism and militarism it is inconceivable that any Czechoslovak Government could ignore these experiences and light-mindedly hazard with the fate of our country. This can be done even less by a socialist government and we must reject any suspicion in this direction.

As regards our relations with the GFR, it is universally known that the Czechoslovak Socialist Republic, although it is an immediate neighbour of the GFR, was the last to take certain steps towards a partial regulation of mutual relations, particularly in the economic field, whereas other socialist countries adapted their relations with the GFR to this or that extent much earlier without this having caused any fears.

We at the same time consistently respect and defend the interests of the GDR, our socialist ally, and do everything in our power to strengthen its international position and authority. This is also explicitly proved by all the speeches of leading representatives of our party and the State and the entire period after January 1968.

The agreements and treaties linking the socialist countries are an important factor of mutual cooperation, peace and collective security. The Czechoslovak Socialist Republic fully respects its contractual commitments and further develops the system of treaties with socialist coun-

6 a
[318]
a

tries which is proved by the new treaties of alliance we have recently concluded with the Bulgarian People's Republic, as well as by the prepared treaty on friendship and cooperation with the Rumanian Socialist Republic.

Like the authors of the letter we shall never agree to the historic achievements of socialism and the security of the nations of our country being threatened and imperialism, by peaceful or forceful means, to break through the socialist system and to change the balance of forces in Europe to its advantage. The main content of our development after January is the actual effort to increase our internal/strength and the stability of the socialist system and thus also our bonds of alliance.

The staff exercise of the allied forces of the Warsaw Treaty on the territory of the Czechoslovak Socialist Republic is concrete proof of our faithful fulfilment of our alliance commitments. In order to ensure its successful course we took the necessary measures on our side. Our people as well as members of the Army welcomed the Soviet and other allied troops on the territory of the Czechoslovak Socialist Republic. The highest representatives of the party and the Government documented by their participation, what importance we attach to it and the interest we have in it. Obscurities and some doubts in the minds of our public occurred only after repeated changes of the time of departure of the allied troops from the territory of the Czechoslovak Socialist Republic after the conclusion of the exercise.

The letter of the five parties also deals with some internal political problems of our present. We accept the assurance that the aim of this interest is not to interfere with the 'methods of planning and management of socialist national economy in Czechoslovakia' and with our 'measures aimed at perfecting the structure of the economy, at developing socialist democracy' and that the 'settlement of re-

a

7 a

lations between Czechs and Slovaks on the sound bases of fraternal cooperation within the framework of the Czechoslovak Socialist Republic' are welcomed.

We agree with the opinion that the strength and the firmness of our ties – which are undoubtedly the common vital interest of us all – depend on the inner strength of the socialist system of each of our fraternal countries. We do not doubt that the undermining of the leading role of the Communist Party would carry a threat of the liquidation of socialist society. However, just for this reason, it is essential that we should understand each other correctly on the question on which the strength of the socialist system and the strengthening of the leading role of the Communist Party depends today.

In the Action Programme of our party we set down the following on the basis of our previous experience:

It is at present especially essential for the party to pursue such a policy that would fully merit the leading role in our society. We are convinced that this is under the present situation the condition for the socialist development of the country...

The Communist Party depends on the voluntary support of the people: it does not implement its leading role by ruling over society but by most devotedly serving its free, progressive socialist development. It cannot impel its authority, but must constantly acquire it by its deeds. It cannot enforce its line by orders, but by the work of its members, by veracity of its ideals.

We do not hide the fact – and we stated this plainly at the May plenum of the Central Committee – that in this country there exist today also tendencies to discredit the party, to deny it the moral and political right to lead the society. However, if we put ourselves the question whether it is correct to judge similar phenomena as a threat to the socialist system, as a decline of the leading role of the

Communist Party of Czechoslovakia under the pressure of
reactionary, counter-revolutionary forces - we come to the
conclusion that this is not the case.

The leading role of our party gravely suffered in the
past by the deformations of the 'Fifties and a policy of
their inconsistent removal by the leadership headed by A.No-
votný. On the contrary, he is responsible for the deepening
of a number of social contradictions between the Czechs
and the Slovaks, between the intelligentsia and the workers,
between the young generation and the older generations. The
inconsistent solution of the economic problems has left over
to us a situation in which we cannot solve a series of justified economic demands of the working people and when the
effectiveness of the entire national economy is seriously
impaired. Under that leadership, the confidence of the masses
in the party was declining and there were expressions of criticism and resistance, but all this was solved by interference from a position of power against justified dissatisfaction against criticism and against attempts to solve social problems consistently in the interests of the party,and
of its leading position.

Instead of a gradual and well considered removal of
faults, further errors and contradictions accumulated as a
result of subjective decision making in the years when it
was objectively possible to gradually develop socialist democracy and to apply scientific management, subjective deficiencies sharpened social contradictions and difficulties.

Outwardly it seemed that everything was in order in
the Czechoslovak Socialist Republic, it was made to appear
that developments were without conflicts, the actual decline
in confidence in the party was masked by outward forms of
directive party management. Although this regime was presented as being a firm guarantee of the interests of the
entire socialist camp, problems were accumulating within
whose real solution was suppressed by forceful measures
against those advocating new and creative approaches.

a

9 a

Any indication of a return to these methods would evoke the resistance of the overhelming majority of party members, the resistance of the working people, the workers, cooperative farmers and the intelligentsia. Precisely by such a step the party would imperil its political leading role and would create a situation which would really lead to a power conflict. This would really threaten the socialist achievements of the people and also our common interests in the anti-imperialist front of the socialist community.

We agree that it is one of the primary tasks of the party to thwart the aims of right-wing and anti-socialist forces. Our party has worked out its tactical political plan for this matter at the May plenum of the Central Committee and is solving these problems according to it. This plan consists of a system of measures which can be successful only if we have the conditions to gradually implement them in the course of several months.

We consider as the condition for success that the realization of the Action Programme and the preparations for the party congress are not endangered by any false step which would cause a power-political conflict in our country. The May plenum of the Central Committee of the Communist Party of Czechoslovakia stated this quite plainly in its resolution:

'Under the present situation the party considers it as the basic problem that it be made impossible to threaten the socialist character of power and the social system from any side - either from the side of right-wing, anti-Communist tendencies, or from the side of conservative forces which would welcome to return to the conditions existing before January 1968 and which were unable to ensure the development of socialism.'

Our party has laid down the following main aims and stages of political work:

1) To consistently dissociate the party as a whole from the deformations of the past for which concrete persons of the old party leadership are responsible: these concrete people are being justly called to task.

2) To prepare the 14th extraordinary Party Congress, which will evaluate the development and the political situation after the January plenum and will in accordance with the principles of democratic centralism in the Party lay down the binding line for the entire party, adopt a political standpoint on the federative set-up of the Czechoslovak Socialist Republic, approve the new state and elect a new Central Committee so that it has the full authority and confidence of the party and the entire society.

3) After the 14th congress to launch an offensive for solving all the fundamental internal political questions: for the construction of a political system based on the socialist platform of the National Front and social self-administration for the solution of the federative constitutional set-up, for the elections to the representative bodies of the State (federal, national and local) and for preparing the new constitution.

At present we are at the stage of the political fight for the implementation of the line of the May plenum of the Central Committee of the Communist Party of Czechoslovakia. It is a real fight and we therefore are scoring not only victories but we have also setbacks: however, it is never possible to judge the result of the entire fight according to the results of individual battles. Despite this we nevertheless believe that since the May plenum the political situation is being successfully consolidated.

The extraordinary district and regional conferences in the past few days have clearly shown that the party is becoming unified on the line of the Action Programme. Delegates have been elected to the congress and their composition is a guarantee that the future line of the party will

a

11a

not be decided by representatives of extreme views, but the democratically entrusted progressive core of our party. The representatives of the new leadership of the Communist Party of Czechoslovakia which is linked with the line of the Action Programme and the May plenum of the Central Committee were all proposed by the regional conferences for the new Central Committee. A certain stabilization is thus going on in the party and the basic steps for preparing the congress proceeded successfully.

In conformity with the resolution of the plenum of the Central Committee of the Communist Party of Czechoslovakia a politically binding socialist platform of the National Front is being created on the initiative of Communists. On June 15, 1968, all the political components of the National Front adopted a programme statement which clearly accepts the historically won leading position of the Communist Party of Czechoslovakia and which expresses the principles of a socialist system, of an internal and foreign socialist policy. The National Front is just these days discussing the proposal for its statute, which is a binding organization norm ensuring the socialist political orientation of all parties and organizations.

By the law on judicial rehabilitations we are basically solving the painful problem of the illegal repressive measures against innocent people which took place in the past years. This step has clearly helped that the attention of the wide public and also of the media of information no longer concentrates on these questions.

In September, immediately after the party congress, certain new important laws will be discussed: the constitutional law on the National Front which is to confirm the permanent existence of the system of political parties on the forum of the National Front and further the law on the right of assembly and association which will determine legal regulations for the creation and the activities of various

voluntary organizations, associations, clubs, etc. This will
make it possible to effectively counter attempts of anti-
Communist forces to gain an organizational basis for public
activities.

Communists are also in accordance with the resolution
of the May plenum of the Central Committee of the Communist
Party of Czechoslovakia solving with initiative important
questions of the work of the trade unions and enterprise
workers' councils. On the whole, the party managed in connection with these questions to counter political demagogy,
which attempted to take advantage of legitimate demands of
the workers in order to disorganize our system and to fan
an uncontrolled movement in the name of 'workers demands' so
as to make the economic and political situation in the country
more difficult. At the same time, however, we are solving,
according to the means at our disposal, some burning social
political problems such as the raising of low pensions and
urgent adjustements of wages. The Government is gradually
dealing with the fundamental economic problems of the country
in order to provide a new impulse for the development of production and so as to make it possible to move over to further
improving the living standard of the people.

We have taken the necessary measures to safeguard the
security of our state borders, the party fully supports the
consolidation of the Army, the security body, prosecutors
and the judiciary. The party has also taken a clear stand
on the question of the People's Militia whose statewide meeting
has given full support to the new leadership of the Communist
Party of Czechoslovakia and the Action Programme. The importance of this step was, as is known, directly welcomed by
the working people not only in this country, but also in the
USSR.

We consider all these steps to be important result
in the implementation of the line adopted at the May plenum
of the Central Committee of the Communist Party of Czecho-

a   13 a

lovakia important features of the consolidation of political conditions and of the strengthening of the not only declared but the really leading influence of the party in our
country.

In spite of this we see and do not want to conceal
that we are not fulfilling all conclusions drawn at the May
plenary session of the Central Committee of the Communist
Party of Czechoslovakia satisfactorily. It happens also at
present that now and then there appear at public meetings and
in media of information voices and tendencies which bypass
the positive endeavours of the party, the state bodies and
the National Front.

We consider the solution of this question to be more
long-term task and are guided by the resolution of the May
plenary session of the Central Committee according to which
'political management cannot be applied by the old, administrative power structures'.The Presidium of the Central Committee
of the CPCz, the Government and the National Front unequivocally rejected the appeals of the statement of 'Two Thousand
Words', which induce to anarchist acts, to violating the
constitutional character of our political reform. It must be
noted that, following these negative standpoints, similar
acts did not in fact occur in practice anywhere in our country and that the consequences of the appeal 'Two Thousand
Words' did not threaten the party, the National Front or the
socialist state. A negative feature of our actual conditions
are still the campaigns and unjustified slander directed
against various functionaries and public officials - including members of the new leadership of the Communist Party of
Czechoslovakia - which are conducted from extreme positions
both right and left. The secretariat of the Central Committee of the Communist Party of Czechoslovakia and leading
comrades have in concrete cases come out unequivocally also
against these methods.

We know that this situation is made possible by the
fact that we have abolished censorship in our country and

14 a

a

enacted freedom of expression and of the press. What in tne past was spread only in the form of 'whispered propaganda', etc. can now be expressed in public.

However, if we put ourselves the question whether it is correct to evaluate such phenomena as forfeiture of the leading political role of the Communist Party of Czechoslovakia under the onslaught of reactionary, counter-revolutionary forces - we reach the conclusion that this is not the case. For all this is only part of our present political situation. There is also another, and in our opinion the decisive part of this situation. The growth of the authority of the new, democratic policy of the party in the eyes of the broadest masses of the working people, the growth of the activity of the absolute majority of the population. The abolition of censorship, freedom of expression are supported by the absolute majority of the people of all classes and straty of our society. The Communist Party of Czechoslovakia is trying to prove that it is capable of a different political leadership and management than by means of the condemned bureaucratic-police methods, mainly by the strength of its Marxist-Leninist ideas, of its proxram, its correct policy supported by all the people.

Our party can prevail in the difficult political struggle only if it is made possible to implement the tactical line of the May plenum of the Central Committee and to settle basic political questions at the extraordinary 14th congress in the spirit of the Action Programme. We therefore consider all pressures trying to impose another course on the party, that is to settle basic questions of policy at another time and elsewhere than at the 14th congress, as the principal danger to the successful consolidation of the leading role of the party in the Czechoslovak Socialist Republic. Such pressure is being brought to bear by domestic extreme forces from the right as well as from conservative dogmatic and sectarian positions, endeavouring for a return to conditions before January 1968.

a

15a

The evaluation of the situation as contained in the ter of the five parties as well as the undoubtedly sincere-meant advice for our further course do not take into account the entire intricacy of the dynamic social movement as it was analyzed by the May plenum of the Central Committee of the Communist Party of Czechoslovakia and the complexity of the conclusions adopted by this plenum. Our policy, if it wants to remain a Marxist-Leninist policy, connot be based exclusively on superficial phenomena which do not always accurately reflect the profound causes of social development but must understand the substance of the development and be guided by it.

The fraternal parties can at present serve the interests of socialism in our country primarily by expressing confidence in the leadership of the CPCz and full support of its policy.

This is why we have proposed, as a prerequisite of successful joint discussions, bilateral meetings of the representatives of our parties so that the joint talks may proceed from deeper mutual consultations and factual information.

We sincerely regret that these proposals put forward by us were not implemented. It is not our fault that the meeting in Warsaw was held without our participation. We discussed the proposals of the five parties for holding this meeting at the Presidium of the Central Committee of the Communist Party of Czechoslovakia twice – on July 8 and 12 – and each time we immediately conveyed our view on the method of preparing this meeting in the way which we considered to be most correct. Unfortunately, our discussion of July 12 was already superfluous because, notwithstanding its outcome, the meeting had already been convened for July 14, as we learned only through ČTK in the afternoon of July 13, at a time when the representatives of the five parties were already on their way to Warsaw.

16 a   a

In no standpoint that we sent to the five parties did
we refuse on principle to take part in a joint conference.
We only voiced our own view concerning its suitability at
the present time and on the method of its preparation so
that it may be really factual and based on more profound information about our complex problems. From the contents of
the letters of the five parties, sent to us between July 4
and 6, 1968, we actually judge that such information is absolutely vital if talks are not to be held whose success would
be threatened in advance by one-sided and sparse information
of the great majority of the participants in the conference
about the real situation in Czechoslovakia.

This is the purpose of our proposals for preliminary
bilateral talks. We were guided not by an effort to isolate
ourselves from the community of our parties and countries,
but on the contrary, by the effort to contribute to its consolidation and development.

We think that the common cause of socialism is not
advanced by holding conferences at which the policy and activity of any fraternal party is judged without the presence
of its representatives. We consider as permanently valid the
principle expressed in the declaration of the Government of
the USSR of October 30, 1956, which says: "The countries of
the great community of socialist nations, united by the common ideals of the construction of a socialist society and
the principles of proletarian internationalism, can build
their mutual relations exclusively on the basis of complete
equality, respect of territorial integrity, national independence and sovereignty and mutual non-interference in internal affairs. This principle, as is well known, was confirmed by the conference of representatives of Communist
parties in Moscow in November of 1957 and was generally accepted. In all our acivities we want to further strengthen
and develop the deep internationalist traditions which, in
our view, must include both understanding of the common in-

a   17a

terests and goals of the progressive forces of the world as
well as understanding of specific national needs.

We do not want our relationships to further deteriorate and are willing to contribute on our part towards coming
down the situation in the interest of socialism and the unity
of the socialist countries on our part we shall do nothing
that would be at variance with this aim. We expect, however,
that the other parties will help these efforts of ours and
will show understanding for our situation.

We consider it an important task to be able in the
nearest future to hold the bilateral talks we proposed and
which would assess, among other things, also the possibilities of a common meeting of the socialist countries and at
which it would be possible to agree on its programme and the
composition, the place and the time of its convening. We
consider it decisive that we agree within the shortest time
on positive steps which would ensure the continuation of our
hitherto firendly cooperation and which would convincingly
demonstrate our common will to develop and strengthen mutual
friendly relations. This is in the interest of our common
fight against imperialism, for peace and the security of nations, for democracy and socialism.

SUMMARY

THE reader who has followed me up to this point will recognize an apparent contradiction in what I have said. In introducing these documents I advanced the thesis that the intervention which occurred on August 20th was prompted by a fear on the part of the Soviet Union and its Warsaw Pact Allies—excluding Rumania, of course—that events in Czechoslovakia had reached the point where they posed a significant threat to the survival of Communist rule in that country and, indirectly, to the survival of the bloc itself. In the individual commentaries on each document, I have consistently argued that Dubček and his supporters had decided that the time had come to initiate change; that having made this decision they further decided that the CCP—and only the CCP— would preside over the process of implementation; and that as a result they and the system would be better off for the effort.

If I am correct in my interpretation of the underlying cause of the intervention and if, moreover, I am also correct in my assessment of the motives which prompted the initiation, and then guided the subsequent implementation of the changes that took place in Czechoslovakia after January, 1968, then the question which remains to be answered is how, given the unwillingness of the CCP to permit its position to be threatened, the situation reached a point where the Soviet Union felt that only prompt military action could prevent a political disaster?

There are, of course, a number of possible answers to this question. First, it might be argued that the Soviet Union had simply decided to revert to a process of change and accommodation similar to that which characterized intra-bloc relations during the Stalinist era; that having decided to do so, the Soviets simply seized upon Czechoslovakia as a convenient place to begin the reversal. Such an argument, however, hardly seems plausible in light of the changes that have occurred in the bloc during the period since 1953. Nor does it conform with what we know of the events which both preceded and followed the intervention. Viewed in the context of these events, there can be little doubt that the

U.S.S.R. was genuinely concerned about the liberalization taking place in Czechoslovakia and that having tried unsuccessfully to remedy the situation by the application of more subtle pressures, turned to force only as a last resort.

Secondly, it might be argued that Dubček and the CCP had decided the time had come to put an end to Communist rule in Czechoslovakia; that having discovered the "error of their ways" they deliberately set about creating a new political order based on the principles of liberal democracy. As I have tried to indicate, such an argument—no matter how comforting to those who view the triumph of democracy as inevitable—simply cannot survive a close reading of these documents.

The answer I am proposing is somewhat more complex. To begin with, it appears to me that, initially at least, neither the Soviet Union nor the Czechs themselves perceived the danger that lay ahead. The Soviet Union, for its part, seems to have accepted the fact that Novotny had blundered badly and that in light of the economic crisis and growing intellectual unrest his removal was both necessary and desirable. If this is so, then Moscow probably also was prepared to accept change within Czechoslovakia; provided that the change in no way jeopardized either the position of the CCP, or the integrity of the bloc. Dubček and his supporters within the CCP probably shared these views.

On at least two points, however, there may well have been a divergence of opinion. There was, in the first instance, the question of how much and what kind of change was needed. Given the differing perspectives of the two, it is not unreasonable to assume that whereas the Czechs, because of their intimate knowledge of the situation, were inclined to consider a broad range of reforms, the Soviets, for their part, were probably inclined to a more conservative estimate. Secondly, there was the question of the ability of the CCP to retain the initiative for change. Here too, one can only speculate as to whether the estimates of the two sides varied and, if so, how much. Considering the history of animosity between the Czech and Slovak wings of the Party and the seeming inability of Dubček to eliminate all of the pro-Novotny elements from positions of authority within the CCP, it is quite likely that Moscow had some reservations about the internal strength of party leadership—reservations which were probably shared, although to a lesser degree, by the leadership itself.

Be that as it may, in the months immediately following the downfall of Novotny both sides appeared to have accepted the need for accommodation. The U.S.S.R., for its part, continued to play up the theme of continuity of leadership in the CCP. The initial reforms were accorded favourable coverage in the Soviet press and Moscow refrained from expressing whatever private misgivings it may have had about the ability of the CCP to preside over the course of developments in Czechoslovakia. The CCP, for its part, moved quickly to correct some of the more oppressive features of the system. At the same time it also cautioned against moving too quickly.

It was during these early months following the change of leadership in Prague that a new element appears to have entered the picture. The CCP which for so long had felt the animosity of the Czech people, suddenly found itself the centre of public acclaim. To say, as Dubček does, that the popular reaction to the initial reforms and to the promise of more to come was surprising is, I think, an understatement. For a party that had grown used to an atmosphere of public hostility, the response was probably overwhelming.

In any event, the sudden popularity of the CCP seems to have convinced the leadership in Prague that the reforms, rather than constituting a threat to the Party, actually served to strengthen its position vis-à-vis the "masses." This, at least, is the impression conveyed by these documents. From the standpoint of the Soviet Union the growing popularity of the CCP, accompanied as it was by adoption of the Action Programme, the promise of even greater liberalization, and expressions of anti-Soviet sentiment, must have been a disquieting development—so disquieting, in fact, that in the period after the adoption of the Action Programme the Soviet Union began to express some reservations about the motives of the CCP. As already suggested, their reservations, although initially stated in rather mild terms, grew in intensity as the months passed.

Here, I suspect, is the key to why the reforms got out of control. On the one hand we have the sudden popularity of the CCP which, it would appear, convinced Dubček and his supporters that their policies were in no way endangering either the position of the Party or the future of the Soviet Bloc. On the other hand, there were the pressures brought to bear by the Soviet Union—pressures which would have made any curtailment of the liberalization process appear to be a bowing of the CCP to the will of Moscow.

The situation can probably best be understood in terms of a specific reform, i.e., the end of press censorship. Initially, the decision to relax controls over the press seems to have met with widespread public approval. It also seems to have been followed by a short period of restrained criticism. In time, however, the criticism became more strident as reflected in the publication of the so-called "Statement of 2000 Words." Confronted with this and other critical statements which appeared in the press during June and July, the CCP must have had second thoughts about the original decision. Yet, its popularity with the people was growing every day. So too, of course, was Soviet opposition to the liberalization. Consequently, since the attacks in the press did not seem to pose a very serious threat to the position of the Party and since, moreover, a reimposition of censorship would have appeared as a concession to the Soviet Union, the CCP did nothing, with the result that the criticism continued.

If this assessment is correct, then it is easy to see how the reforms initiated after the January plenum were permitted to get out of control. The CCP, enamoured as it was by its new-found popularity among the "masses," does not seem to have viewed the situation as a threat to its own position. Although the Soviet Union appears to have taken a somewhat different view, by bringing pressure against the CCP it only seemed to further blunt the Party's instinct for survival. The more pressure Moscow applied, the more it must have appeared to the leadership in Prague that a reimposition of controls would be interpreted by the Czech people as subservience to the dictates of an external power.

Whether the CCP actually viewed these pressures as an unwarranted intrusion into the internal affairs of a "fraternal country," or whether it simply felt that the pressures were unjustified in light of the improved relationship between the Party and the people, is difficult to say. The point is that once the differences between Prague and Moscow assumed the character of an inter-nation rather than an inter-party dispute, resistance apparently became a matter of "national honour." Consequently, the Party would have found it difficult to impose controls, even if, as seems unlikely, it had felt such controls were necessary.

Under the circumstances, the intervention was all but inevitable. Confronted by a Party that, initially at least, *would* not act to correct what appeared to be a potentially dangerous situation, the Soviet Union and its allies undertook to pressure the CCP into curbing the excesses of the liberalization process. In doing so, however, they only succeeded in creating an even more dangerous situation: one in which the Party *could* not act without being thoroughly discredited in the eyes of the Czech people. In a sense, then, the Soviet Union is correct when it says that it intervened in Czechoslovakia to save the CCP from itself. What Moscow fails to add, however, is that it was pressure from the Soviet Union and other members of the bloc which, in the final analysis, seems to have placed the CCP in such an untenable position.

APPENDIX

ON December 21, 1968, Alexander Dubček delivered his last major speech of the year. His audience was the plenary session of the Slovak Communist Party's Central Committee. In spite of the situation when it was delivered, with Soviet forces still in occupation of the country, Dubček's speech is basically optimistic. He appeals for "realism" in the face of the situation imposed by Moscow. Nevertheless, he makes it clear that the Party still stands by the basic principles of the Action Programme. The mention in his speech of the November and December plenums refers to the sessions of the Czechoslovak CP Central Committee where the Action Programme was redrafted to adhere to the demands made by Moscow. Although there was considerable public dissatisfaction about these sessions, particularly because of the lack of information released, it is clear from Dubček's speech to the Slovak Central Committee that he had not yielded the basic points of the reform, except—and it is an important exception—the principle of unrestricted freedom of expression. But above all, Dubček repeated in this last speech of the year his promise that there would be no return to the police state. The most significant passage of his speech is that in which he declares:

"We must, as a permanent positive feature of the post-January policy, consistently ensure fundamental civil rights and freedoms, observe Socialist legality and fully rehabilitate unjustly wronged citizens."

Alexander Dubček's Speech
DELIVERED ON DECEMBER 21, 1968 [1]

People are always asking us the question: What is the sense of their work, what guarantees do they have, what are their prospects? They were convinced that we were proceeding on the correct road and they want to orientate themselves as to whether there are any changes in this policy and what these changes are. The common denominator of these misgivings are meticulous worries, doubts or even distrust as to whether it

[1] The text is reprinted by permission from the B.B.C. Monitoring Service's Summary of World Broadcasts.

is truly possible and realistic to preserve the essential characteristics of the post-January policy, and whether room will be preserved for the purposeful solution of the accumulated problems through the socialist initiative and involvement of the Communists, other elements of the national front, people without Party affiliation, and of all the basic strata of our society—features which were the substance of the programme of the Party's policy formulated after January.

These important questions and misgivings we can and we must answer again and again, patiently but in a principled manner and truthfully, and explain the meaning and goals of our actions as expressed by the November resolution and the tasks laid down by the December plenum of the Central Committee of the CPC. We must also greatly improve the level of information. When we explain and give the reasons for the tasks and course of action laid down, words alone will not be enough. There must first of all be deeds. This I want to stress particularly. From our work and its results it must be clear that the whole Party as the leading political force of the country continues to feel fully responsible for the further development of our country, for the solution of the vital questions of our citizens, and that we intend to continue fully to serve these interests and needs also in the future.

To this prevailing striving for an honest search for the meaning and direction of further activities come even today, naturally, concomitant phenomena which disturb this process of unification and which we must actively oppose. The Party's policy and fundamental tasks are damaged by all tendencies and speeches which in one way or other contradict the tasks laid down by the November and December plenums. This could greatly weaken attention to the tasks which we face in the immediate future and which are our main aim. I am referring to viewpoints which persist in opposing the post-January policy and opposing the spirit and the specific tasks of the further development as laid down by the Central Committee of the CPC and the Government of the Republic.

The Party is not helped by these various rumours and fabrications which maintain tension and uncertainty. Nor is it helped by illusions or tough gestures which accuse the leadership of making undue compromises and create the impression that there might exist a different and realistic alternative for preserving the positive results of the post-January development to the course of action chosen by the Central Committee of the CPC.

I do not know of any other variant which is realistic in the present situation except the position laid down in the November resolution, and the positive solution of the tasks set forth by the December CPC Central Committee plenum at which we also have shown clearly in a short time that we want to continue to concentrate the attention and thoughts of the people primarily on the future, that we want to direct Party *aktivs* mainly towards solving topical tasks of our social life, and we want to concentrate the main attention on the future. The December plenum of the Central Committee was a clear demonstration of this, and in the next period we also want mainly to advance and to concentrate the activities of our Party and the whole of society on this. In this I see the main decisive feature from the viewpoint of fulfilling the task which our Party has laid down.

We do not belittle, play down or distort the complexity of the present situation in which we are working. Everybody sees the difficult political situation we are in. We are trying to see, create and demonstrate a realistic and positive way out of this situation, and in this we are ultimately guided by the interests of our people. Either we manage to win over the people for this solution, and we must first of all win the Communists of our Party, or our society will continue to remain in uncertainty and a waiting situation, and this reduces its strength, its will and creative force for a further positive development.

I am convinced that this is today the main task for our entire CPC. In this the Communists in the press and all other mass information media should give more help in the consistent mission of our socialist society.

The problems which have arisen in connection with the application of the resolution are in substance of a political nature. Hence we shall solve them primarily by political means. The most important thing now is that we demonstrate and convince everyone in the Party by concrete action that we are gradually and purposefully implementing the main and decisive content of the post-January policy, as it is stressed in the resolution. The Party as a whole, not only its leadership but all the members of the Party, are bound by the resolution and obliged to the whole of society. In January it was the Party's Central Committee which initiated the solution of the problems which had accumulated. The primary organisations of the Party backed and are still backing that programme and the methods of its implementation, and so did all district and regional committees and the subsequent plenary sessions of the Central Committee.

Appendix

Our society accepted the post-January course with great hopes. It was accepted by all the workers and working people in general—of this we have convincing evidence. It was accepted by our farmers, by the farming co-operatives and by the workers in the State farms, who were at that very time grouping together as a conspicuous and well-organized social force corresponding to their importance in our socialist society. It is also backed by our socialist intelligentsia as was clearly expressed in numerous statements. It has been accepted as a great hope by our youth who rightly demand scope for their political commitment and their natural entry into public life in our socialist society. Hence to withdraw from this policy, to give up its substance would be a political defeat for the Party and the result would be rigid stagnation of our socialist society.

The post-January political movement, which is clearly socialist in its orientation, did not lack shortcomings, obstacles and difficulties. Forces came to the fore which intended to become parasites of that movement. We realized that and opposed it. Despite all the complexity of the development, the Party always had the movement in its hands and thus guaranteed its continued distinct socialist character. The essence of this movement represented the existing forces, as well as the determination to further the needs of socialist development in our country.

Our policy must systematically follow these sound forces, this determination, and these needs, and at the same time must also more consistently defend them against all abuses and, through self-control of its own work, eliminate shortcomings which could harm a healthy development.

If I were to sum up this problem then, putting it briefly: We wish to and we must return to the consistent implementation of the tasks and ideas of January, but we do not want the repetition of those phenomena which diverted us from their implementation, which carried us away, and finally very much complicated our efforts. The present situation, too, will in the end be successfully mastered only by the implementation of the essence of the post-January policy. Whenever we speak of the post-January policy, what we have foremost in our minds is the official policy of the CPC Central Committee and its Presidium.

On the other hand, this novelty, this flourishing of society and the confrontation finds an outlet in extremities which deviate from the conclusions and the policy of the CPC Central Committee—and this

[340]

is the chief danger which under certain circumstances can, in the present situation, throw us far back and can destroy our efforts. The uncritical approach to deficiencies which accompanied and obstructed the activities of the CPC Central Committee on the one hand and the very harmful, biased view of the post-January development on the other are clear-cut and very serious signs of this. The first opens the scope for trends which continue to exert their effect on the creation of mistrust of the tasks that have been set and chiefly on the solutions and, consequently, cripple the Party's ability to act in implementing an active policy. The second ignores the view of the broadest Party and non-Party masses, driving the Party and its leadership into isolation from the masses, and hence leads to unforeseeable consequences.

In addition to this it is also becoming apparent—and it is for the second time that I am experiencing a thing like that—just as the Action Programme was ignored in journalism after it was approved in April, so now the positive ways out of the November resolution are being ignored, concealed and by-passed, the resolution which is backed by the basic postulates of the Action Programme. Quite often—and I would like to emphasise this—resolutions contain demands for the solution of positive problems which have already been solved and lead to the conclusion that the authors of these resolutions back the post-January policy, while the leadership of the Party, Government and State is against it. Who benefits from this?

A variety of campaigns undertaken against the conclusions of the November plenum of the CPC Central Committee are causing the Party and society as a whole immeasurable damage. They contain demands which in the present situation or within the time limit demanded cannot be accomplished by the leadership of the Party, the leadership of the Government, the National Assembly or the President of the Republic, or demands and a course of action which exert pressure on these organs and their representatives both from the Right and Left and mainly drive them back, making it impossible for them to develop their active work, aimed at the future, thus discrediting these organs and the leading representatives in the eyes of the public. Their aim is to force them to adopt more and more undesirable measures—I should like to stress this— and then to misuse this from a Rightest position as proof of their having compromised themselves and deviated from the post-January policy. Quite frequently this is done under the slogan of defending the post-

January policy. This pushes the Party and all of society on a road toward tragic consequences.

In order to prevent this from happening everything must be done to achieve a united course of action by the Communists in safeguarding the tasks of the November and December plenums of the CPC Central Committee. If the development of recent days, resulting from the mentioned tendencies, continues to interfere with the positive solution, then in this situation the leadership of the Party, Government, State and National Assembly will turn to the Party and people with inevitable measures.

It is possible that these measures which we shall adopt will appear to be undemocratic, but they will be in the interest of democracy; they will be in the interest of preventing anarchist tendencies and their initiators from driving this Republic into a situation not only like the one before January but much further back. Naturally, this would then be done by other politicians. I think this is also sufficiently clear. You might think that these are harsh words, but I am convinced that this is the truth and that it is therefore our duty to say it frankly.

We are resolved to defend and implement the post-January policy, because we—or at least the majority of us—have stood at its cradle. In the interest of this we are resolved to foil all tendencies aiming against this policy, opposing this policy. I am convinced that in this we shall find strong support from the overwhelming majority of Party members and citizens. I therefore repeat: I do not know any other realistic starting-point for advance except the united action of the Communists in accordance with the adopted decisions of the Central Committee of our Party.

★　　★　　★　　★　　★

From the post-January programme the economic reform must be consistently put into practice[1], and care must be taken to ensure sound economic developments. Priority must be given to more effective solutions of problems of living standards, namely personal consumption, salaries and wages, housing construction, and the working and living environment.

We must as a permanent positive feature of the post-January policy consistently ensure fundamental civil rights and freedoms, observe socialist legality and fully rehabilitate unjustly wronged citizens. Observance of laws and

[1] This section does not appear in all the broadcast versions of Dubček's speech.

*norms is an urgent task of all Communists, also in intra-Party life. We stand
on the principle that no one must be prosecuted, in the courts or otherwise, nor
harassed, who supported and endorsed, and who backs the position of Party
organs and their decisions,* or for support and active carrying out of the
position and directions of legal State organs. If this principle were
infringed, it would have very grave consequences for our society, which
might grow into arbitrariness impairing the principles of legality of intra-
Party democracy, and thus into weakening of the foundations of
democracy.

Our membership of the socialist community, in the Warsaw Treaty,
our alliance with the Soviet Union, our ties to the international Communist movement—these are things which have always been in the
policy of the Communist Party and the Government of the Republic
beyond any doubt. Czechoslovakia's policy is equally firmly economically orientated to co-operation with the CMEA, with all socialist
States. At the same time, we do not rule out an extension of economic
co-operation with Western States. Such economic relations are being
sought by all socialist countries, especially those who have a great share of
external economic relations in their economies. In developing its economy, Czechoslovakia cannot ignore it either. The principles of Czechoslovakia's foreign policy and economic orientation are firm, and cannot
be changed even after the August events. We are striving to overcome
the consequences which resulted in politics after these events. It is seen
in political and economic contacts with the Soviet Union and the other
socialist countries.

★   ★   ★   ★   ★

We must realize in this context that the Central Committee at the
November plenum laid stress on a positive starting-point for further
advance. The tasks, laid down at the December plenum, also specify this
very positive course of action for our further work.

In all bodies and organizations of the Party, and particularly at the
annual members' meeting, an active and positive programme must be
prepared which will be based on the conclusions of the November and
December plenums of the CPC Central Committee, and on the positive
starting-point for the further work of the Party organizations which
has been laid down. The leading role of the Party must be carried into

everyday life and this will dispel all discord, and efforts must be made for the continual renewal of the confidence of the people in the Party's policy, in society as a whole and also at every place of work. The Party alone will not settle any major social problem unless it wins over the people.

In every organization it is topical, on the basis of Leninist principles, to enhance the participation of the Communists in the creation and implementation of policy and safeguard their active political work among the people. The interest and the sincere striving of the Party to create the conditions for the development of socialist initiative of all non-Party members must become the hub of concrete measures of our Party's organizations.

It is particularly necessary to ensure and implement greater participation by the workers in the management of public affairs and to co-operate with the trade unions in this respect. Great efforts must be made to remove everything that divides workers and farmers from the intelligentsia and to apply in practice the principle that they have an equal interest in the true progress of our society. Such co-operation is the basis of the active socialist unity of our society. We have realized the strength of this unity and hence we are strengthening and directing it so that we can jointly solve all the problems of our development and carry out the work of our socialist reconstruction. Every Party organ and organization must devote particular attention to our younger generation; we must endeavour to understand them, give scope for their commitment, contribute to their political development and regard them as heirs to our efforts. Any other attitude would, in my view, be wrong.

Comrades, the setting up of federal and Czech and Slovak national organs is an important and historic task which we are now approaching after having accepted federalization in the spirit of our Party's Action Programme. In setting up the new federal organs we shall have to carry out basic change not only on the structure but also in the content of their work, so that it is in line with political and administrative tasks in the State and also corresponds to the economic reform.

Comrades, the Slovak Socialist Republic has become a reality. When on various occasions I recall this fact, I try in this joyful mood to grasp the great, vast significance of this fact for the Slovak nation and for its further development, realising all the many things which had to be accomplished in the history of the Slovak nation, as well as how much selfless work was required on the part of national representatives, and also of figures of the revolutionary movement, to ensure that Slovak statehood was created precisely on the basis of the most progressive social principles and that it was created as the result of a popular movement and of a genuine national awareness. When Federation was solemnly declared, we spoke of the days of routine work which lay ahead. We must fully appreciate what a far-reaching impact this constitutes in State power and administration and what a movement and trend in management this will bring about in both parts of the Republic.

The fact that we are able to master all these problems shows that the Party is truly able to lead and guide our society. Naturally, the creation of the Federation, an event made possible by the Party's post-January policy, does not reduce but increases the work of the Party, adds to its importance, to the weight of its decisions, to its leading role and its ability and duty to integrate. We must consistently implement what has been frequently stated on solemn occasions: that the Party is the decisive element of integration, the bearer of the idea of Czechoslovak Statehood, the advocate of the alliance of Czechoslovakia and its revolutionary movement with the revolutionary movements of the world.

In the past year we have made progress in the awareness and understanding, but also in the practical implementation, of the principle that the Party's authority throughout the entire State can only be based on and enhanced by enjoying authority among the workers, farmers, the intelligentsia and the nations and nationalities, and by correctly understanding the complex movement of social and national interests of both nations and of all nationalities. We have based the Party's leading position at the present stage on the effort to achieve a correct scientific Marxist-Leninist expression of the present status and movement of society. In the past few years—even though it is impossible to underrate the positive results—nationality problems in particular have ranked among the most sensitive issues.

The incorrect and sometimes insensitive attitude of some members of the Party's leadership before January towards the problems of Slovakia and towards the nationality problem as a whole increased tension and failed to solve and overcome the old nationality problems which appeared in all spheres of our social life. I believe that because in Slovakia all problems were interwoven with the nationality problem, they contributed to the fact that at the end of last year the most concentrated criticism of the administrative and bureaucratic methods arose in Slovakia, as well as criticism of the failure to understand the existing state of our socialist society.

But it was also Slovakia from where the great support came for the progressive ideas which had been ripening for years in the Party and in our Republic. The Czech Communists and the Czech public appreciate this initiative, which has become the source for a real understanding of the Slovak problems among the Czechs. This was a valuable contribution towards the creation of relations between our two nations on the basis of mutual confidence. Let us remember that already in the years before January we endeavoured, not without difficulties, to make all that was good and valuable in the history of the Slovak nation a part of the present development for the benefit of socialism. All this was really very difficult and many of you who at that time worked with me know this well. We proceeded from Lenin, who, after five years of experience with the nationality problem, wrote: "Our experiences fill us with the firm belief that only close attention to the interests of the various nations will eliminate conflicts and will create confidence, particularly among workers and farmers speaking different languages. Without that confidence neither peaceful international relations nor progress of all that is valuable in the present civilization are possible."

Comrades, allow me to make in conclusion a personal statement: The Christmas and New Year holidays are approaching. In this period I am again receiving many greetings and wishes from all parts of the Republic. Let me tell you frankly that I appreciate this confidence. I say quite openly that in these difficult conditions it is not easy to carry out the work in the Party so that our people, the working people and the whole Party emerge successfully from this situation. I want to use this opportunity to express my gratitude to Party members and all our citizens for their work, for their political attitude and socialist involvement, for everything they have achieved and repeatedly carried out this year. I want to wish them all a real rest over the holidays, that they spend the holidays in a cordial family environment, and in fine human relations.

For the future we all wish to take a further step next year on the basis of our work this year, towards an improved social system and better prospects for our citizens, towards the better fulfilment of the material and cultural needs of our people and towards the expansion of scope for social and political involvement, for the participation of the people in the administration and direction of our social questions. These are aims which we are persistently pursuing in the interest of a better life for the people and to which we want to devote our strength also in the coming period as well. Our Czech and Slovak nations, combining their forces, gifts and industriousness, together with their socialist convictions and loyalty to socialism, will be able to build a fine home in their fatherland and to strengthen in it those securities about which all of us are concerned. I am convinced that the Slovak Communists and working people will also in the future constitute an active force in the Republic in this effort. The Central Committee and the Party leadership, with Comrade Husak at its head, and the organs of the regions and districts, as well as the State organs, will be the organizing and directing force in Slovakia which will continue to deepen the progressive socialist character of the development in Slovakia. Let all of us hope that this work will be fruitful and beneficial to our people.

Permit me to express the conviction that the CPSI Central Committee, as well as the entire Slovak Party organization, will render full support to the leadership of the CPC in the implementation of our policy. May our work be successful. May the Slovak Socialist Republic and its people celebrate further successes, flourishing in the common fatherland—the Czechoslovak Socialist Republic.

INDEX

Index

Index

Market, see Economy

Militia, see People's Militia

Minister of the Interior, see *CSSR*, Reforms, Government

Minorities, see *CSSR*, Constitutional questions

Moscow Conference of Communist Parties (1957) 329

Moscow Declaration (1965) 329

National Assembly, see *CSSR*, Reforms

National committees, see *CSSR*, Reforms

National front, see Socialist Democracy

Nova Mysl 253

Novotny, Antonin 134, 237, 321

Opinion polls, see Participation

Opposition, see Party
  See Socialist Democracy

Own way to socialism, see *CSSR*, International position

Participation of people 78, 89, 99, 149, 151, 162, 163, 260, 262, 266, 267, 286
  See Cooperatives
  Cooperation with non-Communists 90, 99, 135, 243, 267, 281
  Elections 79, 180, 247, 267, 286, 223
  Enterprise councils 173, 262, 263, 281, 294, 325
  See Press
  Workers 136, 260, 262, 263, 281, 282, 294
  Farmers 264
  Socialist Democracy
  Opinion polls 154

Party:
  Admission of youth and intelligentsia 88, 89, 137, 138, 139, 141, 167, 168, 169, 201, 242, 259, 269, 270, 279, 305, 321, 322
  Apparatus 87, 92, 242, 295
  Central Committee 65, 68, 86, 92, 181, 202, 237, 238, 271, 274, 276, 277, 286, 287, 292, 293, 295, 296, 297, 298, 307, 308, 322, 323, 326, 327
  See Action Programme
  April plenum 222, 271
  January plenum 65, 75, 83, 84, 86, 92, 107, 222, 271, 275, 294
  May plenum 316, 320, 322, 325, 327
  Change of leaders 76, 80, 92, 93
  Congresses, 12th, 13th and 14th: 67, 68, 86, 89, 91, 135, 147, 148, 150, 170, 177, 202, 235, 236, 237, 238, 259, 276, 294, 302, 307, 308, 324, 327
  Communist international unity 107, 108, 209, 257, 258, 259, 277, 292, 316, 317, 328, 329, 330
  CPSU 130, 256, 285, 291, 292
  Conservative forces 134, 149, 150, 229, 230, 327
  Democratization and elections 79, 80, 90, 145, 146, 147, 239, 276
  Democratic centralism 80, 85, 241, 316, 323
  Ethics 82
  History, see *CSSR*, History

Inability to channel reform 66, 68, 71, 85

Intra-party information and discussion 133, 146, 295, 297, 316

Intra-party unity 135, 137, 145, 146, 288, see Split

Leading role 66, 67, 72, 75, 78, 79, 80, 109, 110, 143, 144, 222, 229, 241, 243, 259, 261, 265, 272, 278, 280, 295, 304, 314

Marxism-Leninism 67, 69, 72, 78, 79, 84, 152, 153, 203, 210, 211, 257, 258, 227, 228

Masses, 66, 69, 79, 232, 297, 305, 321, 327

Ideological struggle 155

Opposition 101, 268, 269, 285

Purge 275

Proletarian internationalism 110, 261, 291, 317

Past crimes 127, 128, 223, 243, 274, 275, 321

Rehabilitation of victims 156, 157, 275

Society 84, 88, 144, 145

Split 230, 277

State 92, 126, 133, 138, 151, 244, 246, 247, 265, 266, 290

Style of Party work 78, 79, 80, 81, 145, 146, 155, 223

Trust in Party 80, 99

Working class 73, 128, 135, 153, 229

People's Militia 80, 95, 261, 294, 283, 325

Personality cult and crimes, see *CSSR*, History

Plan, see Economy

Polytechnic education, see Education

Power:
  Monopoly 133, 144
  Personal power 139, 224
  Socialist structure 232, 273, 290

Press:
  Criticism of the press 251, 252, 289, 295
  Dialogue with other ideologies 253
  Freedom of the press 154, 155, 234, 235, 253, 279, 289
  Influence 82, 252, 253, 273, 287, 288, 289
  Participation in the democratic process 251, 253, 254, 287, 289
  See Literarni Noviny
  See Novy Mysl
  See Rude Pravo

Price-system, see Economy

Profit, see Economy

Proletarian internationalism, see Party

Public opinion, see press

Rationalization, see Economy

Reforms:
  See *CSSR*, Reforms
  See Army
  See Economy
  See Education
  See Federalization
  See Party
  See People's Militia
  See Slovak question
  See Trade unions

Rehabilitation, see Party